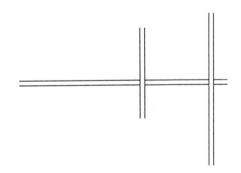

Microsoft® Word 5.5 for the PC

Self-Teaching Guide

Ruth Ashley

Judi N. Fernandez

John Wiley & Sons, Inc.

New York • Chichester • Brisbane • Toronto • Singapore

Publisher: Therese A. Zak
Editor: Katherine Schowalter
Managing Editor: Ruth Greif
Production Services: DuoTech, Inc.

Microsoft, Multiplan, and MS DOS are registered trademarks and Excel is a trademark of Microsoft Corporation. Apple is a registered trademark of Apple Computer, Inc. Lotus 1-2-3 is a registered trademark of Lotus Development Corporation. IBM is a registered trademark of International Business Machines Corporation. AutoCAD is a trademark of Autodesk, Inc. PC Paintbrush is a registered trademark of ZSoft Corporation. HotShot Graphics is a trademark of Symsoft Corporation. Paradox is a registered trademark of Ansa Software, a Borland company. PostScript is a registered trademark of Adobe Systems, Inc.

Recognizing the importance of preserving what has been written, it is a policy of John Wiley & Sons, Inc. to have books of enduring value published in the United States on acid-free paper, and we exert our best efforts to that end.

This publication is designed to provide accurate and authoritative information in regard to the subject matter covered. It is sold with the understanding that the publisher is not engaged in rendering legal, accounting, or other professional service. If legal advice or other expert assistance is required, the services of a competent professional person should be sought. FROM A DECLARATION OF PRINCIPLES JOINTLY ADOPTED BY A COMMITTEE OF THE AMERICAN BAR ASSOCIATION AND A COMMITTEE OF PUBLISHERS.

Library of Congress Cataloging-in-Publication Data

Ashley, Ruth.
    Microsoft Word 5.5 for the PC : self-teaching guide / Ruth Ashley, Judi N. Fernandez.
        p.   cm.
    Includes index.
    ISBN 0-471-53512-5 (acid-free paper)
    1. Microsoft Word (Computer program) 2. Word processing—Computer program. 3. Microcomputers—Programming.
    I. Fernandez, Judi N., 1941-   II. Title.
    Z52.5.M52A83 1991
    652.5 5369—dc20   91-17488
                                                                         CIP

Printed in the United States of America
10 9 8 7 6 5 4 3 2 1

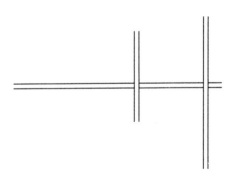

Contents

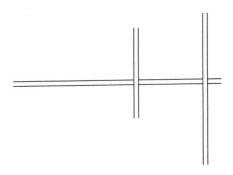

Preface

W̲elcome to the world of Microsoft Word version 5.5. If you have never used a word processor before, you are in for a treat. And if you have used other word processors or earlier versions of Microsoft Word, you'll be surprised and pleased at the wide variety of features and ease of use.

The Purpose/Orientation of This Book

This book provides an easy introduction to one of the widest selling word processors on the market today. Because it has so many different features, it helps to have a guided tour through its menus, commands, and techniques to help you become proficient quickly. The emphasis in this Self-Teaching Guide is on learning by doing. You'll get to practice each feature in detailed steps throughout the text. Additionally, you'll find Self-Check sections that let you test yourself on skills you have just learned. At the end of each chapter, you'll be able to combine the skills and techniques you have learned in that chapter in a comprehensive exercise.

Microsoft Word Version 5.5

Microsoft has released several versions of Word for different computers and systems. This book deals with version 5.5, which runs on an IBM PC or AT compatible computer without requiring Microsoft Windows.

Overview of Things to Come

You won't learn all there is to know about Microsoft Word in this book, but you'll learn enough to use it effectively. And what you learn will enable to you explore Word's remaining features and commands on your own. The material you learn in the early chapters is used heavily throughout this book. Later topics, such as merging files, using graphics, and using macros, can be studied independently.

If you are new to Word, study the first five chapters of this book in order. You can work with the rest of the book in order, of course, but later on you can skip around to get the information you want. If you've used earlier versions of Word, take time to scan the first few chapters and try the guided practice and Self-Checks. You'll be able to turn directly to later chapters if you need help in using this version of Word.

Chapter 1 introduces you to the Word program. You'll learn to start it up, use the menus and commands, type normal text, use the extensive built-in help system, and leave Word. If you need extra help installing Word or making sense out of DOS and its directory structure, you will find it in the appendices.

In Chapter 2, you'll learn to create a file. You'll be able to save what you type and access it again whenever you want. Cursor movement and text insertion and deletion are covered in this chapter, since these features are critical to using Word properly. You'll also learn to tailor the Word screen so that it displays the elements that are useful to you.

In Chapter 3, you'll learn to select text using the mouse and keyboard. You'll also learn to process selected text; you can move it, copy it, or delete it. Searching for text and replacing it are also covered in this chapter.

Chapter 4 deals with printing. You'll see how to make sure Word is set up for your printer and how to print part or all of a document. The Print Preview command lets you see on screen exactly how the printed output will look. You'll also learn to send a file to disk for later printing or create an ASCII file.

Chapter 5 covers the basics of formatting. You'll learn to change the appearance of characters, making them bold or italic, for example. You'll learn to control the alignment, indentation, and spacing of paragraphs. And you'll learn to change the page margins and cause page numbers to appear.

In Chapter 6, we discuss one of Word's unique features. You'll see how to open up to nine files at a time, and work with them in separate windows on the screen. You'll be able to arrange them and change the size and position as needed. You'll even see how to split a single window into two panes to examine different parts of the same file.

Chapter 7 gets back to file management. With this feature, you can determine which files are listed and copy, delete, rename, move, and print them as needed. Many operations you may be used to performing under DOS are really easier to handle under Word.

In Chapter 8 we take another look at formatting. You'll learn to use different fonts, add paragraph borders and shading, and change paragraph positions. You'll also see how to define and control headers and footers for the pages. And you'll see how to use footnotes and annotations through Word. Finally, you'll learn to set up and control a multicolumn format under Word.

Chapter 9 shows you an easier way to handle all your formatting. You'll learn to deal with styles, which format characters, paragraphs, or entire sections of a document. You'll see how to define and use style sheets consisting of all the styles you need for a given type of document.

Chapter 10 covers several more advanced editing features. You can customize tab stops and set up tables within your documents. You'll learn to use glossaries to simplify repetitive text entry. Bookmarks let you move quickly to another part of the document. And outline mode is a great timesaver in developing complex documents.

Chapter 11 covers various Word utilities that you might find helpful as you use Word more. The spelling checker checks for misspelled words and offers suggestions for correcting them. The thesaurus gives you synonyms and similar words for a given word. You can hyphenate your document or sort based on paragraphs or tables. And you can even ask Word to calculate mathematical expressions or total a set of values.

In Chapter 12, you'll learn to use the line draw facility to draw horizontal and vertical lines and diagrams in your documents. You'll also learn to capture screen images using the CAPTURE program. Word lets you insert graphics created by many different graphics and screen capture programs into documents at any point.

Chapter 13 deals with macros, which let you execute a series of Word commands with just a few keystrokes. You'll learn to use a few supplied macros and to record your own as you work with Word.

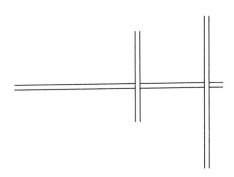

About This Book

We have used some standards to make reading this book and learning to use Microsoft Word as easy as possible. This is a "learn-by-doing" book. Most of your learning comes from actually using Word as you work through this book. You'll see numbered lists of very detailed steps in most topics. Just follow through the steps at your computer and you'll see what happens on the screen. Several times in each chapter, a Self-Check gives you a guided exercise covering topics you have already tried in the detailed numbered steps. The Self-Checks won't give you as much direction; you'll start using Word itself as your instructor. If you don't remember what command to use, you can check through the menus until your memory is jogged or use the online help system. You can also try things on your own; that helps you learn. The Exercise at the end of each chapter involves most of the commands and techniques covered in that chapter. This gives you still another chance to use Word as you develop your skills. Following each Self-Check and Exercise, detailed suggestions are provided in case you had problems working on your own.

Any information in this book that you are supposed to type is shown in **bold** type. References to fields in dialog boxes are also shown in **bold**. Each reference to a command or menu has initial caps. A command reference always includes the menu name as the first word, so you will know how to find it on the screen. Enjoy the book and Microsoft Word while you are learning. Try things out at your computer as you read. Make up your own exercises when a feature looks especially useful. In no time at all, you'll find that Microsoft Word is like a second language, and one that you speak very well.

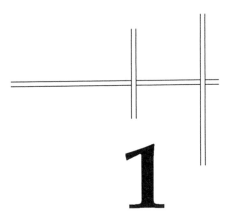

Getting Started

So you are ready to start learning to use Microsoft Word. Word lets you do many things with your documents; so many, in fact, that it's hard to keep all the information in your head at one time. That's why you have menus to help you find what you need. There are also a great many things you can do without using the menu structure. Learning the basics of Word isn't really all that difficult. But you want to learn more than the basics. You want to be able to speak Word almost as a second language. This chapter gets you started learning the ins and outs of a new environment. In each chapter, you'll add to your knowledge of Word. In this chapter, you'll learn how to:

- Start up Word
- Use the mouse and keyboard keys to choose commands and buttons
- Drop down menus to see commands
- Choose commands
- Use the mouse and keyboard keys to move through text in windows
- Use DOS commands from within Word
- Use the Word Help system
- Find information through Help
- Exit Word

What Is Microsoft Word?

Microsoft Word version 5.5 is one of the most advanced word processors available. It has many more commands and features than you'll need to use at first. Because Word has so many features, it is a bit complicated, so we break it down into meaningful chunks for you.

Word Overview

As a word processor, Word handles all the fundamental features of word processors: you can enter text, edit it, move and copy blocks of text within a document and from one document to another. You can search for text, replace text, and jump around in the text. You can format pages with margins, indentation, tab settings, and spacing. Word also lets you check spelling, reference a thesaurus, do arithmetic calculations, and sort your document.

Documents can contain headers and footers, page numbers in almost any form, and annotations. You can include text that doesn't appear on the screen or even in the printed document. Word lets you store text in a form for easy insertion wherever you need it. And you can create macros that perform a series of Word commands with just a few keystrokes.

In addition, Word has many features that make it useful for desktop publishing. You can control fonts and type size, for example. And you can use points and picas as measurement instead of inches if you prefer. Word will create a table of contents and an index for a document. And the documents can contain graphics and line drawing components.

Word has even more features. You'll learn to use most of them as you continue working through this Self-Teaching Guide.

The Word Interface

Microsoft Word version 5.5 is designed to be used with a mouse or by pressing keyboard keys. The screen design, or interface, is much like that of Microsoft Windows. Whether you have a mouse or not, you'll be able to get full use out of Word. If you do have a mouse, you'll find that you frequently use the keyboard keys instead since they are more convenient while you are typing.

If you have a mouse, be sure you read through information for the keyboard; this will be useful to you. And if you don't have a mouse, scan the information for the mouse as well; you may decide to try one! A mouse isn't expensive and expands your options, in Word as well as in many other applications.

Before You Start

You can't use Word without any previous knowledge at all. You need to know a bit about the computer. And Word must be installed. Appendix A has some useful information for you if Word is not yet installed on your computer.

Knowing about the Computer

Your computer is a tool that lets you use Microsoft Word. Computers come in various styles and configurations; we can't teach you how to use yours here, but if you can accomplish these tasks at your computer, you are ready to start learning Word:

- Turn the computer on and off.
- Reboot by pressing Ctrl+Alt+Del (hold down the Control, Alt, and Delete keys simultaneously).
- Find the arrow keys and the NumLock key.
- Insert a diskette if Word isn't on the hard disk.
- Change to the directory containing Word if it is on the hard disk (usually you type **cd \word**).

As you are probably aware, there are many more things you do with your computer, but these are enough to let you get started using Word. If you don't have at least this level of knowledge, you might find it useful to ask your dealer, check with a colleague or neighbor, or read the first few chapters of an introductory book on your particular version of DOS.

Knowing about Word

Before you start, you must know where Word is installed. Most people put Word on their hard disk or a high-density disk. In either case, all the Word program files and your documents can fit on the same diskette, so the process is pretty much the same. We'll assume that you have one of these setups throughout the main text of this book. Appendix B includes special information for those who use Word on a 360K diskette. When a feature is handled differently with this arrangement, the text will direct you to the Appendix for further information.

Wherever it is installed, Word works the same; any differences result from the lower amount of storage space on diskettes. If Word is on a hard disk, it is probably in a separate directory; it is usually named \WORD.

If Word is not installed yet, be sure to check Appendix A and install it. None of the exercises or commands will work until the program is installed.

Starting Word

Starting Word is very simple; you just type **word** at the appropriate prompt. Several steps may be necessary to get to that prompt, however. In any case, your computer must be turned on.

Tip || Throughout this book are lists of steps to guide you through the command or feature being discussed. Try them out on your computer.

1. Turn your computer on in the usual way.

When it is on and ready for a command, you'll see a prompt that indicates the drive (and perhaps the directory) that is active.

If Word Is on the Hard Disk

If Word is installed on the hard disk, the WORD directory may be included in your system's path; that means the computer can find Word whenever you issue the command. But for now you want to be in the WORD directory. To do that, type **cd \word** at the prompt. This makes the WORD directory current. If you get a message like "Invalid directory," your directory has a different name or the Word program is located somewhere else. Find out what it is called and where it is located, then make that directory current.

If Word Is on a Diskette

If Word is installed on a diskette, you may have to insert the diskette. If your boot diskette contains Word, you are all set. If not, switch the diskettes. Most people use the Word diskette in drive A: and reserve B: for a document diskette. If the prompt doesn't show A>, type **cd a:** at the prompt to switch to that drive after inserting the Word diskette into that drive. Now the diskette containing Word is current.

Tip || Refer to Appendix B for more information about starting Word from a 360K diskette.

The Actual Start

Once the drive or directory that contains Word is current, just type **word** at the DOS prompt. You can use either uppercase or lowercase letters. Then press ↵ to tell DOS to process the command.

2. Make the drive or directory that contains Word current.
3. Type **word** at the DOS prompt and press ↵.

It may take several seconds for DOS to find the Word programs and start it up. You'll see a copyright screen that shows the Word version (5.5) with the personalized name added during installation. Then you will see a screen like the one shown in Figure 1.1. Your screen may have some differences, especially if someone else has been using Word on your computer. That's no problem; in fact, it assures you that Word is in good working condition!

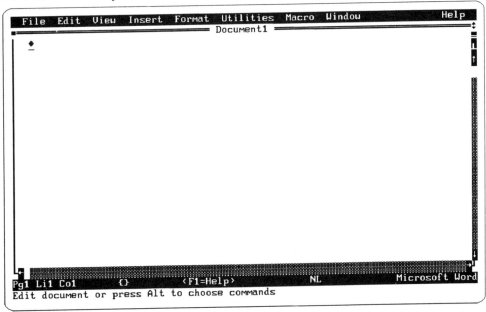

Figure 1.1. Main Word Screen

If you don't get this screen when you start up Word, you have a problem. If you get the message "Bad command or filename," Word isn't in the current directory on the current drive. Check again to find out where it is located and make sure it is installed. For any other problem, check with your dealer or with another Word user.

Tip || Don't go on until you can get into Word. This book depends on your using Word as you read.

Interacting with Word

Microsoft Word version 5.5 provides you with many ways to communicate with it. You can use the mouse or the keyboard. The interface is much like that of the well-known Windows. If you have used any other program with a Windows-like interface, then you can start using Word very easily. Even if you haven't used this style interface before, you'll adapt quickly as you see how easy and even logical it is. If you haven't worked with drop-down menus, dialog boxes, scroll boxes, and the like before, you'll need a bit of extra practice.

In the next section, you'll explore the Word interface and learn what the obvious elements can do for you. Next you'll see how to use the keyboard keys and/or the mouse to manipulate these elements.

Tip || Even if you have a mouse, be sure to read about keyboard functions. While you're typing text, you might not want to switch your hand to the mouse.

Elements on the Main Screen

The main screen is where you do your typing and editing of text. Probably 90 percent of your time in Word will be spent with this screen displayed. Its menus provide a gateway to all the other functions of Word.

The Menu Bar. The top line of the main screen shows the *menu bar*. Each word in the menu bar is the name of a menu that contains a list of commands. Each command performs a function. You'll be able to look at some menus shortly.

The Document Window. The large rectangle that occupies most of the screen is the *document window*. Whatever document you are currently working on appears here. The small diamond in the upper-left corner is the end-of-document mark; since this document is empty, the end-of-document mark is the

ment mark; since this document is empty, the end-of-document mark is the first character in the file. The underscore character just below it is the cursor; it blinks on the screen. As you type, characters appear at the cursor and push the end-of-document mark to the right. You'll get a chance to try this shortly.

The name of the current document appears in the top border of the document window. Since the current document hasn't been saved as a file, it shows the generic name Document1.

Scroll Bars. The bars on the right and bottom borders of the document window are *scroll bars*. You use them with a mouse to move through the document, either vertically (the scroll bar on the right) or horizontally (the scroll bar on the bottom). You'll see how to use scroll bars later in this chapter.

Status Bar. The line below the horizontal scroll bar is the *status bar*. It gives you information about the status of Word and your document. The left edge of the line shows the current page number (Pg1 in Figure 1.1) and the column number (Co1) in the current document. You can add the current line number as well. The curly braces ({ }) indicate information that you can easily insert; you'll learn to use that in Chapter 3. The reminder that pressing F1 gets Help always appears in the status bar. Several different two-letter indicators may appear in the next part. NL means that the NumLock key has been pressed. That's important if your keyboard's arrow keys are on the numeric keypad. You can press the NumLock key to let you use numeric characters from the keypad or use the other numbers when you need the number characters.

1. See if NL appears in the status bar.
2. Press NumLock. Did NL disappear or appear?
3. Press it again.
4. If NL is not in the status bar, press NumLock again to put it there. That's how you want to work most of the time.
5. Press CapsLock. Notice that CL appears in the status bar.
6. Press CapsLock again to remove the indicator.

The Message Bar. The very bottom line of most Word screens is a *message bar*. It contains special messages when a command is selected or in progress. The standard message appears in Figure 1.1. When you see the "Edit document..." message, you are in edit mode and can type or edit your document or issue any commands. The message also tells you one way to choose commands: just press the Alt key to get started.

Tip || If you press Alt by mistake and the menu bar lights up, just press it again to turn the menu bar off.

Typing Text

Typing characters into a word processor is much like using a typewriter. You press a key, and the corresponding character appears. You'll see it on the screen. If you make a mistake, you can backspace right away to remove it.

In word processing, you don't have to press a carriage return. You'll use the ↵ key instead; this key is often called the Enter or Return key. But you don't have to use it after every line. Word uses *wordwrap* to start the next line when one line is full. If you are typing paragraphs, you'll just have to press ↵ at the end of the paragraph. If you are typing short lines, you'll press ↵ at the end of each. Try it out:

1. Type your name, then press ↵.

As you type, notice how the cursor and the end-of-document mark move toward the end of the document.

2. Type your mailing address, pressing ↵ at the end of each line.
3. Type a paragraph explaining why you are going to learn Word. Don't press ↵. Type until at least three or four lines are shown. (Don't worry, no one will see this but you.)

If you make mistakes during typing, just use the backspace key to remove them. But don't worry too much. You are really just getting the feel of your keyboard and seeing how Word puts characters on the screen.

Using Menus

The key to making Word do what you want is its commands, and you reach those through the menus. In this section, we'll overview the menus. You'll learn to pull down the menus using either the keyboard or the mouse in this section.

Using a Mouse. If you have a mouse, you must be able to do two things to see the menus: point and click. *Pointing* is placing the mouse pointer (either an arrow or a rectangle) on the item you want. *Clicking* is depressing a button briefly, then releasing it. In almost all cases, you'll click the left button. If you should use the right, we'll emphasize that in the text.

To pull down a menu using the mouse, point to the menu name in the menu bar, then click. To pull down a different menu, point to its name and click. To release a menu without choosing a command, point to anything outside that menu and the menu bar and click. Figure 1.2 shows how the screen looks when the File menu is pulled down.

1. If you have a mouse, point to the File menu name and click the left button.
2. Point to the Help menu name and click the left button.
3. Point to the empty area of the screen and click again.

The menu should be off the screen.

Using the Keyboard. Pulling down menus from the keyboard isn't quite as easy as with a mouse, but you have more ways to do it. They all start with pressing the Alt key. Once you press Alt, the menu bar is activated and the cursor leaves the document window. The first menu name (File) is highlighted. You'll see that one character in each menu name appears in a different or highlighted letter; this is called its *key letter*. The key letter is the first letter in the menu name except for the Format menu, where the key letter is T (the File menu has key letter F). When the menu bar is activated, you have several ways to pull down a menu.

- Press the key letter (either case). The menu appears.
- Press ↵ or ↓ to drop down the highlighted menu.
- Press → or ← to move the highlight to the next menu name or to change to the adjacent pulled-down menu.

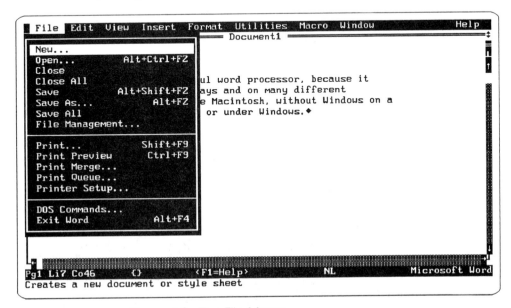

Figure 1.2. The File Menu

The expression Alt,A means to press and release the Alt key, then press A. The expression Alt+A means to press both at the same time. In key press combinations, we use the comma to indicate sequence, one after the other. The + symbol means to press the keys together.

To release the current menu without choosing a command, you can press Alt or Escape. If you press Alt, the menu disappears but the menu bar remains active; pressing Alt again returns the cursor to the document window. Pressing Escape when a menu is pulled down releases the menu and returns the cursor to the document window immediately.

Tip Try out these keyboard practices even if you have a mouse. Sometimes the keyboard is more efficient.

1. Press the Alt key.

The cursor is no longer in the document window. The menu bar is activated. The File menu name is highlighted and you can see all the key letters.

2. Press ↵ or ↓ to see the File menu.
3. Press Alt to remove the menu.

Notice that the menu bar is still activated.

4. Press → twice so that the View menu name is highlighted.
5. Press ↵ or ↓ to see the menu.
6. Press ← to see the Edit menu appear.
7. Press Alt to release the menu.
8. Press the key letter of the Help menu (H) to drop it down.
9. Press Escape.

The menu is released and the cursor returns to the document window.

Dealing with Accidents. Sometimes you might hit Alt accidentally and unknowingly activate the menu bar. If you continue typing, you might pull down a menu, even choose a command accidentally. If this happens, just press Escape repeatedly to get rid of whatever strange menus and dialog boxes appear on your screen.

If you press Alt and then hit a key that is not a key letter, however, Word isn't sure what you want it to do. So it beeps at you. If you hit another key that it doesn't want, it beeps again. So what do you do? Look at the screen. If the menu bar is active, just press Escape to return the cursor so you can continue typing. Or you can click anywhere in the document window. Try it out.

1. Press Alt.
2. Press B.
3. Press C.
4. Notice that the menu bar is activated and press Escape.

Now you can continue typing because the cursor is back in the document window.

1. Drop down the Utilities menu.
2. Change to the Window menu.
3. Release the menu.
4. Press Alt,Z, then release the error.
5. Drop down the Edit menu.
6. Release the menu.

You can click on the word Utilities in the menu bar or press Alt,U to drop down this menu. Then click on Windows or press → twice to switch to the Windows menu. Use Esc or click anywhere in the document window to release the error. Click on Edit or use Alt,E to get the Edit menu.

Commands

Each menu contains a list of commands. In this book, we always include the menu name as part of the command. If we refer to the Print command on the File menu, for example, we'll call it the File Print command or just File Print. The first word of every command indicates the menu on which it is found.

Once a menu is displayed, a key letter in each command indicates that it is available. If a command can't be used for some reason, it is dimmed and its key letter isn't apparent. If a command is followed by an ellipsis (three dots), choosing it brings up a special dialog box that requests further information or action on your part. If there is no ellipsis, choosing the command performs the action immediately. As with dropping down menus, choosing commands with the mouse is different from the keyboard method.

Using the Mouse. To choose a command with the mouse, just point to it and click. The command is performed or a box appears for further information.

1. Point to the Utilities menu and click.
2. Point to the Word Count command and click.

Notice that the total word count of your current document appears on the message line and in the status bar. The message goes away as soon as you click or press a key, but the word count remains enclosed in braces in the status bar.

Using the Keyboard. When a menu is dropped down, the key letters are visible. To choose a command, you can just press the key letter. You don't even have to wait until the menu is dropped down; you can use the File Print command by pressing Alt,F,P, for example.

In a dropped-down menu, one command is always highlighted. You can choose the highlighted command by pressing ↵. To highlight a different command, just use ↓ and ↑ to move it. The highlight cycles around the menu, so if you press ↑ when the first command is highlighted, the last one is highlighted next.

Tip | | Be sure to try the keyboard method even if you have a mouse. You'll find that being able to do it both ways speeds your work no end.

1. Press Alt,U to drop down the Utilities menu.
2. Press W to choose the Utilities Word Count command.

Notice that the menu is released and the word count appears in the message line.

3. Press Alt,U to drop down the Utilities menu again.
4. Press ↓ repeatedly until the Spelling command is highlighted again. Then press it some more until the Word Count command is highlighted.
5. Press ↵.

Notice that the effect is the same both ways.

Key Combinations. Many commands on the menus show a key combination (sometimes called a *shortcut* or a *hotkey*) on the right. You can press this key combination instead of choosing the menu and command. Once you have chosen the menu, the key combinations won't work. The key combinations that involve function keys (F1 through F12) are shown on your Word keyboard template. The Help system can let you know about others. Complete key combination information is in the documentation. We'll introduce the shortcut key combinations as the commands are covered throughout this book.

Tip ||| You can't use these key combinations once the menu is pulled down so you can see what they are! You can use them only when the menu bar is not active.

Menu Overview

Since the menus give you access to the world of Word through its commands, a brief overview is in order. Some of these menus and commands are not covered until much later in this book. If you know what type of commands are on each menu, you can do some learning on your own if you like. As we walk through this section, pull down the appropriate menu on your screen.

The File Menu. The File menu contains commands that let you handle files. The top group of commands lets you create, open, save, and close files. You'll probably use one or more of these commands in every Word session. The File Management command lets you perform many functions, such as copying and deleting files on your disks. The middle group of commands deals with printing documents. The bottom group lets you enter DOS commands without leaving Word or allows you to leave Word. You'll learn to use the last two commands later in this chapter.

The Edit Menu. The Edit menu contains commands that let you do power editing. The top group lets you undo or repeat an action, as well as cut, copy, and paste text. You'll learn to use these in Chapter 3. The second group lets you do search and replace operations or move to a particular location in your document. The last command lets you edit a glossary for easy insertion of text in your document.

The View Menu. The View menu lets you control the content and layout of the main Word screen. The first group lets you use outline mode or change the layout to see how nonstandard elements are positioned on the screen. The second group lets you specify whether the ruler, the ribbon, and the status bar should be displayed. By default, Word shows the status bar, but not the ruler and ribbon. You'll learn to use those a bit later in this book. Notice the dot before Status Bar. That means the status bar is included on the screen. Try choosing the View Status Bar command:

1. Click or use Alt,V to pull down the View menu if it isn't visible.
2. Click on the Status Bar command or press ↓ until it is highlighted and press ⏎ to choose the command.

Notice that the menu is released and the status bar is missing from your screen. To put it back:

3. Click or use Alt,V to pull down the View menu.
4. Click on Status Bar or press ↓ until it is highlighted and press ↵ to choose the command.

The Insert Menu. The Insert menu lets you insert items into your document. The first group inserts such features as breaks, files, and page numbers. The other group inserts more complex elements such as indexes or graphics.

The Format Menu. The Format menu contains commands that help you format your document. The first two groups control basic document formatting, such as character fonts, bold type, spacing, margins, and tabs. The last group lets you use styles to format documents; these are more complex but make formatting easier when you use the same format for many documents.

The Utilities Menu. The Utilities menu contains commands that let you use such features as the spell checker and the thesaurus. Many useful features such as sorting, word counting, and calculating are included. The last command lets you customize your Word program so that it better meets your needs.

The Macro Menu. Macros are time or effort-saving functions that use just a few keystrokes to perform a series of Word commands. Word provides some macros, and you can develop your own. Macros are introduced in Chapter 13.

The Window Menu. The commands on the Window menu let you work with several documents on the screen at once. For now, we'll stick to just one. The last group of items on this menu lists the documents in active windows. Your Window menu probably includes Document1 as the last item. The dot next to it shows that it is in the current window.

The Help Menu. Word has an extensive Help system that you can access in several ways. The Help menu is only one way. The Help Index gives you access to most of the help system through an alphabetized list. We'll cover the Help system in detail later in this chapter.

Leaving Word

One operation that you'll perform often is getting out of Word. The File menu contains the File Exit Word command.

Choosing the Command

To choose the File Exit Word command with a mouse, just point to the File menu name and click. Then point to the Exit Word option and click again.

To choose it from the keyboard, press Alt,F to pull down the File menu, then press X to issue the Exit Word command. Or you can press the Alt key and hold it while pressing F4. In this book, we'll refer to it as the File Exit Word command (Alt,F,X), but you can use the key combination any time you prefer.

1. Choose the File Exit Word command (Alt,F,X or Alt+F4).

If your document hasn't been saved, you'll see a simple dialog box like the one shown in Figure 1.3. We'll cover more complex dialog boxes in the next chapter, where you'll also learn to save files. If your document has been saved or if you haven't made any changes to it, Word is terminated immediately and you're back at the DOS prompt.

Pressing Buttons

When you see a dialog box, you read the text and tell Word what to do next by choosing the appropriate button. Each item enclosed in angle brackets is a button. With a mouse, just click on the button you want. With the keyboard,

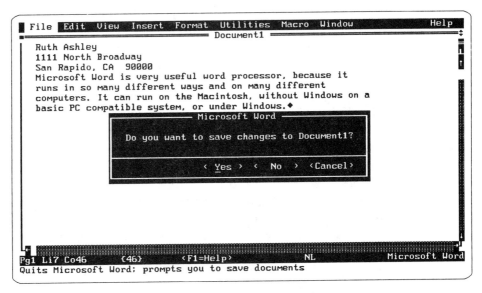

Figure 1.3. Result of File Exit Word Command

notice that a key letter may be present in the buttons. If it is, just press Alt followed by that key. Also notice that one set of angle brackets is colored like key letters. That button is active; if you press ⏎, it takes effect. You can use the Tab key to move from one field or button in the dialog box to the next. When the one you want is indicated, press ⏎.

2. If you see a dialog box, choose the <No> button.

In this dialog box, pressing the <Yes> button causes Word to save the file; you'll have to provide more information if you choose Yes. Pressing the <No> button causes Word to terminate without saving the file. If you choose the <Cancel> button, the File Exit Word request is canceled and you are back in the document window.

1. Start up Word.
2. Type your name in the document.
3. Pull down the Utilities menu.
4. Choose the Count command.
5. Exit Word without saving the file.

Choose the Utilities Word Count command by clicking on the Utilities menu name, then clicking on the Word Count option. With the keyboard, press Alt,U,W. To exit Word, click on the File menu, then on the Exit Word option with the mouse. With the keyboard, press Alt,F,X or Alt+F4. Remember that commas indicate sequence; press each key and release it before pressing the next. The plus sign means to hold the Alt key down while pressing F4.

Using DOS Commands

Sometimes you will want to run a DOS command while you are in Word. While you could exit Word, use DOS, then start up Word again, that seems a waste of time, and you lose your place in the document. In this section, you'll see how you can use DOS commands without leaving Word.

The File DOS Commands command is available on the File menu. To choose it with the mouse, just click on the file name, then on the command option. With the keyboard, press Alt,F,D to choose the command.

The Dialog Box

When you choose the File DOS Commands command, you'll see a dialog box like the one shown in Figure 1.4. This dialog box has two buttons: <OK> and <Cancel>. You'll see these two choices in most dialog boxes. Pressing ↵ is always equivalent to choosing the active button; when the angle brackets around <OK> are distinctive, it is active. Pressing the Escape is always equivalent to choosing <Cancel>.

1. Choose the File DOS Commands command (Alt,F,D).
2. Press Esc to remove the dialog box.
3. Choose the File DOS Commands command (Alt,F,D) again.

This dialog box has a text field (labeled **Command**) in which you can type. The default value COMMAND appears there originally. If you want to get the DOS prompt so you can enter a series of DOS commands, choose <OK> or press ↵. The screen looks something like Figure 1.5. Type DOS commands at the prompt as usual. When you are ready to return to Word, type **exit** as a command. You'll be prompted to press any key to return to Word.

4. Choose <OK> or press ↵.
5. Type **dir** and view the result.
6. Type **date** and view the result.

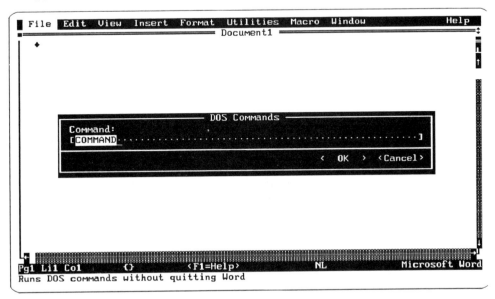

Figure 1.4. The File DOS Commands Dialog Box

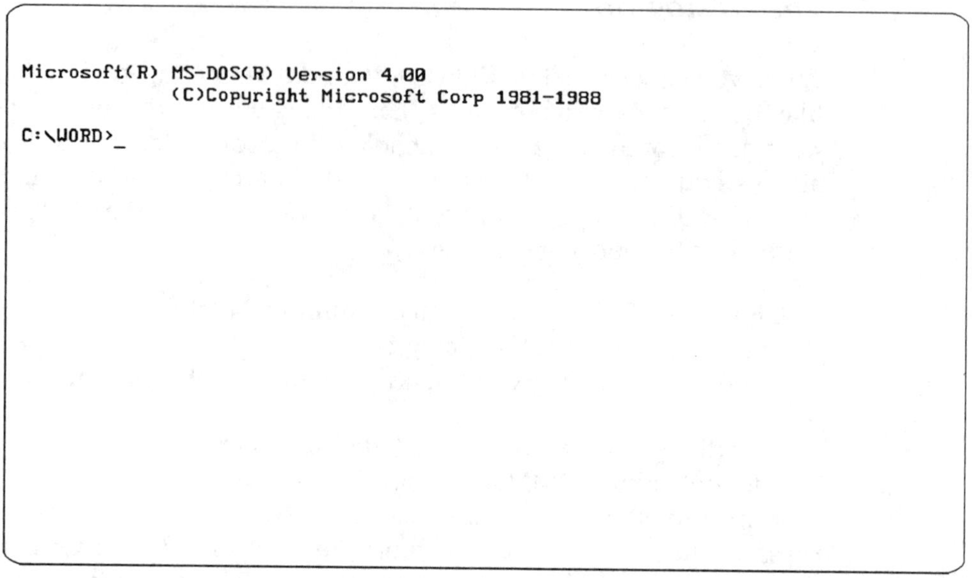

```
Microsoft(R) MS-DOS(R) Version 4.00
          (C)Copyright Microsoft Corp 1981-1988

C:\WORD>_
```

Figure 1.5. DOS Commands in Progress

7. Press ↵ to keep the displayed date.
8. Type **exit**.
9. As prompted, press any key to return to Word.

Running a Single Command

To run just one DOS command, don't choose <OK> before typing the command you want. You don't have to delete COMMAND; when you type, it is automatically removed. For example, if you want to see the current directory, just type **dir**. Then choose <OK> or press ↵. You'll see the directory on a DOS style screen, followed by a prompt to press any key to return to Word.

1. Choose the File DOS Commands command (Alt,F,D).
2. Type **dir** and press ↵.
3. As prompted, press any key to return to Word.

1. Run the single DOS command **type \config.sys**.
2. Run this series of DOS commands:

> **dir **
> **vol**
> **ver**

3. Return to your document window.

Click on the menu and command or press Alt,F,D to get the DOS Commands dialog box for items 1 and 2. In item 1, type the DOS command in the **Command** *field before choosing <OK>. It item 2, choose <OK> first, then enter the commands one at a time at the DOS prompt. Use the command* **exit** *to return in item 3.*

Word's Help System

Word has an extensive online Help system that you can use as you work to get answers to many of your questions. You can find out how to use the current command or how to fill in the current dialog box. You can get a summary of all the keyboard instructions. You can get definitions of common terms. In fact, you can even tap into a complete tutorial. In this section, you'll learn to get information through the Help menu as well as by pressing F1 for context-sensitive help.

Help Windows

Help information is presented to you in help windows, which are much like the document window. You can page through the information with the arrow keys or using PgUp and PgDown. Or you can use the scroll bars to move through the information using a mouse. You can just press Esc or click on the close box (upper-left corner) to close a help window. Each help window also includes buttons that you can use to reach other parts of the Help system or to return to the document window.

Figure 1.6 shows the result of pressing F1 on the standard editing window. This help window includes some features that will recur in many windows. These features appear in most document windows as well.

Notice that the window has three buttons at the top. One gets you to the index, the next backtracks through your help session, and the third leaves the Help system, returning you to wherever you first requested help. These three buttons do not scroll with the text. You'll have to page or scroll back to the top of the help text to choose a button.

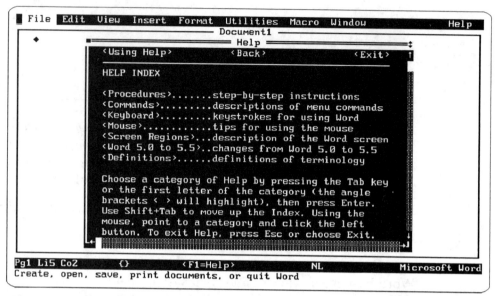

Figure 1.6. Help Window with Scroll Bars

Using the Mouse. Many help windows have scroll bars on the right and at the bottom of the window. In addition, the top border has an icon on each end, just as in the document window. Both the icons and the scroll bars are for use with a mouse.

The small black box on the upper-left corner of the window is the close box; you can click on it to close the window. The small double-headed arrow on the upper-right corner of the window is the maximize icon; you can click on it to make the help window occupy as much space as possible. To restore the previous size, click on the maximize icon again.

With the scroll bars, you can move through the text. If you click on the down arrow at the bottom of the vertical scroll bar, you'll see the next line of the text at the bottom of the window. If you click on the up arrow at the top of the scroll bar, you'll see the previous line of text at the top of the window. If you click and hold the button down on either arrow, you'll set up continuous scrolling in that direction.

Notice the dark box on the scroll bar; this has many names, but Word calls it a *scroll box*. If you click on the scroll bar above the box, you'll see a screen nearer the beginning of the text; if you click on the scroll bar below the box, you'll see a screen later.

You can *drag* (click and hold down the button while moving the mouse) the scroll box to another location on the scroll bar to see an approximate location in the text.

1. Click on the <F1=Help> button in the status bar.
2. Click on the Maximize icon (the double-headed arrow in the upper-right corner of the help window).
3. Click on the Maximize icon again.
4. Click twice on the down arrow at the bottom of the vertical scroll bar.
5. Drag the scroll box to the top of the bar.

You won't have to use the horizontal scroll bar at the bottom of the window in most cases. But if you do, it works much like the other scroll bar, dealing with text wider than the window.

Using the Keyboard. If you don't have a mouse, you can move through the text with the arrow keys or with PgUp and PgDown. You can close the help window by pressing Esc. And you can select buttons just as in dialog boxes; type its key letter or use Tab to select one and press ↵. Later in this book, you'll learn to use a command to maximize a window.

1. If no help window is shown, press F1.
2. Press PgDown.
3. Press PgUp.
4. Choose the <Exit> button.

Moving through the Help System

Moving through the Help system can get quite involved. Some windows give you special help; they have buttons or the top line tells you to click or press ↵ for instructions. Others give you additional ways to find what you need. You'll see a few of these in the next sections.

Context-Sensitive Help

You can press F1 to get help at any time. With the mouse, you can click on the <F1=Help> button if you prefer. What kind of help you get depends on what is going on. If a menu is dropped down, one command option is always highlighted; pressing F1 gets you information about that particular command. If a dialog box is displayed, such as the one resulting from the File DOS Commands command, pressing F1 gets information about how to fill it in.

1. Type a few words into your empty document.

2. Choose the File Exit Word command (Alt,F,X or Alt+F4).
3. When the dialog box appears, press F1 or click on the help reminder in the status line.

The resulting help window tells you what your choices are and offers the single <OK> button. You can remove the help window by choosing the button, pressing ↵, or pressing Esc.

4. Choose the <OK> button.
5. Choose the <Cancel> button in the dialog box.

Some context-sensitive help offers you more choices, as shown in Figure 1.4.

1. Choose the <F1=Help> button in the status line.
2. Choose the <Exit> button to remove the resulting help window.

The Help Menu

You can access help and other information easily through the Help menu. One of its commands, Help About, shows you what version of Word you have and provides its unique serial number.

1. Click or press Alt,H to drop down the Help menu.

Notice that the About option includes three dots, so it results in a dialog box.

2. Click or press A to choose the Help About option.

Notice that the resulting dialog box gives a bit of information and has only one button. You must choose <OK> to remove the box and continue; you can click on it or press ↵ (actually, pressing Esc removes it as well).

3. Choose <OK>.

Help Using the Help System

One of the Help menu commands gives you information about using the Help system. Try this on your system:

1. Choose the Help Using Help command (Alt,H,H).

2. Press ↵ to get instructions.

The dialog box you see, like the one in Figure 1.7, tells you that you can click on the item you want information about or use the Tab key until it is selected and then press ↵. It tells you that the <Back> button can be used to trace your path backward through the Help system. And it tells you how to get out of Help.

3. Choose <OK>.
4. Press ↓or click to choose <Moving around in Help>.
5. Read all the information, then return to the top of the window and choose <Exit>.

You can read through other parts of Help Using Help at your leisure.

The Help Index

The Help Index can take you to any part of the help system. In fact, choosing Help Index (Alt,H,I) brings up the very same Help window as pressing F1 on the basic document window. The window you saw in Figure 1.4 is the first Help Index window. And choosing the <Index> button from any help window gets the same result.

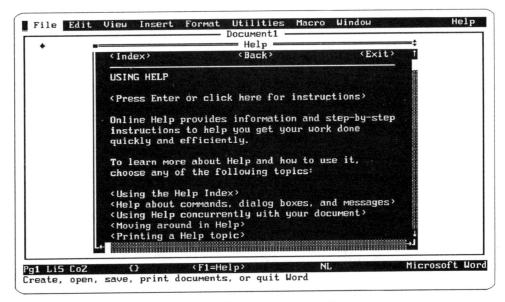

Figure 1.7. The Help Using Help Window

You use this window just like other help windows. Click on the button you want or use Tab (or Shift+Tab to go backwards) to select the button you want.

Help on Procedures. The <Procedures> button brings you an alphabetical list of procedures, with step-by-step instructions. For example, to learn to run DOS commands from within Word, you could follow these steps:

1. Choose the Help Index command.
2. Choose the <Procedures> button.
3. Press D to move to the procedures starting with D.
4. Choose DOS (by clicking or by highlighting it then pressing ↵).
5. When you have read it, press Esc or click on the close box.

Help on Commands. The <Commands> button brings you a list of all commands; you can select any command from any menu and Word gives you more information about what you can do with it. To get more information about the Utilities Word Count command you could follow these steps:

1. Choose the Help Index command.
2. Choose the <Commands> button.
3. Press U to move to the first Utilities menu command.
4. Choose the Utilities Word Count command.
5. When you have read it, you can choose the <Index> button to return to the index or press Esc or click on the close box to return to your document.

Help Using the Keyboard and the Mouse. Pressing the <Keyboard> button brings you a list of various functions such as Editing, Formatting, and Moving in a Document. Just select the one you want and you get detailed information about how to accomplish that function using keyboard keys. The <Mouse> button brings a similar list that lets you get information about using the Mouse.

Tip || You can choose the Help Keyboard command directly to get the same information more quickly.

Help Understanding the Word Screen. The <Screen Regions> button brings up a miniature model of the main Word screen. You just click on the part you want information about, and it pops up. (This works only with the mouse. If you don't have a mouse, you'll be directed into the Word tutorial.) If you have a mouse, try this:

1. Choose the Help Index command.

2. Choose the <Screen Regions> button.
3. Click on the close box in the upper-left corner of the miniature.
4. Choose <OK>.
5. Click on the vertical scroll bar.
6. Choose <OK>.
7. Press Esc to remove the help window.

Getting Definitions. If you have trouble understanding all the jargon involved with word processing and Word, you might want to get some help. Choosing the <Definitions> button brings up a list of definitions, much like the list of procedures. You can press a letter to move to a particular initial letter, or just page or scroll through the list. Click on any word you want to see defined or highlight it and press ⏎.

Other Help Commands

Other commands on the Help menu let you find out how Word 5.5 differs from Word 5. If you are upgrading you will need this information. But if Word 5.5 is your first experience with Word, you don't need this information.

The Help Learning Word command leads you directly into a tutorial that should help you get comfortable with Word quickly. It covers some of the common uses of Word.

1. Look up the definition of scroll bar in the Help Index.
2. Look up either the keyboard help or the mouse help, depending on which you use the most. Read some of the information.
3. Look up information on the View Status Bar command.
4. Return to the document window and terminate Word.

You can get all the requested information by pressing F1 or choosing the Help Index command. For item 1, choose the <Definitions> button, press S, then select <Scroll bar>. Press Esc or click outside the help window to return to the document window. For item 2, choose the appropriate command from the Help menu. For item 3, you can highlight the command on the View menu and press F1 or locate it through the <Commands> button of the Help Index.

Exercise

This chapter covered methods of getting into Word, typing text, choosing commands and buttons, using Help, and getting out of Word. In this exercise, you can practice most of these commands and features.

1. Start up Microsoft Word.
2. Type several lines into the window.
3. Turn caps lock on and type another line. Turn caps lock off.
4. Turn the status bar off, then restore it.
5. Run the DOS command **dir** to see what files are in the current directory.
6. Look up information about how to use Help.
7. Look up information about how to exit Word, then exit Word without saving your document.

To start up Word, type **word** *at the DOS prompt; you may have to change to the directory that contains the Word program. The letters CL appear in the status bar when caps lock is on. The View Status Bar command turns the status bar display on and off. The File DOS Commands results in the DOS Commands dialog box, from which you can run DOS commands such as* **dir***. Pressing F1 or using the Help menu accesses Word's Help system. The File Exit Word command terminates Word; choosing the <No> button when asked if the changes should be saved abandons any changes you made.*

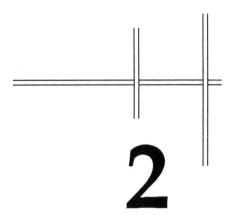

2

Your First File

By now you should have a fairly good idea how Word looks on screen and how to control its menus and choose commands. In this chapter, you'll learn more about entering and editing text. You'll also learn to save your text as a file and reopen it later for more editing. In the process, you'll learn to use more complex dialog boxes.

Once you start using files, you'll probably want to tailor your screen a bit to suit your own working style. You can control the screen appearance and some Word features using the commands covered in this chapter. In particular, you'll learn how to:

- Use the keyboard and mouse to move the cursor in the document window
- Insert and delete characters
- Use both insert and overtype mode while editing text
- Insert a nonbreak space to prevent word wrap
- Save new and existing files
- Use the Edit Repeat command to repeat text
- Use complex dialog boxes
- Change to a different directory within Word
- Open and close files
- Control the screen appearance with the View Preferences command
- Customize Word features work with the Utilities Customize command

Moving the Cursor in the Document Window

Whenever you type text into the document window, it appears at the cursor. So in order to use the document window effectively, you must be able to move the cursor quickly and efficiently. You can use keyboard keys to do this at any time. If you have a mouse, you can use it as well. In order to practice moving the cursor, you will need a fair amount of text in your window to work with.

1. Start up Word.
2. Type **Practice Paragraph** on the the first line and press ⏎ twice.
3. Type four or five lines of text, allowing wordwrap to occur. Then press ⏎ to end the paragraph.

The cursor is on a new line following the end of the paragraph. Now you have some text to practice moving the cursor in. To move the cursor on the screen with the mouse, just click where you want the cursor to be.

4. If you have a mouse, point to any character in the first line of the longer paragraph and click with the left button. Notice that the cursor is now positioned where you clicked.
5. If you have a mouse, point to the last character in the paragraph and click.

Using the Arrow Keys

Whether or not you have a mouse, you'll use the keyboard keys to move the cursor a great deal of the time. They're more convenient than the mouse when you are using the keyboard to type text. Table 2.1 lists the cursor movement keys and their effects. They are all explained in the following sections.

Your keyboard includes four arrow keys, one pointing up (↑), one down (↓), one left (←), and one right (→). In fact, it may have two sets of arrow keys. If you have only one set, they are on the numeric keypad; you'll have to turn NumLock off to use the arrow keys.

1. If your keyboard has only one set of arrow keys and your status bar shows NL, press NumLock. The NL indicator disappears from the status bar and the arrow keys will work.

By pressing the appropriate arrow key, you can move the cursor one line up or down or one character to the right or left. When you press ↑ or ↓, the cursor moves up or down, but it stays in the same horizontal location if

Table 2.1. Moving the Cursor with the Keyboard

←	Left one character
→	Right one character
↑	Up one line
↓	Down one line
Ctrl+←	Left to start of current or previous word
Ctrl+→	Right to start of next word
Ctrl+↑	To start of current or previous paragraph
Ctrl+↓	To start of next paragraph
Home	To start of current line
End	To end of current line
Ctrl+Home	To start of document
Ctrl+End	To end of document
PgUp	Scroll up one window
PgDown	Scroll down one window
Ctrl+PgUp	Cursor to first line of window
Ctrl+PgDown	Cursor to last line of window

possible. A line that ends to the left of the former original cursor location causes the cursor to jump to the end of the shorter line. It moves back to its original position when you move the cursor into a longer line.

When you move the cursor, it follows the text. When you press → or ←, the cursor may wrap to the next or previous line, even continuing to the next or previous paragraph. If you try to move the cursor beyond the existing text using any arrow key, you'll hear a warning beep. You won't be able to move the cursor before the first character in the document or after the last.

Tip If the character 4 appears in your file when you press ←, press the Backspace key to remove it. Then press the NumLock key and try again.

1. Press ← to move the cursor into the paragraph.
2. Press ↑ three times. Watch the cursor move.
3. Press → ten times.
4. Press ↓ three times.
5. Press ↑ five times.
6. Press ← six times.
7. Use the arrow keys some more to move the cursor around the document.
8. Use the arrow keys to move the cursor to the very first character in the document.

Moving to Either End of a Line

You can move the cursor quickly to the beginning or end of the current line by pressing the Home or End key. Home moves the cursor to the start of the line it is in. End moves the cursor to the rightmost end of the line.

1. Press End. Notice that the cursor is at the end of the line.
2. Press ↓ three times. Notice the path the cursor takes as it moves down through the text.
3. Press Home. Notice that the cursor is at the beginning of the line.
4. Move the cursor some more and try Home and End again if you like.

Moving the Cursor by Word

You'll frequently want to move to the beginning of the next or previous word. (According to Word, a *word* is a set of characters surrounded by spaces or punctuation marks. It can also be a single character, such as the paragraph indicator produced when you press ↵; you may not see it on the screen.)

To jump the cursor to the beginning of a word, combine the control key with the appropriate arrow key. Pressing Ctrl+→ jumps the cursor to the beginning of the next word. Pressing Ctrl+← jumps the cursor to the beginning of the previous (or current) word. For example, suppose the cursor is under the first *r* in *cursor* in the previous line. If you press Ctrl+→, the cursor moves to the *i* in *is*. If the cursor is back at that *r* in *cursor* and you press Ctrl+←, the cursor jumps to the first character in *cursor*.

Moving the cursor by word doesn't cause a beep at the beginning or end of the document; that effect occurs only with the simple arrow keys.

1. Use the arrow keys to place the cursor under the *g* in *Paragraph* on the first line of the document.
2. Press Ctrl+← to jump the cursor to the first letter in the word.
3. Press Ctrl+← to jump the cursor to the first letter of the previous word.
4. Press Ctrl+→ to jump the cursor to the first letter of the next word.
5. Jump the cursor by word several times in each direction.

Moving the Cursor by Paragraph

You can also jump the cursor by paragraph using the Control key with the other arrow keys. Word defines a *paragraph* as any string of characters that ends with ⏎. If you press ⏎ three times in a row, you have ended three paragraphs.

When you press Ctrl+↓, the cursor jumps to the first character of the next paragraph, just past where you pressed ⏎. When you press Ctrl+↑, the cursor jumps to the first character of the current (or previous) paragraph.

1. Press Ctrl+↑ to jump the cursor to the beginning of the first paragraph of the document. (You may have to press it several times.)
2. Press Ctrl+↓ repeatedly to see the cursor jump to the beginning of each paragraph. Leave the cursor at the very end of the document.

Repeating Text

So far, all the text in your document is displayed on the screen at once, so you've been moving the cursor on the screen. You'll need a longer document in order to see some more effects. The usual way of getting text into a document is to type it. You can repeat your typing by choosing the Edit Repeat (Alt,E,R) command; you can use the Edit menu or press F4. The Edit Repeat command repeats the last command or the last text you typed since a command was used. You can use the Delete and Backspace keys as you type without interrupting the text that will be repeated.

Suppose you need to use a particular paragraph at four different places in your document. Just type it once, then move the cursor to the new location and choose the Edit Repeat command to copy it. You can move the cursor to the next location, then use Edit Repeat again, as many times as necessary.

1. If the cursor isn't at the very end of your document, move it there using the mouse or arrow keys.
2. Press ⏎, type **Practice Text** on a new line, then press ⏎ twice.
3. Type text that extends over eight to ten lines, then press ⏎ to end the paragraph. Don't make any corrections other than pressing Backspace until the paragraph is finished.
4. Choose the Edit Repeat command (Alt,E,R or F4). At this point, the cursor is at the end of your document.
5. Use the arrow keys to examine the entire document, then move the cursor back to the very end of the document.
6. Choose Edit Repeat four more times. The cursor is still at the end of your document, but the document now contains seven headings and seven paragraphs.

Scrolling by Line

The arrow keys let you scroll text on the screen as well as move the cursor by line. When you scroll, the cursor stays in (approximately) the same position on the screen, but the lines of text themselves move. To cause the arrow keys to scroll rather than move the cursor, you have to turn on ScrollLock. When you press ScrollLock, no indicator appears in the status bar, but you see the effect on the screen.

1. Move the cursor up into your document, about ten lines from the end.
2. Press ↑ and see the cursor move up one line.
3. Press the ScrollLock key once.
4. Press ↑ and see the lines move. The cursor stays in the same line on the screen.
5. Press ScrollLock again to restore normal arrow key function.

Scrolling by Page

Your computer's PgUp and PgDown keys scroll by page. The cursor moves to an approximately corresponding position in the next window of information. When you press PgUp, you'll see the previous page in your document—toward the beginning. When you press PgDown, you see the next page in your document—toward the end. You can page through the entire document using these keys.

1. Press PgUp repeatedly until you see the beginning of your document.
2. Press PgDown repeatedly until you see a row of dots across the screen.

A row of spaced dots across the screen shows you where Word will start a new page when you print the document. The page break makes no difference to your typing. The arrow keys and other cursor movement keys just ignore the page breaks. But the Pg indicator in the status line shows the number of the current page. When you insert or delete text, Word rearranges page breaks automatically.

3. If your status bar shows Pg1 at the left edge, move your cursor down past the page break until the status bar shows Pg2. If your status bar shows Pg2 at the left edge, move the cursor up past the page break until the status bar shows Pg1.
4. Press PgDown again until you see the very end of the document.

Moving the Cursor to the First or Last Line of the Window

On the screen, you see the part of the document that fits in one window. You can move the cursor directly to the beginning of the first or last line displayed in the current window. To move it to the upper-left corner of the window, press Ctrl+PgUp. The cursor is immediately positioned at the beginning of the first line of text in the document window. To move the cursor to the lower-left corner, press Ctrl+PgDown; this places the cursor at the beginning of the last line of text.

1. Press PgUp to display an entire window of text. Notice where the cursor is located.
2. Press Ctrl+PgUp. Notice that the cursor is at the first character in the first line of the window.
3. Press Ctrl+PgDown. Notice that the cursor is at the first character of the last line of the window.

Moving the Cursor to Either End of the Document

You'll frequently want to move the cursor directly to the beginning or the end of the document. You can do this by combining the control key with the Home or End key. Pressing Ctrl+Home moves the cursor directly to the first character in the document. Pressing Ctrl+End moves it directly to the last character in the document.

1. Press Ctrl+Home. Notice that the cursor is at the very beginning of the document.
2. Press Ctrl+End. Notice that the cursor is at the very end of the document.

1. If you don't have a document in your window, create one by typing a paragraph. Then use the Edit Repeat command to insert the paragraph four or five times. This Self-Check expects you to use the keyboard combinations to move the cursor.
2. Move the cursor to the beginning of the current window. Then move it to the beginning of the document.
3. Move the cursor to the end of the current window. Then move it to the end of the document.
4. Move the cursor three paragraphs toward the start of the document.

5. Move the cursor by word through the first line, then jump to the beginning of the next paragraph.
6. Move the cursor to the previous window.
7. Move the cursor to the beginning of the document.

Refer to Table 2.1 if you have trouble with these cursor movements. The more you use them, the more likely you are to remember the key combinations.

Using the Mouse

If you have a mouse, it's easy to move the cursor to a location shown in the displayed document window. Just point to where you want the cursor to appear and click the left button; the cursor jumps to that position.

Using Scroll Bars. To move the cursor to a part of the document that isn't on the screen, use the *scroll bars*. Your screen shows a vertical and a horizontal scroll bar. Which one is more useful depends on the document's margins and how you are viewing it. You'll learn to control these factors as you continue.

If you click on the single-headed arrow at either end of either scroll bar, the screen scrolls one line in the indicated direction. Clicking on the single-headed up arrow at the top of the vertical scroll bar, for example, scrolls the document so that one more line appears at the top of the window and one fewer at the bottom.

If you hold the left button down while pointing to either arrowhead, the text scrolls continuously in the indicated direction. The cursor moves with the line it is in. If it scrolls off screen, you can point to the displayed character where you want it to be and click.

Using the Scroll Box. Notice the dark rectangle (called the *scroll box*) in the scroll bar. The position of the scroll box on the scroll bar indicates the approximate position of the displayed window of text in the entire document. For example, if the scroll box is at the very top (just below the up arrow), the displayed text is at or near the beginning of the document. If the scroll box is at the very bottom (just above the down arrow), the displayed text is at or near the end of the document. If the scroll box is two-thirds of the way down, the displayed text is about two-thirds of the way through the file.

To scroll vertically in larger increments than just a line, click on the scroll bar above or below the scroll box. This is similar to using the PgUp and PgDown keys. Clicking above the scroll box displays about a window earlier. Clicking below it displays about a window later. Holding the mouse button down causes a continuous scroll by window. If the scroll box passes the cursor location, it may stop, depending on where you are in the scroll bar.

You can move through a file using the scroll bar even more quickly if you drag the scroll box. Just point to the scroll box, hold down the left button, and move the pointer in the direction you want to go. If you drag the scroll box to the very top of the scroll bar, you see the first window of text in the document.

Scrolling horizontally is similar; click in corresponding positions on the horizontal scroll bar to scroll sideways in increments. This scroll box can be dragged as well.

Positioning the Cursor. After you scroll using the scroll bar, you may want to make sure the cursor is still on the screen. If it isn't, click in the window to place the cursor. If you don't, pressing one of the keyboard cursor or scrolling keys may have an effect you don't expect. For example, if you drag the scroll box to the bottom of the scroll bar, then press ↑ or PgUp, the cursor movement is based on where the cursor was before you dragged the scroll box.

1. Drag the scroll box to the very top of your current document, then click in the window to position the cursor.
2. Click once below the scroll box.
3. Point to the down arrow at the bottom of the scroll bar, then hold the button down to cause continuous line scrollling until the cursor is out of sight.
4. Press ↑ to see the effect.
5. Drag the scroll box to the center of the scroll bar, then position the cursor.

Tip ‖ This Self-Check lets you practice using the mouse to move through a document. Don't bother with it if you don't have a mouse.

1. Make sure you have a reasonably long document in your window, then scroll to the top of the document and position the cursor at the first character.
2. Scroll down about a window.
3. Scroll to the very end of the document by dragging the scroll box.
4. Scroll continuously all the way to the beginning of the document line by line. Then position the cursor near the beginning.

5. Scroll continuously toward the end of the document by window. Then position the cursor in the last paragraph.

To move directly to a position in the file, drag the scroll box. To move continuously by line, click and hold the button on the arrowhead at the end of the scroll bar. To move continuously by window, click and hold the button on the scroll bar above or below the scroll box. If this doesn't seem to work, point to a spot farther from the scroll box.

Simple Text Editing

Now that you can move through a document and place the cursor wherever you want it, you are ready to start editing documents. The simplest form of editing is using the Backspace key to remove errors as you type. Often, however, you don't catch errors as soon as they are made or you change your mind later. The next level of editing involves changing text. In this section you'll see how to delete characters using either the Delete or Backspace key. You'll also learn to insert or replace characters, depending on the current editing mode.

Deleting Characters

To delete the character at the cursor, just press the Delete key. That character disappears and the character to the right slides over to its position. If you hold down the Delete key, characters are deleted as they slide into the cursor position. You can remove whole words, sentences, and paragraphs by holding down Delete.

To delete the character to the left of the cursor, press the Backspace key. The cursor slides to the left and removes the character there. If you hold down the Backspace key, the cursor continues sliding to the left and removing characters. As with the Delete key, you can remove whole strings of characters with the Backspace key.

When you remove characters with either Delete or Backspace, they are gone for good. You can recover the very last character with Edit Undo (covered later in this chapter), but if you want the other characters back, you'll have to type them again.

1. Place the cursor at the beginning of the fourth word in the first line of the second paragraph of your document. (Use Ctrl+Home to get to the beginning of the document, Ctrl+↓ to get to the beginning of the second paragraph, and Ctrl+→ three times to get to the beginning of the fourth word.)
2. Press the Delete key as often as necessary to remove that word and the following space.
3. Press the Backspace key as often as necessary to remove the word to the left.
4. Move the cursor down one line and delete the word containing (or in front of) the cursor.
5. Delete several more words, using both Backspace and Delete.

Insert and Overtype Mode

Normally, Word is in *insert* mode. That means you can insert characters by just positioning the cursor and typing. Existing characters are pushed to the right and the paragraph is reformatted automatically.

Sometimes you will want to replace characters as you type. To do this, you turn off insert mode to establish overtype mode. When *overtype* mode is in effect, the letters OT appear in the status bar. Then you can position the cursor and type, and your new characters overlay the existing ones. The replaced characters are gone.

While you are in overtype mode, you can move the cursor just as in insert mode. You can use the Delete key as usual. But you can't use the Backspace key while in overtype mode. Word will beep if you try. If you must use Backspace, first return to insert mode.

You can switch between insert and overtype mode very easily by pressing the Insert key on your keyboard. Pressing Alt+F6 also changes from one mode to the other.

1. Position the cursor at the beginning of any word and type **This text is being inserted**. Notice that the existing characters are pushed to the right.
2. Press Insert. Notice the letters OT that appear in your status bar.
3. Move the cursor to the beginning of a word in a different line and type your name. Notice that the existing characters were replaced, not shoved over to the right.
4. Try Backspace. Notice the beep.
5. Press Insert again to restore insert mode.

You can use insert and overtype modes to make corrections to a document at any time.

Nonbreak Space

As you type text into a document, Word automatically performs wordwrap at the end of each line. Sometimes you want to prevent this. For example, you might not want to break a line in the middle of a phrase like "Henry VIII" or in the middle of number that contains spaces, such as "444 555 1234". If you put a normal space in either case, Word feels free to break a line there.

To enter what is called a nonbreak space, hold down both the control key and the shift key while you press the spacebar. If you type the characters 444Ctrl+Shift+Spacebar555Ctrl+Shift+Spacebar1234 the value will appear all on the same line. If it doesn't fit on the first line, the entire value is moved to the next line. The nonbreak space looks the same on screen as the normal space, unless you tailor the screen. You'll see how to do that later in this chapter.

1. If you don't have a document in your window, type a paragraph of at least eight lines before continuing.
2. Delete the fourth word on the fifth line.
3. Insert the word **introspection** at that point.
4. Move the cursor up one line, then overtype a word with another of the same length.
5. Move the cursor to the end of a line and remove the space separating the two words. Then insert a nonbreak space there.
6. Insert the phrase (**according to rumor**) in the middle of a paragraph.

The Delete and Backspace keys remove characters from the window. Use the Insert key to turn overtype mode on and off. To insert a nonbreak space, make sure you are not in overtype mode, then press Ctrl+Shift+Spacebar.

Saving a File

In order to get much use out of any word processor, you have to be able to store files on disk and use them again. When you save a file for the first time, you must supply a name for it. Word might ask for additional information as well. Once a file has a name, you can save it again easily. Or you can save it with a new name to provide another version of the file.

File names are limited to eight characters, consisting of letters, numbers, and a few punctuation characters. They can also include a three-character extension, connected to the basic file name with a period. By default, Word uses the extension DOC; any time you don't supply an extension, Word expects to use DOC. To use a different extension, type it as part of the file name. In most cases, just omit both the period and the extension while in Word.

The File Save As Command

When you save a file that doesn't yet have a name, Word asks for the name and initial information. You can do this for a new file (when the window shows Document1) by choosing either the File Save or File Save As command. If you want to save a copy of an existing file with a new name, choose the File Save As command. The effect is the same. Choosing Alt+F2 is the same as choosing the File Save As command.

If you look at the File menu, you'll see that the File Save command is not followed by three dots; it doesn't normally ask for additional information. If you choose it for an unnamed file, however, Word assumes you really want the File Save As command and gives you the dialog box shown in Figure 2.1.

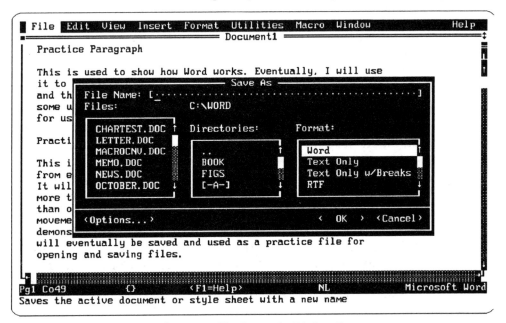

Figure 2.1. The File Save As Dialog Box

Tip This is the first really complex dialog box you've seen. Be sure to read the explanation of how to move around in it.

1. Choose the File Save As command (Alt,F,A or Alt+F2).

Each field in a dialog box can be made active. With the mouse, just point to the field you want and click. With the keyboard, you can use Tab to move from one field to another; use Shift+Tab to move backwards through the fields. Or you can hold down the Alt key and press the highlighted letter in the field name. The letter highlights don't show up in the figure, but they'll be clear on your screen.

Dialog Box. The File Save As dialog box lets you enter the name under which you want to save the file. If the file already existed, the former name (and complete path) appears in the **File Name** field. You type the name you want to use here, including a path if appropriate. The square brackets show you how long the value can be. If you don't include an extension, Word uses DOC.

The central part of this dialog box contains three list boxes. You can click on the list box you want, or use Tab or the Alt key to activate each in turn. Each of these list boxes can be scrolled independently, and you can select any option from within each box. Notice that each has a vertical scroll bar on the right for use with a mouse. You'll use the arrow keys after the field is activated with the keyboard.

The rightmost box shows values for the **Format** field, which determine how the file is stored on disk. To save a file in Word format, leave the first option (Word) selected. You'll learn to use the other options in Chapter 4.

The leftmost list box shows the DOC files that are already stored on the current directory. You can check them out to see what files are there, but don't choose an existing file name as a value for the **Files** field. If you do, you'll see a dialog box like the one in Figure 2.2. Only one file can have a particular name at a time. You'll see the same message if you type an existing file name in the **File Name** field. If you choose <OK>, the existing file is deleted and the name is given to the current document.

The list box in the center shows the available directories. You need to know a bit about directories and paths to use this effectively. (See Appendix C.) The current directory path is shown above the **Directories** field name. You can change the current directory by clicking on the appropriate drive or directory in the list box. Unless you are in the root directory, the top entry is shown as two periods (..), which indicates the parent (or one level up) of the current directory. As you change the directory in the **Directories** list box, the values shown in the **Files** list box change accordingly.

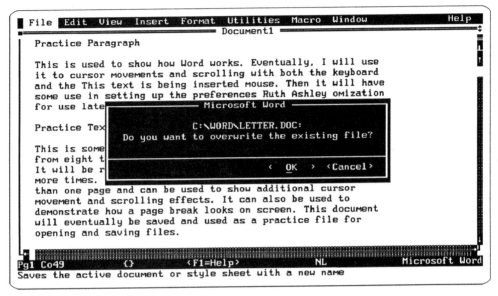

Figure 2.2. Result of Choosing an Existing File Name

2. Tab to or click on the **Files** field and examine what files are already in the current directory.
3. Press Shift+Tab or click on the **File Name** field, then type **prac2**.

Changing the Directory. The <Options> button lets you change the default path for storing files, either for this save operation or as the permanent default.

4. Choose the <Options> button. (Click on it or press Alt+O.)

You can select the directory to use, check the **Always Use as Default** field if you wish, then choose <OK> to return to the standard File Save As dialog box. When you choose <OK> on that box, you may be prompted for additional information you might use to identify the file.

5. Choose <OK> to return to the other dialog box.
6. Choose <OK> to accept the File Save As dialog box.

Summary Information. Your version of Word is probably set up to ask for summary information when a new file is first stored on disk. When summary information prompting is in effect, Word prompts you with the Summary Information dialog box, like the one shown in Figure 2.3, when a new file is established. Later in this chapter, you'll see how you can tell Word to ask for information or to skip it.

You can type a title for the file, the author, and any other information you want. Once the file has a name, it appears in the top border of the box. The date the file was created and last saved show in the lower two fields automatically, even if you don't provide any more information.

7. Type a title for the file, such as **Practice for Chapter 2**. Press Tab or click in the next field.
8. Type your name. Then add any other information you want.
9. Choose the <OK> button.

Once you choose <OK> on this box, the file is saved with the name you provided. You'll return to the document window. Now the name you supplied appears in the top border of the document window, replacing Document1, which appeared before. Later in this book, you'll learn to review and edit summary information as well as to print it.

Saving an Existing File

Once a file has a name and you have established any summary information, you can save it easily. Just choose the File Save (Alt,F,S) command or press

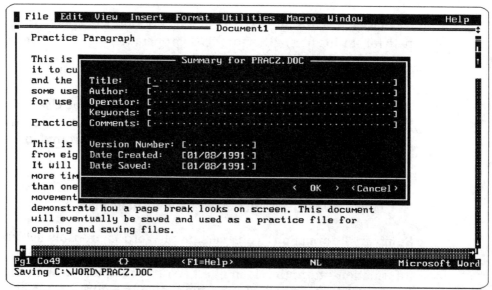

Figure 2.3. The Summary Information Dialog Box

Shift+F12. If your keyboard has only 10 function keys, press Alt+Shift+F2 to save an existing file.

1. Choose the File Save command. Notice the message bar.
2. Move the cursor to a new line.

While the file is being saved, Word displays its full name in the message bar, telling you the file is being saved. Once you do anything to the screen, the message disappears. You can continue to edit the file, since it remains in the current window.

When Word saves an existing file, it actually renames the previously saved version with the extension BAK. The file in its current form is then saved with extension DOC (or another if it was supplied). So your directory always has the current and the previous versions. If, God forbid, your DOC file is destroyed, you can rename your BAK file and recover a great deal of the data. We'll cover renaming in Chapter 7.

Tip   Save your files often. You'll see later in this chapter how to have Word save automatically, but nothing gives you peace of mind like knowing for sure that your file on disk is secure.

Closing Files

The File menu lets you choose File Close to close the current window without leaving Word. When you close a file, you may see other windows under it. We'll cover working with multiple documents in Chapter 6.

If you choose the File Close command or the File Exit Word command when changes have been made to the file since saving it, you'll be asked if you want the changes saved. The File Exit Word command automatically closes any open files.

1. Insert a word at the cursor.
2. Choose the File Exit Word command.
3. In the resulting dialog box, choose <Yes>.

To cause a save during closing or exiting, just choose <Yes> when the dialog box asks you if you want the changes saved. The save is performed, then your other request (close or exit) is processed.

1. Start up Word.
2. Type a sentence into the document.

3. Choose File Close.
4. Type **CHAP2** to use the file name CHAP2.DOC.
5. Choose <OK>.

When all the files and windows are closed, you'll see a screen that looks like the one in Figure 2.4. There is no document window (notice that there is no border) and there are fewer menus. Only some of the commands are available at this time. You can still exit Word or open a file, however.

6. Choose File Exit Word.

1. Start up Word and type three lines into a new file.
2. Save the document as a file named MYFILE.DOC. Provide some summary information when asked.
3. Add a few words to the file, then save it again.
4. Add a few more words, then terminate Word. When asked, have Word save the changes.

The File Save or File Save As command will let you save the file the first time. File Save will do it the second time. Choose File Exit Word and choose <Yes> to save the changes.

Opening a File

When you use Word, you always want to work with a document. That document is usually in, or will be in, a file. So far, you have opened Word and worked with the default document, named Document1. When you were finished, you saved it with a file name. (Earlier in this chapter, you saved files as PRAC2.DOC and MYFILE.DOC.) In this section, you'll see how to open files and create new files.

Starting Word with a File Open

You can start Word with a file open by providing the file name in your Word command. For example, suppose you have a file named JANREPT.DOC. If

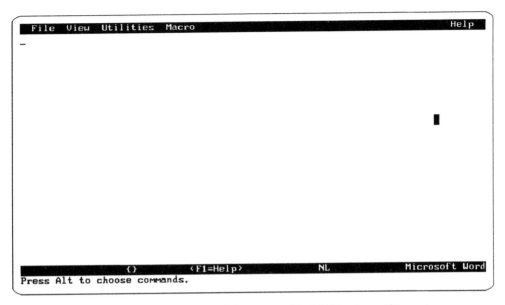

```
 File  View  Utilities  Macro                                    Help
 ▬




                                              ▮




         {}            ‹F1=Help›            NL        Microsoft Word
 Press Alt to choose commands.
```

Figure 2.4. Word Screen with All Windows Closed

you start Word with the command **word janrept**, Word is started as usual and the file JANREPT.DOC is automatically opened. (Remember that Word supplies the DOC extension if you don't provide a different one.) When an existing file is opened, the cursor is always at the first character in the file.

1. At the DOS prompt, type **word prac2**. (If you didn't save PRAC2, type **word readme** to see a supplied file.)
2. When the file appears on your screen, choose the File Exit Word command to leave Word.

You can supply a path with the file name if necessary. For example, to edit an existing file named FEBREPT.DOC in the \REPORTS directory, you would type **word \reports\febrept** at the prompt.

Tip || Remember that DOS doesn't care whether you use uppercase, lowercase, or a combination of both.

You can use this method to create a new file as well. Just type a new file name in the command to start up Word.

1. At the DOS prompt, type **word new2**. You'll see a dialog box that asks if you really want to start a new file.

2. When the dialog box appears on your screen, choose the <OK> button.

The resulting Word screen will look just as before, except the document window will have the file name you used (**NEW2.DOC**) in the top border instead of Document1. When you first save this file, you'll be prompted for summary information, but you won't have to supply the name again.

3. Type your mailing address on three or four lines.
4. Choose the File Save command.
5. Type in some summary information and choose <OK>.
6. Choose the File Exit Word command.

Opening a File Later

If you prefer to start up Word in the usual way (by just typing **word** at the DOS prompt), you can open a file from within it. Just choose the File Open command (Alt,F,O). You can press Ctrl+F12 if you prefer. If your keyboard doesn't have twelve function keys, you can press Alt+Ctrl+F2 to open a file. No matter which approach you use, you'll next see the File Open dialog box, shown in Figure 2.5.

1. At the DOS prompt, type **word**.
2. When the standard Word screen appears, choose the File Open command.

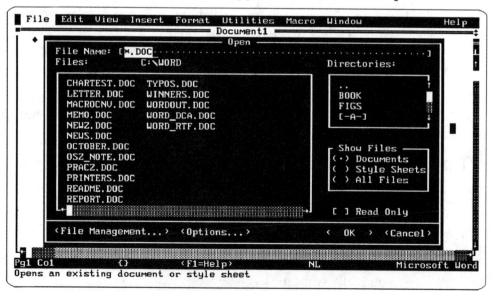

Figure 2.5. The File Open Dialog Box

Tip || This dialog box contains some features you haven't seen before. Be sure to read the details on how to use it.

File Open Dialog Box

The File Open dialog box lets you type a file name, with path if appropriate, or select a file from the current drive and directory. You can even change the drive and directory, much as in the File Save As dialog box.

To open a file, just type the name in the **File Name** text box. If the file extension is DOC, omit the period and extension; Word will supply them. Notice that the default value is *.DOC; it disappears if you start typing anything. To select a file from the **Files** list box, you can double-click on it with the mouse; that selects the file and chooses <OK> in one step. To move to the list box using the keyboard, press Alt+F or Tab to it. When the first file name in the box is highlighted, you can use the arrow keys to highlight the file name you want. Then press ↵ or choose the <OK> button to select it. Notice that this list box has a horizontal scroll bar at the bottom instead of a vertical scroll bar on the right. The list is shown horizontally; if you can't see all the file names, just use the scroll bar to see the rest. Of course, you can use Home, End, PgUp, and PgDown as well as the standard arrow keys to move around in the box.

1. Choose the **Files** list box.
2. Use ↓ to highlight **new2**, then press ↵ or else click on **new2**.

To change to a different directory, select the **Directories** list box (with the mouse, the Tab key, or Alt+D), then use the arrow keys or mouse to select the directory or drive you want. Press ↵ or choose <OK> to change to that directory or drive. The contents of the **Files** list box changes when you change the selection in the **Directories** list box.

The **Show Files** box controls which files are listed in the **Files** list box. This group of fields is an example of what are often called *radio buttons*; they are indicated with parentheses and only one of the group can be on at a time. A dot appears in the parentheses of the current value. You can tab to the group, then use the arrow keys to move the indicator (a bullet) from one button to the next. If you turn on a radio button by clicking or pressing Alt+letter, any other button in the group is automatically turned off.

The **Show Files** group offers you three choices. The default field is **Documents**; all file names with extension DOC are listed. This is the best reason for letting Word supply the DOC extension for your files. The **Style Sheets** button causes only files with extension STY to be listed; Chapter 9 covers these. The

All Files button causes all files in the directory to be listed; this will show you files that have different extensions.

3. Click on the **All Files** field or press Alt+A to turn it on. Notice the change in contents of the **Files** list box.
4. Turn on the **Document** field by clicking, pressing ↑ twice, or pressing Alt+D. The file list is restored to only DOC files.

The **Read Only** field is an example of a *check box*. It is indicated by square brackets. Each check box is independent and can be either on or off. When it is turned on, an X appears in the brackets. When it is off, a space appears there. You can turn a check box on or off with the mouse by clicking on it. With the keyboard, you must select the field by tabbing to it or pressing Alt+letter. Once the field is selected, press the spacebar to toggle the X. If you turn the **Read Only** field on, the file will be opened as read only; you won't be able to edit it. This protects the file from inadvertent changes.

File Open Options

The <Options> button on the File Open dialog box has the same effect as the similar button in the File Save As dialog box.

5. Choose the <Options> button. Examine the new dialog box.

This dialog box lets you change the default directory for this operation or for permanent use. When you start up Word, the default directory is the one you entered from. You can change the current directory by typing the new path or using a **Directories** list box to select it. To convert that directory to the default, turn on the **Always Use as Default** check box to cause the change to be permanent.

6. Choose <Cancel> to remove the dialog box. (Remember you can press the Escape key to remove it.)

File Management

The File Open dialog box includes a <File Management> button. Pressing this button brings you to the File Management dialog box, with extensive features for managing files. We'll covers those features in detail in Chapter 7. For now, if you get the File Management dialog box, just choose the <Close> button or press Esc to get rid of it.

Once the File Open dialog box is set up as you want it, choose OK to open the file. It appears on your screen in a document window of its own.

7. Choose <OK> to open the file.
8. Choose the File Exit Word command to return to the DOS prompt.

1. Open the file named MYOWN.DOC from the DOS prompt. If you didn't save this one, open a file you created.
2. Add a line or two of text to the file, then save it and exit Word.
3. Create a new Word file named MYNEW.DOC from the DOS prompt.
4. Add a few lines to the file, then exit Word and abandon this file.
5. Start up Word as usual, then open the file PRAC2.DOC using the File Open command.
6. Add a few lines, then save and close the file.
7. Open the MYOWN.DOC file, add a word or line, then save it and exit Word.

To open a file while starting Word, type the file name following **Word** *at the DOS prompt; you can omit the DOC extension. To use the File Open command, just choose the command and type or select the file name.*

Tailoring the Screen

So far, you've been working with default screen features. In this section, you'll see how you can change the way it looks by adding elements to the screen or removing them. Some of these features you've already seen.

1. Start up Word and open PRAC2.DOC.

The Ruler and the Ribbon

The View menu lets you turn the ribbon, the ruler, and the status bar on or off. Figure 2.6 shows a screen on which all three are displayed. You've already

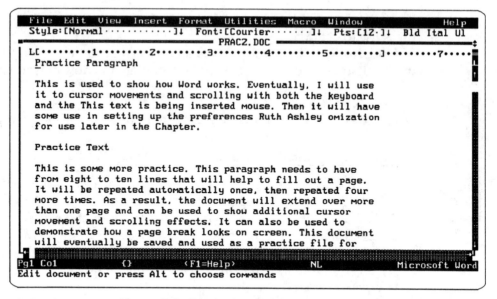

```
 File  Edit  View  Insert  Format  Utilities  Macro  Window              Help
 Style:[Normal···········]↓  Font:[Courier·······]↓  Pts:[12·]↓  Bld Ital Ul
═══════════════════════════════ PRAC2.DOC ═══════════════════════════════
L[········1········2········3········4········5········]·········7····
  Practice Paragraph

  This is used to show how Word works. Eventually, I will use
  it to cursor movements and scrolling with both the keyboard
  and the This text is being inserted mouse. Then it will have
  some use in setting up the preferences Ruth Ashley omization
  for use later in the Chapter.

  Practice Text

  This is some more practice. This paragraph needs to have
  from eight to ten lines that will help to fill out a page.
  It will be repeated automatically once, then repeated four
  more times. As a result, the document will extend over more
  than one page and can be used to show additional cursor
  movement and scrolling effects. It can also be used to
  demonstrate how a page break looks on screen. This document
  will eventually be saved and used as a practice file for

Pg1 Col                 {}          <F1=Help>              NL         Microsoft Word
Edit document or press Alt to choose commands
```

Figure 2.6. Displaying the Ribbon and Ruler

seen how to turn off the status bar by choosing the View Status Bar command. The View Ribbon and View Ruler commands let you turn the ribbon and ruler on and off. With the mouse, you can turn them off and on by clicking on the ruler/ribbon icon (⊥) just above the up arrow on the vertical scroll bar. Use the left button (the usual one) for the ruler and the right button for the ribbon.

The Ruler. The ruler appears just below the top border of the document window. It provides characters that show the positions of characters in that window. A dot appears at each character location. Numbers 1, 2, and 3 indicate the tenth, twentieth, and thirtieth position. The left square bracket ([) indicates left edge of the current paragraph; it's in position 1 in the figure. The right square bracket (]) indicates the right margin or indentation of the current paragraph; it's in position 60 in the figure.

Other settings can also be shown in the ruler; you'll learn to use some of them as you continue.

2. Choose the View Ruler command. Notice how it looks.
3. Choose View Ruler again to turn it off.
4. If you have a mouse, click on the ruler/ribbon icon with your left (usual) button. Click again to turn the ruler off.

You probably won't need to use the ruler just yet, since you are working with default margins. However, feel free to leave it on if you like.

The Ribbon. The ribbon provides a quick way to do formatting of characters and paragraphs in your document. It appears just below the menu bar, above the document window. In Chapter 5, you'll learn to use many of its features.

5. Choose the View Ribbon command. Notice how it looks.
6. Choose View Ribbon again to turn it off.
7. If you have a mouse, click on the ruler/ribbon icon with your *right* button. Click again to turn the ribbon off.

The View Preferences Command

You may want to change other features about your screen as well. Word can display marks that indicate where the Tab key, the Spacebar, or ↵ was pressed. It also lets you display or hide screen elements such as the message bar, the menu bar and window borders. You can even suppress the scroll bars if you wish. This section covers most of the display features you can control after you choose the View Preferences dialog box, shown in Figure 2.7. The <Customize> button is an alternate route to the Utilities Customize command, covered later in this chapter. It puts into effect any changes you've made in this dialog box before transferring you to the next one.

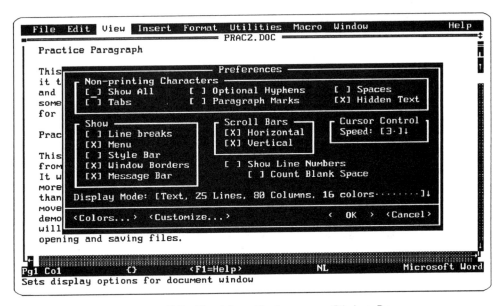

Figure 2.7. The View Preferences Dialog Box

Once you make changes to your viewing preferences here, they stay in effect. If you exit Word, the next time you start up and open a file, the changes will still be in effect. You can make changes again at any time.

1. Choose the View Preferences command (Alt,V,E).

Non-printing Characters. The upper box in the dialog box contains fields for various characters that appear on the screen but don't print. In the **Non-printing Characters** group box are check box fields for various characters you can turn on. By default, the **Hidden Text** field is turned on. We'll cover the use, display, and printing of hidden text in Chapter 5. The use of optional hyphens is covered in Chapter 11.

When the **Spaces** field is turned on, a small dot appears on the screen everywhere you pressed the spacebar. If you use a nonbreak space, a space appears instead of a dot, so you can tell the difference. When the **Paragraph Marks** field is turned on, you'll see a paragraph symbol on the screen at every position where you pressed ↵. When the **Tabs** field is turned on, you'll see a small right-pointing arrow at each point where you pressed Tab.

Figure 2.8 shows two views of the same part of a document. In the upper window, spaces, tabs, and paragraph marks are turned off. You can't tell what keys were pressed where.

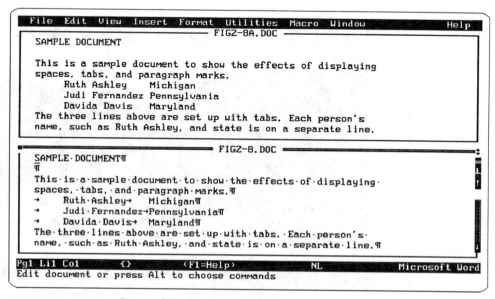

Figure 2.8. Non-printing Characters Display

In the lower window, spaces, tabs, and paragraph marks are turned on. You can see exactly what keys were pressed. Notice that the last line includes a nonbreak space.

You probably won't want to display spaces on a regular basis; they just make the screen too cluttered. Many people find the paragraph and tab marks very useful, however. You can decide, based on your own typing style. You may see these characters in figures as you continue in this book.

1. Choose the View Preferences command, if necessary.
2. Turn on the **Spaces** field, then choose <OK>. Notice the effect in the document.
3. Move the cursor to a space between two words and press delete to remove the space. Then press Ctrl+Shift+Spacebar to insert a nonbreak space. Notice that there is now no dot between those two words.
4. Choose the View Preferences command.
5. Turn off the **Spaces** field, then turn on **Paragraph Marks**.
6. Choose <OK>.

Notice that the dots are gone. Now you can't tell where the nonbreak space was placed. But you can see where each paragraph ends very nicely. A paragraph mark on an otherwise blank line creates a blank line in the document.

1. Move the cursor to the end of the document (Ctrl+End).
2. Type this table, pressing the Tab key before each word on a line:

```
     1        Jane        Blue
     2        Sam         Red
     3        Mike        Black
```

3. Choose the View Preferences command.
4. Turn on **Tabs**. Notice how the tab marks appear in your document.
5. If you want, turn off the paragraph marks and the tabs. You can leave them displayed if you prefer.

What to Show on the Screen. The View Preferences dialog box includes five items that you can check to turn on or off; these are all included in the **Show** group. By default, the **Menu, Window Borders**, and **Message Bar** fields are turned on; you see them in every screen. If you prefer, you can turn these items off to remove them from the screen and show more lines of text. You'll probably want to leave them displayed, however, because they help you use Word effectively. When you are more experienced with Word or just need more lines for text on the screen, you might want to work with these elements turned off.

The **Line Breaks** field is useful when you use a line length that is wider than the screen. While it is turned off, you see all the text on the screen without having to scroll sideways. When this field is turned on, the lines break on screen at the same place they will when printed. That means you can see exactly where each line ends when a document is printed. When it becomes relevant, we'll discuss this field again.

The **Style Bar** shows you what style has been assigned to each paragraph; it appears in the leftmost column of each document window. *Styles* are special formats that you can define and assign to paragraphs. You'll learn to apply styles in Chapter 9. For now, if you turn it on, you'll see an asterisk opposite the first line of each paragraph. We'll discuss the style bar in Chapter 9 as well.

Turning Off the Scroll Bars. The **Scroll Bars** group lets you turn the horizontal and vertical scroll bars on or off. You can tab to the group box, or use Alt+H and Alt+V to toggle these fields. If you don't have a mouse, you might want to get rid of the scroll bars on your screen.

1. Choose the View Preferences command.
2. Click on **Menu** or press Alt+M to turn off the Menu display, then choose <OK>.

Notice that the menu bar is gone! You can restore it temporarily by pressing the Alt key.

3. Press Alt, then choose the View Preferences command again.
4. Turn on the **Menu** bar display by clicking on **Menu** or pressing Alt+M.
5. Turn off the **Window Borders** (Alt+B) and **Message Bar** (Alt+G) fields.
6. Choose <OK>.

Notice that the menu bar is back, but now the message bar and window borders are gone. You can see more lines on the screen now. Let's see the maximum number:

1. Choose the View Preferences command.
2. Turn off the **Menu** field.
3. In the Scroll Bars box, uncheck the **Horizontal** field to remove the bottom scroll bar.
4. Choose <OK>.
5. Choose the View Status Bar command to turn it off.

At this point, your screen has nothing but text from top to bottom. The vertical scroll bar is still on the right edge of the screen. Now restore the screen to its default condition. Feel free to modify these steps to leave the screen set up as you want it.

1. Choose the View Status Bar command to turn it on. (Press Alt first to display the menu bar.)
2. Choose the View Preferences command.
3. Check the **Menu, Window Borders, Message Bar,** and **Horizontal** fields to turn them on.
4. Choose <OK>.

Controlling the Cursor Speed. When you hold down an arrow key, the cursor travels through the text in your document at a particular speed. If you find that speed too fast or too slow, you can modify it in the **Cursor Control Speed** field. Notice that this field has a small down arrow next to it. Clicking on the down arrow or pressing ↓ when the field is selected by tabbing or after pressing Alt+E displays a small list box. You can scroll within it to see the values from 0 through 9. Speed 0 is the slowest and 9 is the fastest. You can set the cursor speed however you want. The default speed is 3.

Displaying the Current Line Number. When you work in Word, the status line by default shows the page number and the column number where the cursor is currently located. You may want to show the line number on the page as well. This helps you tell at a glance where on the page your cursor is. You can tell when you are near the bottom, for example.

The **Show Line Numbers** field lets you specify that the line number will appear in the status line as well. The **Count Blank Space** field causes Word to count lines that occupy the top margin as well.

1. Choose the View Preferences command.
2. Move the cursor to the **Show Line Numbers** field and turn it by clicking or pressing Spacebar.
3. Choose <OK>.

The line number appears as **Li**n, where n gives the line containing the cursor. As you move the cursor, the value changes. If you want the line count to include blank lines preceding text, you turn on the other field as well. Lines containing a paragraph mark do not count as blank lines; they are real.

Setting the Display Mode. The display mode field also has a down arrow following the value; it too has a field menu that you can display by clicking on the down arrow or pressing ↓ when the field is selected by tabbing or pressing Alt+D.

1. Choose the View Preferences command.
2. Drop down the **Display Mode** field menu (click on the field arrow or press Alt+D followed by Alt+↓).

The options available depend on your monitor and what it can display. The general forms of display mode are text and graphics. Other variables are the number of lines, the number of columns, and the number of colors. The choices you have available depend on your system.

The difference between text and graphics mode isn't really apparent yet, except that the mouse pointer is an arrowhead instead of a rectangle. Once you start formatting characters and using more complex layouts and document features, you'll want to use graphics mode occasionally. When you use graphics, the screen response is somewhat slower, but the effects are clearer on the screen. We'll cover using graphics mode later in this book. You can see whether you like the way it looks with more lines if you want.

3. Highlight an option (click or arrow) that wasn't selected originally, then choose <OK>.
4. Examine the result. Then choose View Preferences again.
5. Select the **Display Mode** field by clicking on it or pressing Alt+D.
6. Drop down the field menu by clicking on the arrow or pressing Alt+↓.
7. Select the previous default choice, then choose <OK>.

Colors. If you aren't happy with the colors displayed on your screen, you can choose the <Colors> button in the View Preferences dialog box. This dialog box includes a list box of **Things to Color**, a sample of how that item appears on the screen, and a full color listing showing the colors your screen can produce. You can change the color of the menu bar, for example, of the accelerator keys, or even of the general background or character color. We aren't going to cover this optional feature, but feel free to try it out to see what your screen can do.

1. Turn on the ruler and the ribbon.
2. Turn on the display of spaces, tabs, and paragraph marks. Then examine the screen.
3. Turn on the line count display in the status bar. If it is already on, turn it off.
4. Arrange the screen so that the maximum number of lines of text are displayed. Then examine the screen.

5. Restore the message bar, the menu bar, the status bar, the horizontal scroll bar, and the window borders. Remove the spaces, tabs, and paragraph marks display. Then examine the screen again.
6. Put the screen in graphics display mode if you can. Then restore the default text mode.
7. Set up the screen as you want it.

Use the View menu commands to turn the status bar, ruler, and ribbon off and on. Use the View Preferences commands to do the other tailoring.

Customizing Word

You've seen how you can tailor the Word screen using the View Preferences command. Word also lets you have a bit of control over how it works. You can customize such features as automatic saving, whether Word asks for summary information, and whether the menus show alternate keys. You can change these features by choosing the <Customize> button on the View Preferences dialog box or through the Utilities Customize command. The resulting dialog box is shown in Figure 2.9. Many of these features you haven't heard about so far; we'll cover them at the appropriate points in this book.

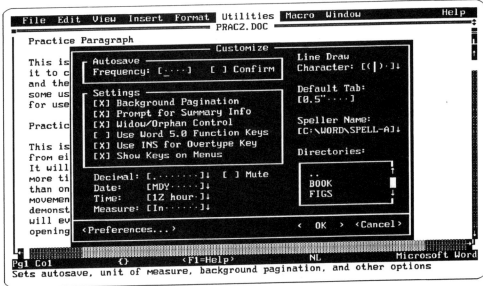

Figure 2.9. The Utilities Customize Dialog Box

When the fields are all as you want them, choose <OK>. To cancel any changes you've made in the dialog box, choose <Cancel>. The <Preferences> button transfers you directly to the View Preferences dialog box; it first processes any changes you've made in this one, so it has the effect of choosing <OK>, then choosing the View Preferences command.

Autosave

Normally, Word doesn't save a file until you tell it to. But you can request that Word save the file at specified intervals so that you can recover it in case of a power interruption or other major problem. If the system goes down while you are using Word, any automatically saved files are present on disk in a special format with extension SVD. The next time you start up Word, it will ask you if you want to recover those files. If you choose <OK>, Word will update the DOC file with the SVD version. You might lose any changes after the last automatic save, but anything before then will be up to date.

When you save a document normally, any SVD files for that file are deleted, so their presence signals to Word that some of your work may have been lost. Once the restoration has been done, you can continue from that point. Be sure to use the File Save command frequently if your system goes down very often.

The first field in the Utilities Customize dialog box is used to set the autosave frequency.

1. Choose the Utilities Customize command (Alt,U,U).

You enter the frequency in minutes; to cause a save every 10 minutes, just type 10 in the **Autosave Frequency** field.

2. Type **5** in the **Autosave Frequency** field.
3. Move to the **Confirm** check box and turn it on.
4. Choose <OK>.

If you turn on the **Confirm** check box, you'll be asked each time the automatic save occurs. (This is very annoying!) Then you have to respond to a dialog box asking you if you want autosave to take effect. Just press ↵ or choose <OK> and the file is saved. Very shortly, you'll see a dialog box asking you to confirm the save. When you do:

5. Choose <OK>.
6. Choose the Utilities Customize command.
7. Change the **Autosave Frequency** field to 15.

8. Uncheck the **Confirm** field.

9. Choose <OK>.

Tip If you want files saved automatically at a different frequency, use Utilities Customize again and set the frequency you want. To prevent autosaves, set the frequency to 0.

Settings

You can establish or change several background settings in the Settings group; these are all check boxes so you can turn any number of them on. When **Background Pagination** is off, Word doesn't show you where page breaks occur in a document until you request it. When **Prompt for Summary Information** is off, Word doesn't automatically display the Summary dialog box when you save a previously unnamed file. **Widow/Orphan Control** affects the location of page breaks; when it is off, most paragraphs can be broken over a page break at any point.

The **Use Word 5.0 Function Keys** field lets you use the function key effects of an earlier version of Word; we aren't dealing with that. Just leave it turned off unless you know the Word 5.0 settings by heart. The **Use INS for Overtype Key** field lets the Insert key work as an overtype toggle. If you turn this field off, the Insert key and several shortcuts using it work as they did in earlier versions of Word. This book assumes it is on; that's the Word 5.5 default.

The **Show Keys on Menus** field controls whether or not shortcuts are displayed on menus. This results in narrower menus, but doesn't save you any time. You'll most likely want to just leave the keys displayed as they are.

1. Look at the Utilities menu. Then choose the Utilities Customize command.
2. Turn off the **Show Keys on Menus** field, then choose <OK>.
3. Look at the Utilities menu again. Then choose the Utilities Customize command again.
4. Turn the **Show Keys on Menus** field on again, then choose <OK>.

Assorted Fields

The Utilities Customize dialog box includes assorted additional fields that you can use to customize your installation of Word. The **Line Draw Character** field (in the upper right) is covered in Chapter 12. The **Speller Name** field is covered in Chapter 11. The **Directories** list box here is associated with the **Speller Name** field.

To select a field, click on it, tab to it, or press Alt+letter. Any field that has a menu (indicated by a down arrow following the value) lets you see the possible values. Just click on the down arrow or press Alt+↓ to see the menu.

Default Tabs. By default, Word has a tab set every 0.5 inches. When you press Tab, a tab character is inserted and the cursor jumps to the next tab setting. In the **Default Tab** field (Alt+F), you can change the default interval by typing the desired interval. If you want tabs to occur every 3/4 inch, for example, type .75 in the field. Any default tabs you've used in the document are adjusted to use the new setting.

The default unit of measurement is inches; you can omit it when you want to use inches. You'll see how to specify other measurements shortly.

1. If your document doesn't contain this table, type it in pressing the Tab key before each word on a line:

   ```
   1      Jane       Blue
   2      Sam        Red
   3      Mike       Black
   ```
2. Choose the Utilities Customize command.
3. Move the cursor to the **Default Tab** field and type **1** to change the tabs to one inch apart.
4. Choose <OK>. Notice the change in the table lines.
5. Choose the Utilities Customize command.
6. Move the cursor to the **Default Tab** field and type **.5** to set the default spacing, then choose <OK>.

The default tab settings affect the entire document or section. In Chapter 10, we'll cover setting individual tabs for separate paragraphs.

Decimal Character. The default decimal character is the period. If you are preparing documents for a country that uses the comma instead, you can change the character in the **Decimal** field (Alt+L). Once you've changed it, the decimal character affects several other commands. We'll review this field when we get to them.

Canceling the Beep. The **Mute** field (Alt+U) lets you turn off the beep. If you check this field, Word will never make a sound. The screen still lets you know if your commands work and whether you are trying to move beyond the document limits. If you are working in a room with other people, however, you might want to turn off the beep by turning on the **Mute** field.

1. Move the cursor to the top line of your document.
2. Choose the Utilities Customize command.
3. Check the **Mute** field. (Click on it or press Alt+U, then press Spacebar.)
4. Choose <OK>.
5. Press ↑ several times. Notice there is no beep!
6. Choose the Utilities Customize command again.
7. Uncheck the **Mute** field, then choose <OK>.

The Date and Time Formats. Word can insert the date and time into your documents; you'll learn how in Chapter 10. The formats of both are controlled by the Utilities Customize command.

The **Date** field (Alt+A) includes a field menu (notice the down arrow) that shows the two formats for the date. By default, system dates are shown in month, day, year order. If you prefer, dates can be shown in year, month, day order. You can select this from the field menu.

The **Time** field (Alt+T) lets you select a 12-hour or 24-hour clock. The default is a 12-hour clock, but if you are working with military, international, or government documents, you may prefer to select 24-hour time from the field menu.

Default Unit of Measurement. Word's default unit of measurement for settings such as tabs, margins, and indents is inches. You may prefer to work in centimeters or even in points or picas. The **Measure** field (Alt+M) menu gives you the choices for the default horizontal measurement. If you change it here, for example to *cm*, any other default values are adjusted. The default tab spacing of 0.5" will be automatically changed to 1.27 cm.

1. Turn off the display of keys on the menus.
2. Set the default tabs at 3/4 inch.
3. Change the autosave frequency to ten minutes.
4. Enter some data into your paragraph using tabs.
5. Restore the features to the way you want them.

All these functions can be handled through the Utilities Customize dialog box. The tab settings here are in regular increments, so tabs are at 3/4 inch, 1.5 inches, and so on.

Exercise

This chapter has covered basic editing of Word documents, along with saving and opening files. In this exercise, you can practice creating, editing, and saving documents.

1. Save any documents and exit Word.
2. Start Word. Then type a paragraph and repeat it three times.
3. Type a table of three lines of data. Use at least two tab presses in each line.
4. Move the cursor and scroll through the entire document.
5. Insert a sentence in the middle of your first paragraph, then delete a few words from your second paragraph.
6. Save the file as CHAP2EX.DOC. Then reopen it and continue working.
7. Modify the screen appearance so the horizontal scroll bar and the window borders do not appear, but the ruler and ribbon do.
8. Remove the key displays from the menus and change the default tabs back to one-half inch.
9. Restore the defaults and preferences you want to use in your work.

Use the File Save and File Open commands to save and open files. You can use either the mouse or keyboard to move the cursor and scroll. The Delete and Backspace keys can both be used to delete characters. Use the View Preferences command to toggle the appearance of the scroll bars and borders. You can change the ruler and ribbon display through the View menu or by clicking on the icon. Use the Utilities Customize command to change the default tab increment and the appearance of keys on menus.

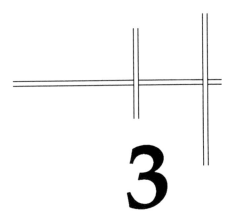

Editing and Modifying Files

Y̲ou have already learned to manipulate Word using several of its menus, commands, and dialog boxes, but it has many additional editing features. You can search for a string of text, replacing it with another string if appropriate. You can select a block of text, then perform an operation on it. You can delete the block, copy it to another location, and insert it as often as you need. You can repeat commands automatically or even undo them using other Word commands. In this chapter, you'll learn to:

- Select text
- Extend or shrink a selection
- Delete a selected block of text
- Undo an editing action
- Move a block of text
- Copy a block of text
- Insert a block of text elsewhere
- Cancel a selection
- Repeat a command
- Search for text
- Replace located text
- Move directly to a page in a document

Selecting Text

Before you can use many Word commands, you must select the text to be affected. For example, to copy characters from one location to another, you must first select them. Other commands select text for you; if you search for a particular phrase, for example, Word selects it when it is found. When text is selected, it is shown highlighted or in inverse video on the screen. The selected portion is often referred to as a *block*.

A selection is always continuous; you can't select three words on this line and one four lines later. There are two general ways of selecting text: from the cursor location or a specific increment. The mouse method is different from the keyboard.

From the Cursor Location

Selecting text from the cursor involves fixing the current cursor location and extending a selection from it. You can extend a selection from the cursor using either the mouse or the keyboard.

By Specific Increments

You can also select text in specific increments using either the mouse or the keyboard. Word defines various increments you can use:

Word	Any group of characters separated by spaces, tabs, dashes, or punctuation, including trailing spaces before the next word. A punctuation mark with its trailing spaces is also a word.
Line	Text stretching from the left margin to the right margin, including any paragraph or new line mark.
Sentence	Any group of characters leading up to a period, question mark, or exclamation point, with any trailing spaces after it. A punctuation mark without a trailing space doesn't end a sentence.
Paragraph	Any group of characters leading up to a paragraph mark, including the mark itself.
Document	The entire document.

Tip || If you don't have a mouse, skip to the "Using the Keyboard" heading.

Using the Mouse to Select from the Cursor Location

Selecting text from the cursor location with the mouse is easy:

1. Point to either end of the block.
2. Press the left button and hold it down.
3. Drag the pointer to the other end of the block.
4. Release the mouse button.

The selected block is highlighted on the screen. It remains selected until you click the mouse again or press any cursor movement or character key. While you are dragging the mouse to select text, the window scrolls automatically in the direction you drag; you can include as much text as you need.

Here's another way to use the mouse to select text from the cursor location:

1. Point to one end of the block.
2. Click the left button.
3. Point to the other end of the block (without dragging), press Shift and click (Shift+Click) the left button again.

The block is selected. This method is often easier when the entire block is shown in the current window.

You can move the second point (the end of the block) to extend or shrink the selection once you have released the mouse button. First press the Shift key and hold it down while you position the mouse pointer and click again to extend or shrink the selection using any of the techniques. If you position the pointer within the selection, Shift+Click shrinks the selection. If you position it outside the selection, Shift+Click expands it.

1. Start Word, if necessary.
2. Open the PRAC2.DOC file if it isn't open yet.
3. Place the mouse pointer in the middle of the first paragraph. Click the left button and drag the pointer down two lines. Then release the button.
4. Click anywhere in the document window to release the selection.
5. To start another selection, click the left button. Then move several lines down the screen, press Shift, and click again.
6. Move the pointer down a few lines, press and hold the Shift key, and click again.
7. Click anywhere in the document window to release the selection.
8. Practice performing additional mouse selections if you like.

Using the Mouse to Select by Increments

Selecting by increments with the mouse depends on the increment. Some selection is done using an invisible screen element called the *selection bar*. The selection bar is located at the extreme left of a document window, just inside the window border. (If the style bar is displayed, it occupies the same part of the window.) Clicking in the selection bar lets you select the line or paragraph at that level, or your entire document. Here's how to select the various elements with a mouse:

Word Place pointer anywhere in a word and click the right button or double-click the left button.

Line Place pointer in the selection bar opposite the line and click the left button.

Sentence Place pointer anywhere in a sentence and click both buttons, or hold down the Ctrl key and click the left button.

Paragraph Place pointer in selection bar anywhere opposite the paragraph and click the right button or double-click the left button.

Document Place pointer in selection bar and Ctrl+Click. (Hold down the control key and click the left button.)

To extend any selection to include several units, you can drag the mouse. To select a dozen lines, for example, just click in the selection bar opposite the first or last line you want, then drag the mouse to the other end. You can adjust the selection however you wish before releasing the mouse button.

To extend or shrink the selection after releasing the mouse button, hold down the Shift key. Then you can use the same method and increment to affect the selection. For example, suppose you want to select a series of paragraphs, but you aren't sure how many. Just place the pointer in the selection bar opposite the first paragraph and click the right button or double-click the left, holding the last click. Then drag the mouse down through the selection bar until all the paragraphs you want are selected. Until you release the mouse button, you can adjust the selection to include more or fewer increments. Once you release the button, you have to press Shift to adjust it, but the adjustments will all be in the increment you used originally.

1. Point to a word in the middle of the screen and click the right button.
2. Point to a word in the middle of any sentence, press the control key, and click.

3. Point to the selection bar opposite any line on the screen and click. Notice that the line is selected.
4. Point to the selection bar opposite any paragraph and click the right button. Notice that the entire paragraph is selected.
5. Point to any location in the selection bar, hold down the control key, and click. Notice that the entire document is selected.
6. Click anywhere in the document window to end the selection.
7. Move to the beginning or end of the document and select the entire document by dragging the mouse through the text or Ctrl+Click in the selection bar.
8. Practice with additional increment selections if you want.

Tip Even if you use a mouse most of the time, be sure to learn to use the keyboard for selecting as well. It is often quicker, especially if you want to modify a previously selected block.

From the Cursor Location with Standard Keyboard Keys

You can select text with the keyboard by holding down the Shift key and pressing any cursor movement key or combination. When you release the Shift key, the selection is set; it remains selected until you click the mouse or press any keyboard cursor movement or character key. All the standard cursor movement keys (shown earlier in Table 2.1) can be used to select text once the Shift key is pressed. You can also extend or shrink an existing selection while Shift is held down.

The cursor is the selection anchor. Actually the cursor's left side is the anchor. If you press Shift+←, the character to the left is selected; if you press Shift+→, the character to the right is selected. You expand the selection by moving away from the anchor point. You shrink it by moving back toward the anchor point. Until you release the Shift key, you can move the free end of the selection freely on the screen. You can use any of the cursor movement keys to extend the highlight through the document, even if an original selection was done with the mouse.

To extend or shrink the selection once you have released Shift to set it, press Shift again and use the cursor key combinations (or mouse) some more.

1. Hold down the Shift key and press ↑ three times.
2. Keep holding Shift, and press → four times.
3. Release Shift, and press ↓. Notice that the selection disappears.
4. Press Shift+PgDown. Notice that most of your window is selected.

5. Press Shift+→ until another complete line or a few more words are selected.
6. Choose the Utilities Word Count (Alt,U,W) command. Notice that the number of words in the selection appears in the status bar.
7. Practice some more with keyboard selections if you like.

By Increments from the Keyboard

You can select certain increments of text with key combinations. The first time you press one of these key combinations, the current increment (the one containing the cursor) is selected. If you press it when a selection is already started, the next unit (toward the end of the document) is selected instead. By repeatedly pressing the key combination, you can select one increment after another.

Word	Alt+F6
Sentence	Alt+F8
Paragraph	Alt+F10
Document	Shift+F10 or Ctrl+5 (in numeric keypad)

These keyboard increment selections select only one increment at a time. If you need to select more, you'll have to extend the selection as explained in the next part.

1. Press Alt+F6 several times to select one word at a time.
2. Press Alt+F8 several times to select one sentence at a time.
3. Press Alt+F10 several times to select one paragraph at a time.
4. Press Shift+F10 to select the entire document.
5. Practice with keyboard increment selection some more if you like.

From the Cursor with F8

When you press F8, Word enters *extend mode;* you can extend the selection from the current cursor location. The EX indicator appears in the status bar. At this point, you can extend your selection using any cursor movement keys. Any text that is already selected remains selected and you can extend it. That means you can do some selecting, then press F8, then use any cursor movement keys or combinations to complete your selection. You can make it smaller as needed. You can even add to your selection in the increments shown in the previous topic. Pressing F8 lets you forget about the Shift key whether you are using the mouse or the keyboard.

If you press F8, then press one of the increment combinations, adjacent units are selected. For example, if you want to select eight words, you can place the cursor in the first word, then press F8, then press Alt+F6 eight times. This time, all the words are selected, instead of one at a time.

Pressing Esc cancels the effect of F8 while leaving the text selected. Using any command also cancels the effect of F8.

1. Press F8. Notice that EX appears in the status bar.
2. Press Alt+F8 three times. (Hold down the Alt key and press F8 three times before releasing it.)
3. Press Esc to end the F8 effect. Notice that EX disappears from the status bar.
4. Press F8 to enter extend mode again.
5. Press ↓ three times.
6. Extend the selection with the arrow keys for several lines and words.
7. Choose the Utilities Word Count command. Notice that the EX disappears from the status bar and the new count appears in the scrap.

F8 to Extend to the End of a Sentence. When you press the period key while extension (F8) is in effect, the selection is immediately extended from the cursor location through the next period followed by a space. To extend a selection three sentences, press F8 if EX isn't in the status bar, then press period three times.

Tip || Pressing F8, period is not the same as pressing Alt+F8. Alt+F8 selects the entire sentence, *not* from the cursor through the next period.

F8 to Extend by Increments. You can press F8 repeatedly to extend your selection by increments, from word to sentence to paragraph to document. The first time you press F8, the EX indicator appears in the status bar, but nothing additional is selected. If you press F8 again, however, the word containing the cursor is selected. Press it again, and the sentence containing that word is selected. Press it once more and the paragraph containing that sentence is selected. And press F8 again, and the entire document is selected.

When the selection is as you want it, press Esc to cancel the effect of F8 or just use the command you are preparing for; either one ends the selection. If you use any cursor movement keys or click the mouse after the selection is set, the selection is canceled.

Shift+F8 to Decrease a Selection. You can use Shift+F8 to downsize your selection in increments. If more than a paragraph is selected, the first time you press Shift+F8, it backs down to a single paragraph—the one that contained the cursor when you started the selection. The next time you press Shift+F8, the selection backs down to the current sentence. Press Shift+F8 once more and the selection backs down to a single word. One more Shift+F8 cancels the selection altogether, leaving the cursor in place.

If extend mode was on before you pressed Shift+F8, it remains on, as indicated by EX in the status bar. You can press Esc or use a command to cancel selection extension.

1. Press F8. Notice the EX in the status bar.
2. Press F8 again. Notice that the word containing the cursor is selected.
3. Press F8 again. Notice that the sentence containing that word is selected.
4. Press F8 again. Now the paragraph containing that sentence is selected.
5. Press F8 again. Notice that the entire document is selected.
6. Press Shift+F8. Notice the selection is downsized to one paragraph.
7. Press Shift+F8 three more times, until only a cursor remains. Notice that EX still appears in the status bar, so press Esc to end it.

1. Use any method you like to select the third or fourth paragraph in the document.
2. Use any method you like to extend the selection to include five more lines.
3. Get a word count on the selection.
4. Select one word in the last paragraph in the document. Expand it to a sentence, then a paragraph.
5. Select the entire document.
6. If you've been using a mouse, use the keyboard to do steps 1 through 5 again. If you've been using the keyboard, try to repeat the steps using other keyboard methods.

You can use any selection methods here. If you have trouble performing these selections, read over the chapter sections again. Take time to try each set of numbered steps so that selecting text becomes a snap. You'll have to be able to select text often, but you don't have to remember all the ways to do it.

Deleting a Block

To delete a block of selected text, just press the Delete key; the selection is gone and the cursor remains in that position.

1. Use any method to select a sentence in your document.
2. Press the Delete key.

Notice that the sentence is gone and nothing is selected. If you used F8 three times to select the sentence, extend mode is turned off.

The Edit Undo Command

The Edit Undo command will "undo" your most recent action in Word. It will undo the latest text you entered or most commands, but it must be used immediately after the action you want to undo. If you use the Delete key to remove a series of characters, Edit Undo restores only the last character deleted. If you use the Backspace key to remove a series of characters, Edit Undo restores the entire series. If you type in overtype mode, you can use Edit Undo to restore all the overlaid characters since you pressed Insert to change modes, as long as you don't use any cursor movement or commands.

One common use is to undo a simple block delete. If you select a block of text and press the Delete key, the text is deleted. If you then choose the Edit Undo command, however, the block is "undeleted" and put back in the document in exactly the same location. Repeated use of Edit Undo toggles the action. Pressing Alt+Backspace has the same effect as Edit Undo.

1. Choose the Edit Undo command. Notice the sentence reappears.
2. Press Alt+Backspace. Notice the sentence is gone again.
3. Move the cursor down a few lines, then use Edit Undo or Alt+Backspace again. Notice the sentence is back in its original location.

Edit Undo also will remove the text you've typed since the last command, since that is considered to be one action (if you didn't interrupt it with any cursor movement or commands). If you have just typed a paragraph and aren't sure if you want to use it, press Alt+Backspace and it's gone. Press it again and it's back. But be careful. Once you try a command, move the cursor, or type something else, the previous action is lost and can't be undone.

A few commands can't be undone, and never any except the very last one. If you typed some text, then used a command, it's too late to undo the text.

And if you used a command, then typed a few words, it's too late to use Edit Undo to undo the command. You'll get some practice using Edit Undo on commands later in this chapter.

1. Position the cursor and add a sentence to your document.
2. Choose the Edit Undo command from the menu. Notice that the sentence is gone.
3. Press Alt+Backspace. Notice the sentence is back again.
4. Choose the Utilities Word Count command.
5. Press Alt+Backspace again. The sentence is not affected.

Almost any command or typing affects the command that can be undone. In this case, you may notice a difference in the status bar when you choose Edit Undo.

The Edit Repeat Command

You've seen how to undo a command. You saw earlier how to use Edit Repeat to repeat the text typed since the last command. Edit Repeat (or F4) will also repeat the last command. Most cursor movement or scrolling doesn't affect what is repeated, so if you use a command like Utilities Word Count, you can repeat it easily. Here's how you could get the word count of several paragraphs in a row using keyboard commands:

1. Select the first paragraph (Alt+F10).
2. Choose the Utilities Word Count command.
3. Select the next paragraph (Alt+F10)
4. Press F4 to repeat it.

Just repeat steps 3 and 4 until all the paragraphs you want counted are done. If you want to keep track of the word counts, you'll have to make notes. If you miss one, you can use Edit Undo to go back one step. It won't change the selection, but it will show you the previous word count.

1. Select a paragraph, then delete it. Undo the deletion.
2. Select three or four paragraphs and do a word count.
3. End the selection, then use Edit Repeat to do another word count.

4. Select a sentence in the last paragraph, then delete it. Undo the deletion twice.
5. Type four or five words in the last paragraph, then use Edit Repeat to put them in the previous paragraph as well.

You can use any method of selecting text for this exercise. Be sure to do Edit Undo or Edit Repeat immediately after the command is finished or the text is typed. You can move the cursor before repeating, but not before undoing an action.

Moving and Copying Text

In word processing, you'll often want to move or copy text from one location to another. When text is *moved*, it is placed in a different location and removed from the original location. When text is *copied*, it is placed in a different location and left in the original location as well. These are often called *cut-and-paste* operations.

The Edit menu includes commands to cut a block of selected text and to copy a block. A cut is the first step in moving text; it deletes the text from its original location and saves it in a temporary location. A copy is the first step in copying text; it doesn't remove any text, but duplicates it in the temporary location. For both operations, the next step is to place the cursor where you want the text to be placed and paste it there.

Using the Scrap

Once a block of text is cut or copied, it is stored in an area of memory called the *scrap*. Once it is in the scrap, you can paste it in as many locations as you want in any open document.

The status bar includes an indication, enclosed in braces ({}), of what is in the scrap; this is the same place you see the result of a word count. Since the space is limited, you'll see only the first three and the last two or three characters. No matter how much text is in the scrap, you'll only see a few characters. For example, if the phrase "universal brotherhood" is cut, the scrap indicator looks like this: {uni...ood}. Invisible characters are replaced by symbols, which you may see in the status line. Many of these are the same ones you'll see on the screen if non-printing characters are displayed. You'll see a paragraph mark in the scrap if one is near the beginning or end of the text there. You'll see a dot for each space. And you'll see an arrow for a tab. You won't see these unless the special character is within the first few or last few characters, but their effects will appear if you insert the text from the scrap into the document.

The scrap holds only one chunk of text at a time. Once you place some more there with another Edit Cut or Edit Copy command, the former scrap contents are gone. Using any command that places information in the scrap removes the previous contents as well. For example, the Utilities Word Count replaces the scrap contents. If you use Edit Undo immediately after one of these commands, you can recover the previous contents of the scrap.

Pressing Delete does not place anything in the scrap. You can restore it immediately with Edit Undo, but it isn't available very long. Deleting one character lets you undo one character. Deleting a selected block lets you undo that block.

Placing Text in the Scrap

When you choose the Edit Cut or Edit Copy command, any selected text is placed in the scrap. If you choose Edit Cut when no text is selected, the character at the cursor is placed in the scrap. The Edit Copy command is not available when no text is selected. You'll see a message box telling you that no text is selected, and you'll have to choose <OK> to continue.

The shortcut key for Edit Cut (Alt,E,T) is Shift+Delete; the Delete key without Shift doesn't put the text in the scrap, but removes it completely. The shortcut key for Edit Copy (Alt,E,C) is Ctrl+Insert; you can also use Alt+F3 to copy text to the scrap.

Choosing the Edit Cut command not only places text in the scrap, but it also removes it from the document itself, so the selected text is no longer displayed in the document window. Choosing the Edit Copy command places text in the scrap without changing the document. The text remains selected, but extension (EX in the status bar) is turned off.

1. Select a sentence of text.
2. Choose the Edit Cut command. Notice the scrap indicator in the status bar.
3. Choose Edit Undo. Notice that the scrap is gone (or changed).
4. Choose the Edit Copy command. Notice that the scrap indicator shows the first few and last few characters.

Inserting Text from the Scrap

Once text is in the scrap, you can insert it into the document by placing the cursor where you want the text to be, then selecting the Edit Paste command (Alt,E,P); its shortcut key is Shift+Insert. The Edit Paste command is not available unless some text is in the scrap. The contents of the scrap, no matter how small or large, is inserted at the cursor. It also remains in the scrap, so you can insert it as often as you want and wherever you want. Once you use Edit Cut or Edit Copy again, however, the scrap contents are replaced with the new block of data.

1. Place the cursor after the next sentence.
2. Choose the Edit Paste command. Notice that the sentence is inserted at the cursor, but is still in the scrap.
3. Move the cursor to another location, and choose Edit Paste again (try Shift+Insert this time).

You can also use Edit Paste to place a word count value in the document. Just position the cursor while the scrap contains the result of a word count, and choose the Edit Paste command.

1. Choose the Utilities Word Count command.
2. Move the cursor to the end of your document and type **This document contains**.
3. Choose the Edit Paste command.

When you choose Edit Paste, whatever is in the scrap is inserted into the text at the location of the cursor. If you insert something you don't want, just choose Edit Undo (Alt+Backspace) to remove it.

Tip | Speed moving and copying must be done with a mouse. If you don't have a mouse, you can skip this section.

Speed Moving and Copying

If you use a mouse, you can move and copy text with a speedy operation that doesn't put anything in the scrap. You can use this technique to move or copy something while protecting the scrap contents for later use. Here's how:

1. Select text to move.

2. Point to where you want the text to be pasted. Use the scroll bars to locate other parts of the document.
3. To move it, press Ctrl+Click right mouse button.
4. To copy it, press Shift+Ctrl+Click right mouse button.

Tip || Use Shift+Delete to cut text, then Shift+Insert to paste it. Or use Ctrl+Insert to copy text, then Shift+Insert to paste it. These pairs of commands are easy to remember.

1. Cut an entire paragraph from near the beginning of your document and insert it at the end.
2. Insert the same paragraph at the very beginning of the document. Then remove it with Edit Undo.
3. Copy three sentences from the middle of your document to three other locations in the document.
4. Use Edit Cut to remove four words in sequence.
5. Insert the scrap contents at the very beginning of the document.

Use any method of selecting text for cutting and copying here. Use the menus or the shortcuts to cut, copy, and paste blocks. If you didn't get the effects you expected, you probably managed to change the contents of the scrap before pasting it into the document or didn't position the cursor before choosing the Edit Paste command.

Searching for Text

When you work with a document, you may often have to locate a particular word or phrase. Word helps you search for these with the Edit Search command. Using this command, you can specify a string of characters to search for. Word will find and select the string for you.

Searching for character strings can take a great deal of time in long documents. Ideally, you should enter a unique string so that the first one found is the one you want. If you want to search for a paragraph about Chardonnay in a report about wines, for example, searching for Chardonnay will more likely find it than searching for red or wine. You can keep the search time short by using short strings. Word will find the string "Chard" much more quickly than

"Chardonnay", for example. And unless the document includes vegetables as well, it probably will find the right one.

If nothing is selected when you use Edit Search, the search starts at the cursor and proceeds toward the end of the document. If nothing is located, you'll be asked if Word should continue from the beginning of the document until it reaches the original location. If a selection is in effect, the search takes place only within the selection.

The Edit Search Command

When you choose the Edit Search command, you'll see the dialog box shown in Figure 3.1. The **Text to Search For** field is empty the first time you see this dialog box. Later, it will contain the last text searched for.

To search for a specific string of text, just enter the text in the field; this is called the *search text*. You can type up to 256 characters; the text scrolls sideways if necessary. But you won't often need that many characters. You may choose to search **Up** (toward the beginning of the document) or **Down** (toward the end). The default is **Down**. Once you change it, that direction remains until you change it again or leave Word.

If the text isn't found, you'll see a message box telling you so. When you choose <OK>, the cursor is back where it was before you started the search.

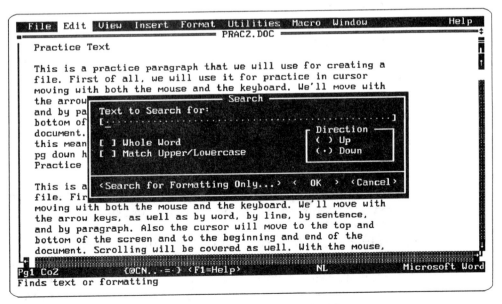

Figure 3.1. The Edit Search Dialog Box

1. Position the cursor at the beginning of your document.
2. Choose the Edit Search command (Alt,E,S).
3. In the **Text to Search for** field, type **the**. Notice that the direction is **Down**.
4. Choose <OK>.

At this point, the letters **the** should be selected on your screen. If they aren't, do those steps again using three or four letters that do appear in your document.

Repeating the Search. Suppose the selected text is not the occurrence you wanted. You could enter a more specific string or you could repeat the search. If you choose Edit Search again, the dialog box reappears with the word you entered before displayed and highlighted. If you choose <OK>, the command is repeated. But this time there is some selected text, so it will search only there.

To make it even easier, you can use Shift+F4 (Repeat Search) to select the next occurrence automatically. Any time you use Shift+F4 the last string searched for will be searched for again. If there is a selection, only the selection will be searched. If not, the search begins at the cursor.

If you want to modify the contents of the **Text to Search for** field, you can. If you press a character, the highlighted text is removed. If you press an arrow key, you can edit what is displayed.

Starting Over. If the search affects the entire document, it may reach the end before the search is done. If so, and if it didn't start at the beginning, you'll see a dialog box like the one shown in Figure 3.2, asking you if it should start over at the beginning and continue searching. Just choose <Yes> to cycle back to the beginning or <No> to stop the search. If you cancel the search, the last occurrence located remains selected.

1. Press Shift+F4. Notice that the next occurrence is selected.
2. Choose the Edit Search command.
3. Type a text string that occurs several times in your document, then choose <OK>.
4. Press Shift+F4 to repeat the search.
5. Press Shift+F4 repeatedly until you are asked if Word should continue from the beginning. Then choose <Yes> and see if another is found.

Controlling the Search. Normally, Word finds the string wherever it occurs. When you use *the* as the string, it locates the word itself, as well as the string in such words as *therefore, Theatre, ATHEISM,* and the like. If you want the search to locate only the complete word, turn on the **Whole Word** check box. Then only the word in the form *THE, The,* or *the* will be found.

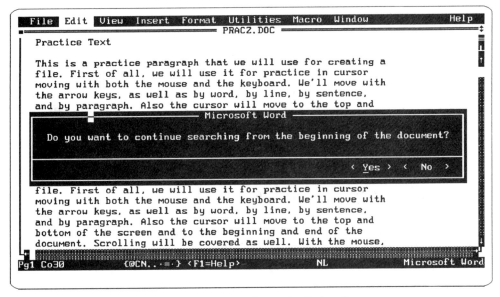

Figure 3.2. Continue Search Dialog Box

You can also control whether or not the found text matches exactly in terms of capitalization. When the **Match Upper/Lowercase** field is turned off, the search finds the characters, no matter what case is used. If you turn this field on, the search locates only exact matches.

When both these fields are turned on, only whole words with exact case matches are found.

1. Add the word Michel to your document. Place the cursor somewhere before it.
2. Choose the Edit Search command.
3. Type **chel**, then turn on the **Whole Word** check box.
4. Choose <OK>.
5. If prompted, choose <Yes> to continue searching from the beginning.

The string wasn't in the file as a complete word.

6. Choose the Edit Search command. Notice the search string you entered is still there.
7. Turn off the **Whole Word** check box, then choose <OK>.

This time the word is located eventually. Notice that it is selected. You could delete it, cut it, or copy it if you want.

Using a Wildcard

Sometimes you don't know for sure what to search for. For example, a name may be spelled Rob or Bob. You can use the question mark to indicate any character at all in the text string. The string **?ob** will find either Rob or Bob. If you type **gr?y**, the search will locate such strings as gray, grey, and even gruy (in Gruyere). You can control the case and whole word fields when you use wildcards just as you can with straight text.

Locating Special Characters

You can search for special characters as well as text. For example, if you want to search for an actual question mark, you need to use a special code. Table 3.1 shows how to specify the special characters you can search for. Notice that the caret (^) precedes the letter indicators. If you want to search for the caret character, you'll need two carets.

Most of the special characters are self-explanatory. If you want to search for two paragraph marks in a row, you would use ^p^p in the search string. If you want to search for a specific number of spaces, however, just type that number of spaces in the search string. The white space character (^w) searches for any number and combination of the other special characters except for ?.

Table 3.1. Searching for Special Characters

Code	Special Character
^s	Nonbreak space
^t	Tab character
^p	Paragraph mark
^n	Newline character
^-	Optional hyphen
^c	Column break (see Chapter 8)
^d	Section mark (see Chapter 5)
^?	Question mark
^^	Caret
^w	White space (any combination of nonprinting characters)

1. Choose the Edit Search command.
2. Type ^p to search for a paragraph mark, then choose <OK>.
3. Press Shift+F4 to repeat the search.

If you want to search for nontext characters, you probably will need the <Search for Formatting Only> button. That is covered in Chapter 10.

Replacing Text

Sometimes you just want to locate text to see it in context. But often you'll want to change it. Suppose you typed a client's name as Sphinx when it is actually Spinks, for example. Word lets you change every occurrence in the document. You can also remove a string wherever it occurs. Just specify the string and use nothing at all to replace it with.

The Edit Replace Command

When you choose the Edit Replace command, you see the dialog box shown in Figure 3.3. Notice that it is like the Edit Search dialog box, with the **Replace with** field added.

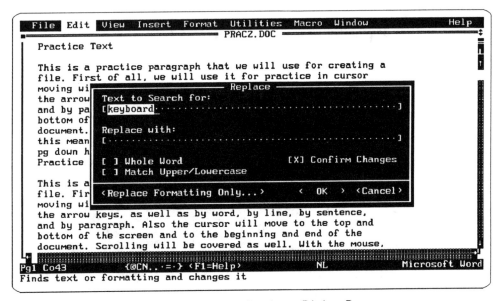

Figure 3.3. The Edit Replace Dialog Box

All the options and buttons have the same effects as in the Edit Search dialog box. You can limit the search to whole words or to matching case if appropriate. You can also deal with only the formatting codes.

Type the search string in the **Text to Search for** box, using any special characters or wildcards that are appropriate. At this point, be sure not to press ↲; that means <OK> to Word. If you choose <OK> and the **Confirm Changes** check box is turned off, the text will be located and replaced with whatever is in the **Replace With** field, which is nothing until you add something there. The effect is to delete every occurrence of the search text.

If **Confirm Changes** is turned on, you'll see the selection in context along with a dialog box like the one in Figure 3.4. The dialog box doesn't show you what the replacement string is, so you are better off choosing <No> if you aren't sure.

If you choose <Yes>, the replacement is done, Word finds the next occurrence, and you see the dialog box again. If you choose <No>, the replacement is not done, Word finds the next occurrence, and you see the dialog box again. If you choose <Cancel>, the replacement is not done, and the operation is canceled.

Use the Tab key or click to get to the **Replace With** field and type the replacement string. You can't use a wildcard (?) in the replacement string, but you can use all the special characters shown in Table 3.1 except for ^W.

If you accidentally replace a string you didn't want to replace, you can use Edit Undo to undo the entire Edit Replace operation. You can interrupt a

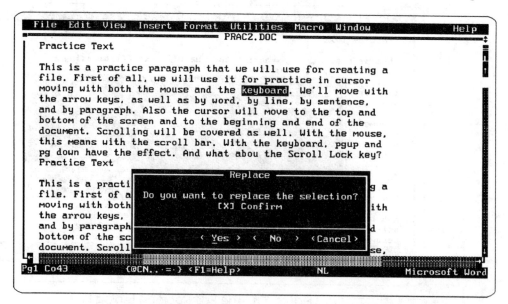

Figure 3.4. Confirming Changes

global (without Confirm) replacement by pressing Escape, then choose Edit Undo. In either case, the document returns to the way it was before the replacement started.

Confirming the Replacement

If the **Confirm Changes** field is turned on (the default), the process stops each time the search text is located. You'll be prompted to approve each replacement before it occurs. When this field is turned off, all the occurrences are located and changed without asking your approval. When all the replacements are done, Word lets you know how many changes were made.

You have to be careful about this. Suppose you want to change the word labor to labour throughout a long document. It might be safe to turn off **Confirm Changes**, but maybe not. The words belabor and laboratory would be changed to belabour and labouratory as well. Be absolutely sure your global change won't change anything it shouldn't affect before you do this.

Searching in a Selection

As with the Edit Search command, the replacement process takes place within a selection if any text is selected. Otherwise it starts at the current cursor location and goes toward the end of the file. If it reaches the end before it is canceled, you'll be asked if it should continue at the beginning of the file. When the operation stops, the cursor is back where it was when you started the Edit Replace command.

1. Choose the Edit Replace command.
2. Type **Practice** in the **Text to Search for** field.
3. Tab once, then type **Experience** in the **Replace with** field.
4. Make sure **Confirm Changes** is turned on, then choose <OK>.
5. When the confirmation dialog box appears, choose <Yes> each time until all the replacements are finished.
6. Choose Edit Replace again.
7. Type **Experience** in the **Text to Search for** field, then tab and type **Practice** in the **Replace with** field.
8. Turn the **Confirm Changes** field off, then choose <OK>.

All the changes are made automatically. You'll see a dialog box only to get back to the beginning of the document.

Customizing the Replacement

If you want to replace only exact case matches of the search string, turn on the **Match Upper/Lowercase** field. Then only exact case matches are found, as in Edit Search, and the case of the replacement will be exactly as you type it. If you want to replace any case string with a particular string, turn this field off. Word will still try to match the case in the replacement, however. Suppose you use *exemt* as the search string and *exempt* as the replace string. Strings *exemt, Exemt, EXEMT, EXemT,* and *exemT* will all be located. The replacement strings will use all uppercase if the located string was all uppercase, or initial caps if the located string had an initial cap. The strings above would be replaced with *exempt, Exempt, EXEMPT, Exempt,* and *exempt*.

Moving to a Page

You are now able to move through a document using either the keyboard keys or a mouse. Word provides a command to go directly to a particular page, as indicated on the left end of the status bar. When you choose the Edit Go To command (Alt,E,G), you see a dialog box like the one in Figure 3.5. You can also press F5 to get it instantly. You'll learn to use other parts of this box later, but for now, the default radio button setting of **Page** is what you need.

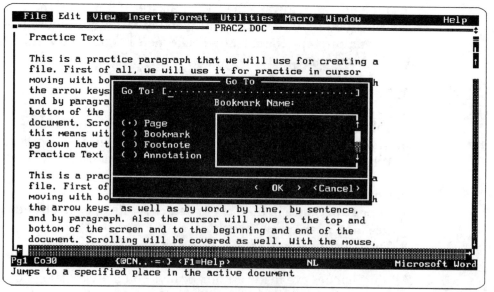

Figure 3.5. Edit Go To Dialog Box

1. Move the cursor to the end of the document.
2. Choose the Edit Go To command.

When the dialog box appears, the **Go To** field is empty. You type the page number you want there, choose <OK>, and your document scrolls to the top of that page. If you don't enter a page number, it goes to the top of the next page. If you happen to be on the last page, you'll be notified that there are no more pages in the document.

3. Type **1**.
4. Choose <OK>. Notice that the cursor is at the top of page 1.
5. Press F5 to choose the Edit Go To command. Notice that the cursor is now at the top of page 2.

If your document has only one page, you saw a message box instead. Don't worry about it.

1. Make sure you have a document with more than a page of text open.
2. Search for a word that you know is in the document. Then press Shift+F4 to repeat the search.
3. Replace every occurrence of another word you know is in the document with a phrase of several words. Don't confirm the changes.
4. Add a line to your file that contains three tab presses. Then select the line and replace the tab presses with four spaces each.
5. Use the Edit Go To command or F5 to move to another page of the document.

Use the Edit Search command to locate text and Edit Replace to locate and replace it. Turn off the **Confirm Changes** *field before starting the replacement. Use ^t to indicate a search for a tab.*

Exercise

This chapter has covered many useful commands that you can use in editing and typing documents. Selecting text is required before moving or copying it, and useful if you want to search or replace text in only part of the document. You can practice these commands and techniques in this exercise.

1. Make your document longer by selecting the entire document and copying it to the end three times.
2. Select four successive paragraphs and cut them to the scrap. Then delete another paragraph without affecting the scrap.
3. Paste the cut paragraphs at the end of the document.
4. Search the entire document for the word *paragraph*.
5. Replace the word *paragraph* everywhere it appears with any capitalization (except for the second time) with *group of sentences*.
6. Search for one occurrence of the phrase *group of sentences*, then copy it to the scrap and insert it three more places in the document.
7. Select several paragraphs and count the words. Then insert the word count into the document.
8. Use the Edit Go To command to move to a different page in the document.
9. Save the document as CHAP3EX.DOC so you will have a long one to work with before continuing.

To copy the entire document, select it with Shift+F10 or Ctrl+Click in the selection bar. Then use Edit Copy to place it in the scrap. Cancel the selection by pressing Esc or clicking anywhere, place the cursor at the end of the document, and choose Edit Paste three times.

Use any method to select the four paragraphs and use Edit Cut to put them in the scrap. Use the Delete key to delete a paragraph without affecting the scrap. Edit Paste places the scrap contents at the cursor.

Edit Search and Edit Replace locate text. When text is located and selected, you can use Edit Copy or Edit Cut. Any selection is counted when Utilities Word Count is chosen. Edit Go To moves the cursor to the page number you type.

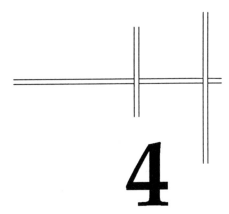

Printing

You've learned to do quite a bit of editing and manipulation of documents. The end product of any word processing, however, is printed output. In this chapter, you'll learn to print your documents, as well as to use many of your computer's print preparation and operation features. What features are available to you depends to some extent on your monitor and to a great extent on your printer. In Chapter 7, you'll learn to print files from disk. In this chapter, you'll learn to:

- Print the current document
- Make sure your printer is set up properly
- Select the appropriate print options
- Print multiple copies
- Print file summary information
- Print selected pages or text
- Print in the background so you can continue to use Word
- Preview a file on screen to see how it will print
- Save a printer file to disk for later printing
- Create an ASCII version of a file on disk

Printer Preparation

If your printer is used by other applications, it is undoubtedly connected correctly. If you have a new system, you'll have to make sure. Check out these aspects of your printer before you try to use it:

- Is it plugged in?
- Does it have paper?
- Does it have a ribbon, cartridge, or inkjet?
- Is it connected by a cable to the computer?
- Is it turned on? (Look for an on/off switch.)
- Is it online? (Look for an online/local or select/unselect switch.)

When Word was installed on your computer, it was set up for one or more specific printers. Most computers only have one printer; that makes it simple. But you might have installed two or more printers. You'll be able to use any printers that were installed.

Word prepared a file with extension PRD (it stands for "printer driver") for each printer defined at setup time. If you use a hard disk, any PRD files you'll need are in the WORD directory. If you have 1.2 M or 1.44 M diskettes, your PRD file is on the program diskette. If your computer supports only 360K diskettes, you'll have to copy the PRD file for any printer you want to use to the document diskette.

When you get ready to print a file, you'll be able to see what printers are installed and select the one you want to use. Word lets you choose a printer based on the available PRD files.

Printing a Document

If your printer is prepared according to the checklist above and has been installed by the Word Setup program, you should be able to use it immediately. To try it out, bring up Word if necessary and open a short file, preferably a document that you created earlier. We'll look at the options and variations later, but first follow these steps to print your document.

1. Choose the File Print command (Alt,F,P).
2. Choose <OK> (↵).

Tip || The shortcut key Shift+F9 invokes the File Print command.

You won't be able to use Word until the printing is finished, so just wait a moment until your page(s) appear or you see a message box on screen.

If a message box appears, your printer is not set up as you expected. The message should tell you what the problem is. If not, just get rid of the message box and continue with this chapter. If you haven't figured out the problem by the end of the chapter, you'll have to check with your dealer or with the Microsoft hotline.

If nothing prints and no message box appears, try to move the cursor. If the system is hung up, you'll have to solve the problem right now or reboot. The most common problems are that the printer is not connected to the specified port or that it isn't turned on. Word just keeps trying to send the file to the port you specified. If it is hung up, try to locate the problem and fix it. If you can't, you'll have to reboot and try to identify the problem before you request another print operation.

Stopping Printing

After you tell Word to print, it initializes the printer, then displays a message in the message line that tells you which page is being printed. The message also tells you to press Esc to <Cancel>. You won't be able to use your computer until this message is gone.

If you press Esc to <Cancel> the printing, you'll see a dialog box to confirm your request. Your choices are <OK> and <Cancel>. If you choose <OK>, printing continues. If you choose <Cancel>, the print job is canceled and you can use Word again.

Once printing is complete, the message changes to tell you how many lines and words were printed. The message might be "9 lines and 79 words counted" for a short document, or "490 lines and 4596 words counted" for a longer one. As soon as you move the cursor, start typing, or choose another command, that message disappears and the normal one is shown.

Printing Choices

In order for you to print a document using File Print, it must be current; that is, the document to be printed must be on the screen and contain the cursor.

When you tell Word you want to print, you see the dialog box shown in Figure 4.1. The upper part of the dialog box tells what sort of printer will be used and the name of the PRD file. In the figure, a standard postscript printer on the first serial port (COM1) uses POSTSCRP.PRD as its driver. The dialog

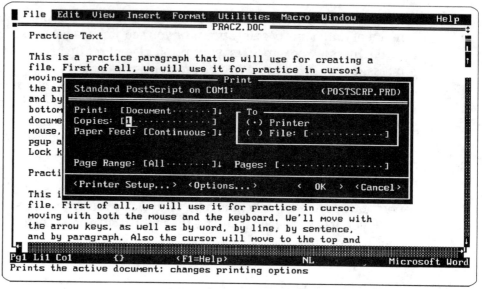

Figure 4.1. The File Print Dialog Box

box you see gives information relevant to your printer. The <Printer Setup> button lets you change how the printer is installed or request a different printer that has already been installed.

The fields in the dialog box let you request different settings for several items. The **Print** field drop-down menu lets you choose from several options:

Document	prints the current document
Summary Info	prints summary information for current document
Glossary	prints the current glossary
Style Sheet	prints the current style sheet
Direct Text	lets you type characters to be printed directly

If you want to type all or part of the current document, use the Document option (the default). The value in this field always reverts to Document after you print. Most of the time, you'll want to leave Document as the **Print** field selection.

If you want to print only the summary information, choose **Summary Info**. The summary information for the current file will be printed on a separate page. This makes a good title page and provides helpful information if you put useful data in it. If you didn't supply any summary information, you'll still get default information, including the complete file name with path, the dates it was created and last saved, and the size of the file. In Chapter 7, you'll learn to update and modify the summary information.

You'll learn to use glossaries and style sheets later in this book; you print the current one by selecting it here. Printing direct text has a few special applications that are explained later in this chapter.

The **Copies** field lets you specify how many copies you want printed. If you type 3, the entire document is printed once, then again, and finally a third time. A complete copy is printed before the next one begins.

The **Paper Feed** field lets you choose from at least these options:

Continuous	paper is fed continuously, either on continuous forms or through a feeder
Manual	paper is inserted manually, so the computer should pause after each page

In most cases, you'll use continuous feed, whether your computer uses continuous form paper or a sheet feeder. You might use manual feed when you want to hand feed an envelope or a special preprinted form. If your printer supports other options, such as separate paper trays or bins, they'll be listed here as well.

Specifying How Much to Print

If you aren't printing a document, you'll probably want to print the entire item. With documents, however, you may not want the whole thing printed each time. The **Page Range** field lets you specify three options:

All	print all pages
Pages	print the specified pages
Selection	print whatever is currently selected

This field keeps its value after printing, so you have to check it each time. If you want to print only some of the pages, select Pages or just type the page numbers you want in the **Pages** field; Word automatically selects Pages in the **Page Range** field if you type a page number.

You can list individual pages, separated by commas, as in 4,6,8. Or you can list ranges of pages separated by a colon or a dash, as in 9:12 or 5–8. You can combine both types to specify exactly what pages are to be printed, as in 1,4–5,7,10:19,22. You don't have to list the pages in chronological order, but Word will print them in order, from the lowest page number to the highest.

The page numbers you enter remain in the **Pages** field. If you select All again later, the numbers still remain but the full document is printed. That lets you select Pages again from the **Page Range** menu and reprint the same pages again later on. You can delete the page numbers in the dialog box to get rid of them if you wish, but they don't affect the output unless Pages is selected on the **Page Range** field menu.

When you select Selection, any numbers in the **Pages** field have no effect. When you choose <OK>, the selected text is printed, starting at the top of a new page.

Tip || The **Page Range** options affect other types of printing as well. You can use them any time they are appropriate.

Printing Direct Text

You might want to print direct text to add notes to a page, to address an envelope, or for some other reason. The effect is to use your keyboard and printer as a typewriter. What you type in this mode doesn't get placed in a document; it goes directly to the printer.

To print directly from your keyboard, select Direct Text from the **Print** field menu and press <OK>. A dialog box appears with room for one line of text and two buttons. Type the first line of direct text in the dialog box, then select the <Print Text> button. Type the next line and press <Print Text> again. When you have processed the last line, select the <Cancel> button.

On most printers, you'll have to eject the paper from the printer manually. Most printers have a page eject button. If your printer is a laser printer that doesn't have an eject button (such as the Apple LaserWriter Plus), you have a problem! There is probably a command you can send the computer to eject a page; check your printer documentation.

Tip || If your printer didn't work earlier, don't try this exercise yet. The next section includes information that may help you get it going.

1. Choose the File Print command (Alt,F,P).
2. If the cursor isn't in the **Copies** field, move it there. Then type **3**.
3. Move the cursor to the **Pages** field and type **2**. Notice that the **Page Range** field value changes to Pages.
4. Choose <OK> to print three copies of page 2.
5. Select the entire second and third paragraphs (at least 12 lines).

Tip || If you have a laser printer and don't know how to eject a page, don't try the next steps. You don't want to tie up your printer waiting for a page eject signal that never comes.

6. Choose the File Print command (Alt,F,P).
7. Move the cursor to the **Page Range** field. Choose Selection on the field menu.
8. Choose <OK> to print the selection.

---

1. Close the current document and open one that contains several pages. Use the file named README.DOC if you don't have another one.
2. Print just the first page.
3. Print just the summary information.
4. Print pages 2 through 4 and page 6, if the file is long enough.
5. Print 3 copies of pages 2 and 3.
6. Select two adjacent paragraphs on the first page and print them.
7. Restore the default settings and print the entire document once.
8. Close the file without saving any changes you may have made.

---

*You can achieve all these effects with the File Print command (Alt,F,P or Shift+F9). Select Document in the **Print** field for all items except 3, when you want Summary Info. Choose Pages from the **Page Range** menu for items 2, 4, and 5. Choose Selection for item 6 and All for item 7.*

Printer Setup

You can examine or change your printer setup by choosing the File Printer Setup command (Alt,F,R) or by selecting the <Printer Setup> button on the Print dialog box. In either case, you'll see the dialog box shown in Figure 4.2. You can examine the current values and change them if appropriate.

The name of the PRD file for the current printer appears in the **Printer File** field in the upper left. The **Files** list box includes PRD files for all printers installed through Word Setup. To change to a different printer, just select the driver you want from the **Files** list box. If your PRD files might be in another directory, you can change the directory in the **Directories** list box, just as when you are opening a file.

The **Printer Name** list box includes the names of printers that use the associated printer file. If your printer wasn't working right, you might want to scan through this list and see if a different name is more appropriate. The selected name appears in the Print dialog box as well as in this one.

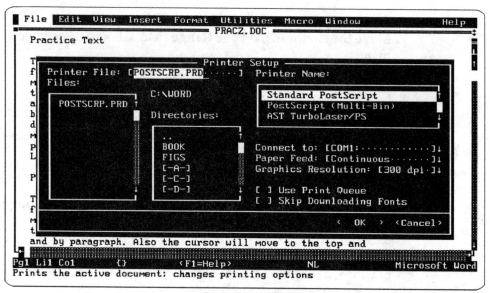

Figure 4.2. Printer Setup Dialog Box

The fields at the lower right show how the printer is set up. The **Connect to** field indicates the port. Its menu lets you choose from all the possible printer ports: LPT1 through LPT4 and COM1 through COM4. It should indicate the port your printer is attached to. A parallel printer is always attached to a parallel port; if you have only one parallel printer it is attached to LPT1. A serial printer might be attached to any serial port, but not the same port a mouse is connected to.

Tip If your print requests hang up Word, the port connection might be wrong. Try different port connections to see if you can locate the correct one.

The **Paper Feed** field here lets you choose from at least Continuous and Manual; it has the same effect as the similar field in the Print dialog box. If you use manual feed occasionally but continuous feed most of the time, you would select Continuous here in the Printer Setup dialog box. On the occasions when you need manual feed, just change the field in the Print dialog box. Any paper tray specifications here should be the ones you use most of the time. When you make a change for a single print job, change it in the Print dialog box.

The **Graphics Resolution** field menu lets you choose from different resolutions your printer can handle. If it can't handle any, you won't have any choices. If it handles only one, as PostScript does, that's the one you'll see. If several are available, you can choose the one you want from the menu. A lower resolution prints faster in most cases, while a higher resolution gives a clearer printed result. We'll deal with graphics in more detail later in this book.

The last two check boxes control completely different things. The **Use Print Queue** field sets up background printing, which means you can continue to use Word while printing is in effect. The **Skip Downloading Fonts** field saves time when your printer doesn't need those fonts. Fonts are covered in more detail in Chapter 8.

Using Background Printing

When a print queue is in effect, Word writes the printed output to a temporary file on disk, then prints it automatically from there. After the actual printing is done, the temporary file is erased. While the file is being stored on disk, you'll see the usual print message on the message line, telling you what page is being printed. While this is going on, you can press Esc to stop the process.

Once the file is written to disk, actual printing starts. The usual message is restored and you can continue working in Word. The screen response may be slower while printing is going on, but you may be able to function. Word gives priority to the printing operations, so your keypresses may not appear immediately. The speed of your system and your printer configuration will affect this.

While background printing is going on, don't keep pressing the same key if you don't get a screen response. Word remembers a few keypresses. Have faith and wait, or keep typing until Word catches up with you. If the computer beeps, stop and wait. The beep means the area that holds keypress information is full. When the screen catches up with you, start typing again.

You can send several print jobs to the queue. Word prints the documents in the print queue in the order in which they are placed there. To set up background printing, turn on the **Use Print Queue** field in the Printer Setup dialog box. Then whenever you use the File Print command, Word automatically uses the queue. To stop sending print jobs to the queue, turn off the field and choose <OK>. The next print request will be printed immediately instead of being sent to disk first.

1. Choose the File Printer Setup command (Alt,F,R).
2. Turn on the **Use Print Queue** field, then choose <OK>.
3. Make sure you have a longer document file open (try README.DOC if you haven't created one).
4. Choose the File Print command (Alt,F,P or Shift+F9) and choose <OK> to print the document.

If you want to make any changes to what is printing from the print queue, choose the File Print Queue command (Alt,F,Q). You'll see a dialog box like the one shown in Figure 4.3.

5. When the standard Edit document... message appears in the message bar, choose the File Print Queue command (Alt,F,Q) and choose <OK> again.
6. Notice the number of files in the queue. Choose <OK>.

The upper part of the box shows the current status and tells how many files are in the queue. It shows which file is currently being printed. You can't find out what the other files in the queue are. And you can affect only the current one. The first file in the queue may be a printer initialization file. For many printers, Word inserts an initialization file in the queue before each file, so when the queue shows the message in Figure 4.3, it is printing the named file (that's one) and has two more files; one of those two is an initialization file and one is another document file.

Use <Pause> to stop printing temporarily; you might do this to stop the noise for a phone call, for example, or to let you change the ribbon or paper. The effect may not be immediate; it depends on what size buffer (internal memory) your printer has. Many printers automatically invoke the queue pause when something goes physically wrong, such as running out of paper.

Printing will start again at the same location in the file when you use <Continue>. If you press <Restart File> after pausing the queue, printing

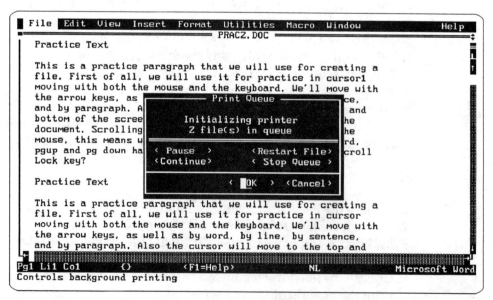

Figure 4.3. The Print Queue Dialog Box

starts again at the beginning of the file that was interrupted. You might do this if the ribbon breaks or if the paper gets out of alignment, for example. You might have to adjust the paper position in the printer to make sure it starts at the top of a page.

1. Use File Print to print three more copies of the same long file.
2. Choose the File Print Queue command (Alt,F,Q) again.
3. While the file is printing, press the <Pause> button, then choose <OK>.
4. When printing has paused, choose the File Print Queue command (Alt,P,Q) again and press the <Continue> button, then choose <OK>.

If you want to stop printing a file, press the <Stop Queue> button; the current file is stopped. If your queue contains several files, the next file in the queue is printed.

5. When printing resumes, choose the File Print Queue command (Alt,P,Q) and press the <Stop Queue> button, then choose <OK> or <Cancel>.
6. Choose the File Printer Setup command (Alt,F,R).
7. Move the cursor to the **Use Print Queue** field and turn it off.

1. If any of the Printer Setup options should be changed for your system, change them now. Try a standard print of any document to see if the printer works.
2. Turn on the print queue.
3. Send your complete document to the queue.
4. When the standard message returns, send the first four pages of the document to the queue.
5. When the standard message returns, send the summary information to the queue.
6. Pause the queue. When printing stops, start it up again.
7. <Cancel> the current document that is printing.
8. Turn off the print queue function.

Use the File Printer Setup command to turn background printing on and off. Use the File Print Queue command to monitor the printing. <Continue> resumes printing at the same spot, while <Stop Queue> cancels the current document.

Printer Options

You can set a few more options for your printer by selecting the <Options>
button in the Print dialog box. Figure 4.4 shows the resulting dialog box. Once
you set these options, they stay in effect until you change them again. Many
of them have counterparts in the File Print dialog box for temporary changes.

Printing Mode

If your printer can handle two print modes, Draft is the lower resolution. If
it's available, you can turn it on for faster printing. If your printer can print on
both sides of a page, you can turn that feature on with the Duplex field.

Controlling Graphics Resolution

The **Graphics Resolution** field here offers the same choices as in the Printer
Setup dialog box. You can change it in either place. Use your usual value in
the Printer Setup box. If you need to make a change for an occasional document, change it here in the Print Options dialog box. In general, a lower

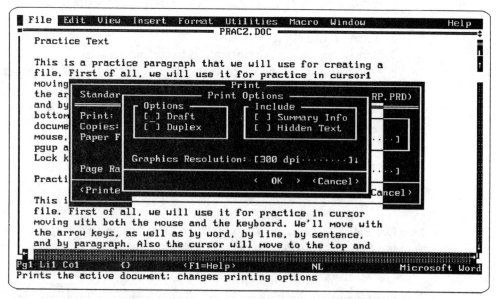

Figure 4.4. The Print Options Dialog Box

resolution prints faster, and a higher resolution produces clearer printed output. We'll cover graphics in more detail later in this book.

Including Summary Information

If you want to print only the summary information for a file, you already saw that you can select it in the main Print dialog box instead of using Document as the **Print** field value. If you want to print the document and include the summary information as well, turn on the **Summary Info** field in the Print Options dialog box. The summary information will be printed first, on a separate page, followed by the document or whatever you chose to print.

1. Choose the File Print command (Alt,F,P or Shift+F9).
2. Choose the <Options> button.
3. Move the cursor to the **Summary Info** field and turn it on.
4. Choose <OK>.
5. In the Print dialog box, set it up to print the first page of the current document.
6. Choose <OK>.

The printed output includes a page containing the summary information, followed by the first page of the document.

Hidden Text

If you include hidden text in a file (you'll see how to do this in the next chapter), you generally do it for the purpose of not having it print. If you want to print it for some reason, turn the **Hidden Text** field on here. You might want to print the hidden text if it includes notes on what you want to do next, for example, in a copy of a document that is for your eyes only.

Print Preview

Word provides a way for you to see on screen what a document will look like when it is printed. When you choose the File Print Preview command (Alt,F,V or Ctrl+F9), Word shows the current page in preview mode. It shows the margins, any headers or footers, page numbers, even graphics, that you don't see in standard editing mode. Many of the features of Print Preview you won't appreciate until later in this book, but even now you can see how a document will look after it is printed. In the next chapter, you'll be able to examine formatting effects before printing.

In preview mode, you may not be able to read the text in the pages (if you don't have VGA), but you can always see the layout, the margins, and the page break locations. You can't make any changes in preview mode; you have to return to edit mode to do that.

The Preview Screen

When you choose File Print Preview (Alt,F,V or Ctrl+F9), Word formats the pages and shows you the current page in the current view mode on the preview screen. You can view pages one at a time, two at a time, or facing pages, which includes an even-numbered page on the left and an odd-numbered page on the right. Figure 4.5 shows two pages at a time.

The preview screen has a status line and a message line, just like the standard edit screen. The status line shows the numbers of the pages displayed. If only one page is previewed, its number is at the left end of the line. If two pages are previewed, the number on the left indicates the page shown on the left while the number just to its right indicates the page shown on the right. The file name and <F1=Help> button also appear on the status line.

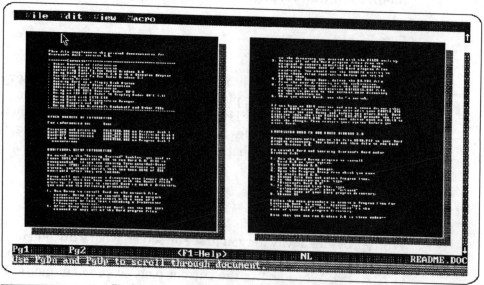

Figure 4.5. Print Preview Screen–Two-up

Preview mode has four menus. The Macro menu is the same as in edit mode. The View menu gives you three choices: View 1-Page (Alt,V,1), View 2-Page (Alt,V,2), or View Facing Pages (Alt,V,F). The Facing Pages option looks much the same, but shows pages as they would appear in a two-sided bound document. The one-page display shows a single page, centered. It's no larger than one of the pages in a two-page display.

The Edit menu has a single command, Go to (Alt,E,G); pressing F5 has the same effect here as in edit mode. You can use Edit Go to to move to any page in the document within preview mode. You can also use the PgUp and PgDown keys to page through. Ctrl+Home and Ctrl+End move directly to the first or last page in the file, just as in edit mode. If you use a mouse, the scroll bar on the left moves through the file, much as in edit mode.

The File menu offers an exit (Alt,F,X) from preview mode (or you can just press Esc), and it lets you print the file as well. The standard File Print (Alt,F,P) and File Printer Setup (Alt,F,R) commands can be chosen just as from edit mode. They have exactly the same effects here as when printing from within edit mode.

Tip || The shortcut key Ctrl+F9 switches to preview mode from the keyboard.

1. Choose the File Print Preview command (Alt,F,V).
2. Examine the screen. Then pull down the View menu and check out the other views. Leave it in 2-Pages.
3. Page through the file with the PgUp and PgDown keys.
4. Change the view to 1-Page and press Ctrl-Home, then Ctrl-End to see the first and last pages.
5. Try the Edit Go to command (Alt,E,G), then type 2 and choose <OK> to go to page 2.
6. Press Esc to return to the document in edit mode.

Notice that you return to the document at the page you left current in preview mode. When two pages are displayed, the one on the left is usually considered current. However, if you were on page 6 when you started preview and didn't change the pages, you'll be returned to page 6.

1. If you haven't done so yet, set up the printer for your use.
2. Make sure you have a fairly long document (such as README.DOC) current, then preview it.
3. Examine it in all views, then set up facing pages.
4. Move to the beginning of the document (scroll bar or Ctrl+Home).

5. Move to the end of the document.
6. Print the document from preview mode.
7. Return to edit mode.

Setting up the printer depends on what your system has. If your printer is already working fine, you won't have to do much here, but do examine the settings. In preview mode, most commands work just as in edit mode. You'll get the same print dialog box as before.

Printing to Disk

Sometimes you want to create a file on disk instead of printing immediately. You might want to do this to print it later under another program, to deliver the diskette to a system that uses a different printer or typesetter, or you might just need a file in a different format for some other reason. The File Print command lets you save a file in a fairly generic format or in print format for the current printer. Be sure to do any printer setup or option selection before you print a file to disk.

For Later Printing

In the Print dialog box (see Figure 4.1), you can choose to print to a file rather than to the printer. When you do, you supply the file name in the dialog box as well. You can include a path here as well. The **File** field looks small, but it scrolls sideways as you type. If you don't include a path, the file is written to the current directory.

The file name you supply here must meet DOS standards. If you include an extension, use a period and from one to three alphanumeric characters. The file can be printed later using other software.

1. Choose the File Print command.
2. Move the cursor to the To group box and turn on the **File** field.
3. Type **testfile.out** in the field, then choose <OK>.

The file is written to the current disk. If that disk happens to be full, you'll see a message and nothing is sent to the disk. But if your File Print command finishes satisfactorily, you can print the file later using the other software.

To Create an ASCII File

Sometimes you need an ASCII file that contains no formatting codes at all. Your computer may contain special AUTOEXEC.BAT and CONFIG.SYS files, which are used in the booting process; these must be ASCII files. You may need an ASCII file to transmit over telecommunications or to use on another computer or with different software.

To create an ASCII file, use the File Save As command (Alt,F,A). When you do, the **Format** list box offers you a choice of saving the file as a Word file (the default), Text Only, Text Only w/Breaks, or as RTF. Text Only and Text Only w/Breaks both create pure ASCII files. An RTF file (Rich Text Formatting) is also in ASCII format, but it tries to maintain the format.

An ASCII file contains a carriage return at the end of each line. Both Text Only and Text Only w/Breaks strip out any Word formatting. The Text Only option saves the file without any carriage returns added, so every paragraph occupies a single line. If the resulting file will be used in another type of word processor or by a desktop publisher, this might be the style you want. Text Only w/Breaks results in a carriage return at the end of each line. Most telecommunication methods require ASCII files to have lines no more than 80 characters long, so including breaks lets you achieve this.

1. Save the file as it is (File Save or Shift+F2) before continuing this exercise.
2. Choose the File Save As command (Alt,F,A or Alt+F2 or F12).
3. Change the file name to ASCII.OUT, then select the Text Only option in the **Format** field and choose <OK>.

You may see a message box warning you that your file will lose any formatting. This is only a problem if you neglected to change the file name; in that case, choose <Cancel> and start the list again.

1. Print the current file to disk as SELF4.OUT; put it in a different directory if you can.
2. Create an ASCII version of your file with a new extension, with a paragraph mark at the end of every line. Examine the output under Word.
3. Create another ASCII version without any added carriage returns. Examine this version under Word as well.
4. If you created new files, just leave them for now.

Be sure to provide a new name for each disk file you create. To print the document to disk, use the File Print command and choose the **File** *radio button instead of* **Printer**. *To create ASCII files on disk, use the File Save As command and select the appropriate type in the* **Format** *list box.*

Exercise

This chapter has covered setting up your printer, printing documents on your printer, and printing files to disk. In this exercise, you'll get a change to practice these operations.

1. Exit Word, then start it up again. Open CHAP3EX.DOC or another reasonably long file, such as README.DOC. Print it.
2. Print the first three pages of the document.
3. Select about four paragraphs spanning two pages, then print it.
4. Examine the file in preview mode. Go directly to page 6 in preview mode, then try paging or scrolling.
5. Create an ASCII version with no added paragraph marks named READASC.OUT.

Use the File Print (Shift+F9) command to create printer or disk output of documents. Type **1-3** *in the* **Pages** *field to get the first three pages. Use File Print Preview (or Ctrl+F9) to see on screen how the printed pages will look. Paging works the same under preview as on the document window. Use File Save As to create a Text Only ASCII version.*

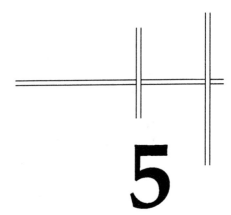

5

Basic Formatting

So far, you have been using the default format in your version of Word. But Word can do much more. You can modify the appearance of any character or series of characters to make it bold, italic, subscript, etc. You can modify the appearance of any paragraph, changing its alignment, spacing, and indentation. And you can modify on a larger scale, changing the margins or adding page numbers. In fact, you can even control how the entire document is paged. In this chapter you'll learn to:

- Make characters bold
- Make characters italic
- Make characters underlined
- Apply a double underline
- Use a subscript or superscript
- Convert characters to uppercase or small capitals
- Make characters show strikethrough
- Use hidden text
- Change paragraph spacing
- Change paragraph alignment
- Change paragraph indentation
- Change section margins
- Use page numbers
- Insert page breaks and change pagination

Formatting Characters

Word lets you format characters in many different ways. You can work with just a single character or with a series of adjacent characters. Later in this book you'll learn to change the font itself, to modify how the characters look and what size they are. For now, you'll see how you can change the appearance of the characters in the default font. Word offers several ways to do this. You can use the menus, you can use speed formatting at the keyboard, or you can use the ribbon for the most common character formatting.

What you see on the screen when you apply character formatting depends on your monitor and the display mode you are using. If your monitor supports graphics mode and you have graphics turned on, you'll see the full effect of any character formatting on the screen immediately. If you are working in text mode, you'll see shading, highlighting, or colors to indicate that character formatting is in effect. If your monitor supports graphics mode, you'll want to use it during this part of the chapter. To check your current mode, follow these steps:

1. Choose the View Preferences command (Alt,V,E or Alt+F9).
2. Examine the **Display Mode** field. If it shows Graphics, you'll be able to see formatting on the screen.
3. If it shows Text, click on the field menu arrow or press Alt+D,Alt+↓.
4. If Graphics is an option, select it.
5. Choose <OK>.

If you changed to Graphics display mode, the screen now looks somewhat different, but not substantially. The cursor will move more slowly, but that won't be a problem during this chapter.

Character Formatting Effects

Figure 5.1 shows many of the print effects Word can create through character formatting. Bold characters make text stand out on the page. Italic characters are often used for emphasis, foreign expressions, and titles. Underlining has many uses. Double underlining may be new to you, but you might find applications for it in your work.

The strikethrough effect is useful in showing what parts of a document have been changed. All uppercase can be achieved by using CapsLock when you first prepare the text, of course, but it is convenient to be able to convert text with a single command. If you convert text to uppercase with character

This line shows **bold characters.**
This line shows *italic characters.*
This line shows underlined characters.
This line shows double underlined characters.
This line show the ~~strikethrough~~ effect.
This line shows ALL UPPERCASE characters.
This line shows characters in SMALL CAPITALS.
This line shows superscripts in $a^2 + b^2 = c^2$.
This line shows a subscript in H_2O.

Figure 5.1. Character Formatting Effects

formatting, you can restore its previous appearance by turning off the formatting. Small capitals give you another way to make text distinctive; they are frequently used for A.M. and P.M. To use small capitals, you must type the text in lowercase letters. If you use uppercase, they stay that way. This allows you to use a word like DUOTECH, for example.

Subscripts and superscripts let you vary the position of the characters with respect to the line. Subscripted characters start just below the baseline of adjacent characters, while superscripted characters start just above the normal baseline. If you have never used many of these effects, don't let it bother you. The same techniques are used for all of them, so you can just use what you need. If the occasion ever arises for another type of character formatting, you'll already know exactly how it works.

Your printer may not support all these features. You may not even see them on your screen. You'll probably want to try all the options on your printer to see if they are effective. Later you'll learn to use different fonts your printer may have available; some other fonts may support more effects than your default font does.

Changing Case without Formatting

Word knows that you may want to change the case of a string of characters fairly often, so another way is provided for you to do this. Just select a string of characters and press Shift+F3. This key combination cycles through three case settings: uppercase, initial caps, and lowercase. If you select the string "changing the case", for example, pressing Shift+F3 once makes it appear as "CHANGING THE CASE", a second time changes it to "Changing The Case", and a third time makes it all lowercase. These are actual changes to the characters; you can make additional changes on an individual character basis.

If the selected string includes some nonstandard capitalization, it will be lost. If some of the words have initial caps and some don't, for example, they will all be the same style when you stop using Shift+F3.

1. Bring up a document with several pages.
2. Select a string of five or six words.
3. Press Shift+F3 three times, watching the selected string.
4. Select a different string that includes at least one word with initial cap and one without.
5. Press Shift+F3 until all the characters are lowercase.
6. Select a word that is all uppercase. (You may have to type one first.)
7. Press Shift+F3. Notice that the first step goes to initial caps this time.

Using the Format Menu

The Format Menu, shown in Figure 5.2, lets you accomplish most character formatting tasks without your having to commit any new commands to memory. The first command on the menus is Character; the ellipses indicate a dialog box.

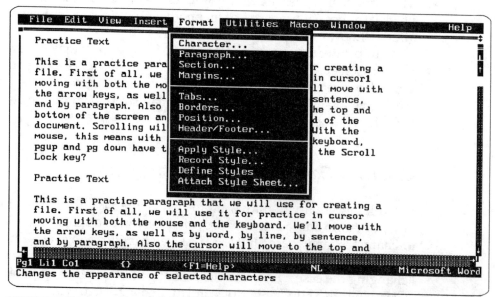

Figure 5.2. The Format Menu

When you choose the Format Character command (Alt,T,C), you'll see the dialog box shown in Figure 5.3. Pressing Ctrl+F2 is a shortcut that results in the same dialog box.

The fields near the top of the box are concerned with the font and size; you'll learn to control those later in this book. The list of formats on the left lets you choose how the selected characters will look; you can choose as many as are appropriate. A check mark appears in each selected format. The position list on the left lets you choose only one position; the same character can be in only one position at a time.

Tip

Since the character formatting options are all listed in the dialog box, you don't have to remember what is available. Just choose the Format Character command and check the list.

Applying a Format. To apply a format to already typed characters, you must first select the characters to be formatted. Then choose the Format Character command and check the options you want applied. Then choose <OK> and you'll see the result on the screen. The actual formatting effect will be displayed in Graphics mode; special color or highlighting indicates the characters in Text mode. You'll see the actual formatting of the characters when you print the document if your printer supports them. You might be able to see some of them in print preview mode if your screen has enough resolution.

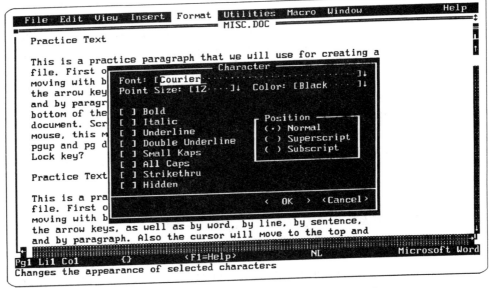

Figure 5.3. The Format Character Dialog Box

1. Select a two- or three-word phrase.
2. Choose the Format Character command with the mouse or keyboard (Alt,T,C or Ctrl+F2).
3. Turn on the Bold option, then choose <OK>.
4. Select a different word.
5. Choose the Format Character command.
6. Turn on the Small Kaps option, then choose <OK>.
7. Select two characters in a larger word.
8. Choose the Format Character command.
9. Turn on the Italic option and the Superscript option, then choose <OK>.

Now you can see now what the formatting looks like on your screen.

1. Choose the File Print Preview command (Alt,F,V or Ctrl+F9). See if you can identify the formatting.
2. Choose the File Print command. Examine the printed results.

Tip

If you aren't sure what features your printer supports, add lines like the ones in Figure 5.1 to your file. Format a few words in each line. Then print the file. You'll have a permanent record of what your printer can and can't do.

Removing a Format. If the selected text already includes formats, the Character Format dialog box shows those formats turned on in the list on the left. Just select them again to turn them off. If the selected text includes some characters that have a format and some that don't, the field shows a hyphen. If you select a format when it applies to some of the characters in the selected text, it is applied to all of the characters. You'll see shortly how to restore text to normal, unformatted state.

If the text was formatted with a position format, you can restore it to normal by selecting the **Normal** field in the **Position** box on the right. A selection that includes superscripted or subscripted text along with text in normal position does not have any position location marked in the dialog box. Selecting any of the three position options, however, sets that position for all the selected characters.

Using the Ribbon

So far, you haven't really had any use for the ribbon, an optional screen element. The ribbon, which you saw in Figure 2.6, provides shortcuts to the most used formatting features. There are two ways to turn it on:

1. Choose the View Ribbon menu command (Alt,V,B)

    or

2. Click the right button on the ruler/ribbon icon (⊥).

The ribbon appears just below the top border of the document window. The rightmost part is used for character formatting. It looks like this:

```
Bld   Ital   Ul
```

When the ribbon is displayed, you can select the characters to appear in any combination of bold, italic, and underline formats and click on the format abbreviations. And whenever the cursor is on a formatted character, the ribbon indicator for that formatting style appears in a distinctive color. If the word NEW is formatted in italics and underline, for example, both Ital and Ul will be distinctive when the cursor is in the word NEW. If the selected text contains some characters with the formatting and some without, question marks appear in the ribbon, as in B?? for bold.

Using Speed Formatting

Word provides a method of applying formats quickly from the keyboard using the control key. You hold down the control key and press the appropriate letter. Speed formatting is available for all the character formatting effects. Table 5.1 lists all the character speed formatting keys. Notice that Ctrl+Spacebar sets the selected characters back to the default, no matter how

Table 5.1. Character Speed Formatting Keys

Ctrl+B	Bold
Ctrl+I	Italic
Ctrl+U	Underline
Ctrl+D	Double underline
Ctrl+K	Small caps
Ctrl+H	Hidden text
Ctrl++	Superscript
Ctrl+=	Subscript
Ctrl+space	Normal character
Ctrl+Z	Normal character, except for font

they were formatted. If you want to remove all formatting except font changes, use Ctrl+Z instead of Ctrl+Spacebar.

Whether or not the ribbon is displayed, you can select the characters to appear in any of these formats and press the control key combination. You can apply several formats in succession to the same selection. Like the other character formatting methods, the speed formatting keys toggle the formatting on and off.

Tip If some of the speed formatting keys don't seem to work, someone may have installed other elements that use the same keys. Try pressing Ctrl+A,Ctrl+x, where x is the speed formatting key.

1. Select a word.
2. Press Ctrl+B. If the word doesn't look any different, try Ctrl+A,Ctrl+B.
3. Make sure the word is still selected, then press Ctrl+Spacebar.
4. Select a sentence (press F8 three times). Then Press Ctrl+I. (Use Ctrl+A,Ctrl+I if you don't get the effect you want.)
5. Make sure the same sentence is selected, then press Ctrl+Spacebar.

Formatting as You Type

If you want to apply character formatting as you type, use the speed formatting key at the beginning of the characters to be affected, type the characters, then use the speed formatting key again to turn off the effect. Try it out in your practice file. First move the cursor to the end and start a new sentence.

1. Type **This is an example of** in normal format, then press Ctrl+B to start bold formatting.
2. Type **bold characters**, then press Ctrl+B again to end bold formatting.
3. Type **and also** in normal format, then press Ctrl+I to start italic formatting.
4. Type **italic characters**, then press Ctrl+I again to end italic formatting.
5. Select *italic characters*, then choose the Format Character command.
6. Choose Small Kaps, then choose <OK>. These characters will have both formats.
7. Press Ctrl+Spacebar to restore normal formatting, then add a few normal words to the text.

When you look at the sentence on the screen, you may not be able to see the formatting very well.

1. Select the sentence you just added.
2. Choose the File Print command. Choose Selection in the **Page Range** field and choose <OK> to print it.

After you examine the printed result, take a moment to restore your system to its usual values.

1. Choose the View Preferences command (Alt,V,E).
2. If the **Display Mode** field shows Graphics, drop down the field menu and change it back to Text for the rest of this chapter.

Using Hidden Text

Hidden text is text that appears on the screen and in print only if you have requested it. In its normal default state, Word displays hidden text on the screen when you edit a document, but doesn't include it in printed output. You might want to use hidden text to bury notes to yourself or to your secretary. You can also use hidden text to design forms to receive text for printing on preprinted forms. Word includes control information for such functions as graphics, contents, and indexes in hidden text.

You format text as hidden with the Format Characters command or with the Ctrl+H speed formatting key. It shows on the screen, but when you print the document it doesn't appear. Occasionally, you may wish to print the document with the hidden text in place; for example, you might want to show hidden text while you are in the process of designing a form. You could, of course, reformat the hidden text and turn off the formatting. An easier way is to turn on the **Include Hidden Text** field in the Print Options dialog box. Any text marked as hidden is printed along with the rest of the text. It isn't flagged in any way. Be sure to turn off this field before you print again. If you want to try it out:

1. Select a sentence in the middle of a paragraph and use Ctrl+H to format it as hidden.
2. Select the entire paragraph.
3. Choose the File Print command.
4. If the **Page Range** field doesn't show Selection, move the cursor to it, drop down the field menu, and select Selection.
5. Choose <OK> to print the paragraph.

When you examine the printed paragraph, you'll see that the hidden text does not appear. To make it print without reformatting, try this:

1. Choose the File Print command.
2. Press the <Options> button.
3. Move the cursor to the **Hidden Text** field and turn it on.
4. Choose <OK> to remove the Print Options dialog box.
5. Make sure the **Page Range** field still indicates Selection.
6. Choose <OK> to print the paragraph.

When you examine the printed result this time, you'll see that the hidden text is included. Normally, hidden text on the screen is marked by a dotted underline. If you delete the first or last character of a hidden block, the block may expand. If you don't want hidden text to display on the screen at all, you can modify this effect through View Preferences. Here's how:

1. Choose the View Preferences command.
2. In the **Non-Printing Characters** box, turn off **Hidden Text** by clicking on it or pressing I.
3. Choose <OK>.

The hidden text no longer appears on the screen, but it is still there internally. If you format additional text as hidden, it disappears immediately. The screen display of hidden text is totally independent of the printing effect. Before you can work with hidden text, you have to display it again.

4. Choose the View Preferences command.
5. In the **Non-Printing Characters** box, turn on **Hidden Text**.
6. Choose <OK>.

Take a moment to restore the print options before continuing:

1. Choose the File Print command.
2. Press the <Options> button.
3. Move the cursor to the **Hidden Text** field and turn it off.
4. Choose <OK> to remove the Print Options dialog box.
5. Move the cursor to the **Page Range** field, drop down the menu and select All.
6. Choose <OK> to cause the changes to take effect.
7. When the print message appears, press Escape to cancel it unless you really want a printed copy of your document.

1. Make sure you have a document that contains several paragraphs current. Open README.DOC if you don't have another one available.
2. Make two adjacent words in the first paragraph bold.
3. Make two different adjacent words in that paragraph italic.
4. Make one different word double underlined. Then remove this effect with a speed key (Ctrl+Spacebar).
5. Make two letters in the middle of a long word superscripted.
6. Add the sentence "This is a new italic example" to the end of the paragraph, putting the words "a new italic" in italics as you type.
7. Print the document to see the effects.
8. Close this document without saving any changes, then bring up your practice document again.

You must select existing text before you can apply character formatting to it. After selecting it, you could use the Format Character command, the ruler, or the control characters to format text as bold or italic. You must use the Format menu to make text double underlined or superscripted. Use Ctrl-I to apply italics while entering new characters.

Formatting Paragraphs

So far, you have used single-spaced paragraphs with default indentation and alignment. The paragraphs have been aligned on the left and extended to the left and right default margins. There has been no justification, so the right edge has been ragged. Word lets you control these features through the Format Paragraph command. Figure 5.4 shows the dialog box that results when you choose the Format Paragraph command.

When you choose the Format Paragraph command with the mouse or with Alt,T,P, the paragraph containing the cursor is considered selected. If you want to affect several adjacent paragraphs, select text that extends into all the paragraphs you want to format.

1. Choose the Format Paragraph command (Alt,T,P).

Tip You don't have to select the entire paragraph; if any text in the paragraph is selected or contains the cursor, the whole paragraph will be affected.

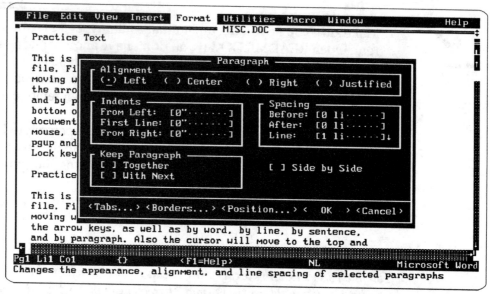

Figure 5.4. The Format Paragraph Dialog Box

We'll cover the Keep Paragraph option later. You'll also learn to use the <Tabs>, <Borders>, and <Position> buttons. These buttons are just alternate paths into other commands you can reach directly through the Format menu. The Side by Side option can get quite complex, so we won't cover it here.

Tip || Remember that Shift+F10 selects the entire document.

Formatting paragraphs individually can be a great deal of work; even formatting them as groups can get to be a drag. Later in this book (Chapter 9), you'll learn to define styles and apply them to your paragraphs with a single command. You'll still have to use all the basic formatting, but only once. Then you can, in effect, copy the format to all other paragraphs that can use it. The first step, though, is to learn to use the basics.

The Formatting Codes

Paragraph formatting codes are stored in the paragraph mark at the end of a paragraph. If you delete that mark, any paragraph formatting is gone and the text becomes a part of the next paragraph and takes on its formatting. If you haven't been working with paragraph marks displayed, you might want to turn them on. You can do this with the View Preferences command, selecting the **Paragraph Marks** field (Alt,V,E,P,↵). You'll see a paragraph mark at the end of each paragraph, marking every place you pressed ↵. These marks don't print, so you may want to have them on whenever you are entering text or working with your files.

While you type, you can format paragraphs. When you press ↵ to start a new paragraph, all the formatting codes that apply to the current paragraph carry over to the next.

Units of Measurement

By default, Word uses inches for most measurements; it uses lines for a few vertical measurements. It uses *in* or " to indicate inches and *li* to indicate lines. If you want the default measurements, you can just type numbers and omit the unit indicator. To use a different unit of measurement, you must type the number followed by the appropriate unit indicator. Table 5.2 lists the acceptable units. Spacing doesn't matter; you can type **4cm** or **4 cm** to indicate four centimeters.

You can change the default unit of measurement for horizontal increments through the Utilities Customize command (Alt,U,U). Just drop down the **Measure** field menu and select the measurement you prefer. The vertical measurement is always lines.

1. Choose the Utilites Customize command.
2. Move the cursor to the **Measure** field.
3. Scroll through the menu to see the options.
4. Choose <Cancel> to leave the dialog box without making any changes.

Table 5.2. Units of Measurement

Indicator	Unit
in or "	Inches
cm	Centimeters
p10	Character positions in font with 10 characters per inch
p12	Character positions in font with 12 characters per inch
pt	Points (72 points is 1 inch)
li	Lines (6 lines is 1 inch; 12 points is 1 line)

Paragraph Alignment

The default paragraph alignment is left; each line starts at the left margin and the right edge is ragged. If you prefer, you can select center or right alignment. With center, each line is centered between the right and left margins; this is useful for title pages, some headings, and even some poetry. With right alignment, each line extends to the right margin and the left edge is ragged; your application will determine if you want to use this.

A justified paragraph extends from the left to the right margin. Word inserts extra space between words and characters to maintain the straight edges. The exact effect depends on your printer and the type of spacing it can handle. Try it out by placing the cursor into a paragraph.

1. Choose the Format Paragraph command.
2. Turn on the **Right** button, then choose <OK>.
3. Notice the result on screen. Examine it in print preview, then choose the Format Paragraph command again.
4. Turn on the **Justified** button, then choose <OK>.
5. Notice the effect, check print preview, then restore **Left** alignment through the Format Paragraph command.

Speed formatting keys are available for paragraph formatting as well. Table 5.3 lists all these keys. As with the character formatting, you may have to use Ctrl+A if one of these doesn't work as you expect.

As you can see, just press Ctrl+C to center a paragraph, Ctrl+L to align it on the left, Ctrl+R to align it on the right, or Ctrl+J to justify the lines. You'll see how to use the other keys as you continue.

Table 5.3. Paragraph Speed Formatting Keys

Ctrl+C	Centered alignment
Ctrl+L	Left alignment
Ctrl+R	Right alignment
Ctrl+J	Justified alignment
Ctrl+Q	Indent from left and right
Ctrl+N	Increase left indentation
Ctrl+T	Hanging indentation
Ctrl+1	Single space
Ctrl+2	Double space
Ctrl+O	Space before paragraph (letter O)
Ctrl+X	Normal paragraph

Tip || Notice that Ctrl+X restores a normal, unformatted paragraph. This parallels the effect of Ctrl+Spacebar, which unformats selected characters.

1. Put the cursor in a different paragraph that is at least eight lines long.
2. Press Ctrl+J to see the justified effect.
3. Press Ctrl+C to see the lines all centered.
4. Press Ctrl+R to see the lines aligned on the right.
5. Press Ctrl+L to restore the default left alignment.

Paragraph Indents

You can cause Word to indent paragraphs from the left margin and/or from the right margin. You can also cause the first line of the paragraph to be indented or hanging-indent style. These options are in the **Indents** group box of the dialog box. The default values are 0 inches, or no indentation. You enter the number of inches of indentation you want.

For example, if you want a paragraph to be indented one and one-half inches from each margin, type **1.5** in both the **From Left** and **From Right** fields. You can include " or *in* if you like, but that's the default so it isn't necessary. If you want a different unit of measurement, you must type its indicator. If you want the normal paragraph line length but want each paragraph to start with a one-inch indentation, leave the **From Left** and **From Right** fields at 0 and type **1** in the **First Line** field. You can also combine the various types of indentation. Try it out, using the same paragraph as before.

1. Choose the Format Paragraph command.
2. Move the cursor to the **Indent** section, then type **.5"** in the **From Left** field and **1.5"** in the **First Line** field.
3. Choose <OK>, then see the effect.
4. Select text in two adjacent paragraphs.
5. Choose the Format Paragraph command.
6. Type **2"** in the **From Right** field, then choose <OK>.
7. Examine the effect.

Hanging Indents. A hanging indent occurs when the first line of the paragraph extends farther to the left than the rest of the lines. To create a hanging indent, you need to indent the entire paragraph from the left and use a negative value for the first line indent. For example, if a paragraph is indented one inch from the left margin and the first line indent value is –1, the result is a hanging indent. The speed formatting key Ctrl+T automatically sets up an indentation of 0.5" from the left and –0.5 for the first line, creating a hanging indentation automatically. Try it out.

1. Put the cursor in a paragraph that does not contain any character formatting. It should be several lines long.
2. Press Ctrl+T.

Notice the effect. The hanging indent is created immediately. You can check it out.

3. Choose the Format Paragraph command.

Notice that the values in the **Indents** box reflect the indentation.

4. Choose <Cancel>.
5. Press Ctrl+X to cancel the paragraph formatting.

Increasing the Indentation. If you are working with the Format Paragraph dialog box, you have to calculate the amount of indentation you want and type it specifically; you can't use +1 to increase indentation 1 inch, for example. A speed formatting key causes Word to do the calculation for you.

To increase the amount of indentation from the left, you can use the Ctrl+N speed formatting key. Each time you press Ctrl+N, the amount of indentation from the left margin is increased by half an inch. If you press Ctrl+N three times while the cursor is in a paragraph that originally had no indentation, it will be indented 1.5 inches.

Tip || You can select as many paragraphs as you want before using a speed formatting key. The effect applies to all of them.

Another speed formatting key lets you indent from both the left and right the same amount. Pressing Ctrl+Q indents both 0.5 inches. It works like Ctrl+N, but affects both margins. You can't decrease the indentation with speed formatting keys, however. If you indent too much, use Ctrl+X to cancel the formatting and start over. Or you can use the Format Paragraph command to modify the indentation.

1. Place the cursor in a typical paragraph.
2. Press Ctrl+Q.
3. Press Ctrl+N.

You have now indented the paragraph one inch from the left and half an inch from the right.

4. Press Ctrl+X to remove the indentation.

Using the Ruler. If you haven't been using the ruler on your screen, you might want to try it. You can turn the ruler on by choosing the View Ruler command or by clicking the left button on the ruler/ribbon icon. The ruler numbers the inches across the screen starting at the left margin of the current section. The location of the left and right indentation for the current paragraph is indicated by [and] in the ruler; these are affected by any indents. The location of the first line indent is shown as a vertical bar.

Turn on your ruler if it isn't on yet, then try it out.

1. Move the cursor to an unformatted paragraph and examine the right and left margin indicators.
2. Press Ctrl+Q and examine the right and left margin indicators.
3. Press Ctrl+N twice, then check the ruler line indicator.
4. Move the cursor into the next paragraph and press Ctrl+T. Check the ruler line when the cursor is in the first line, then when it is in the second.
5. Select all the text in your document (Shift+F10 or Ctrl+Click in the selection bar).
6. Choose the Format Paragraph command.
7. Type **0** in each field in the **Indent** section to restore the default paragraph formats.

Tip   You can press Ctrl+X to unformat the paragraph instead of using the command suggested in items 6 and 7.

Paragraph Spacing

Paragraph spacing has two different effects; you can control spacing between lines or spacing at the beginning or end of the paragraph. The abbreviation *li* in the dialog box indicates lines; remember that's the standard line size assuming six lines per inch. Alternatively, you can select Auto from the **Line** field menu, which lets Word select the line spacing based on the largest character in the paragraph; we'll deal with this later.

Remember that when you type a value, you don't have to type **li**. You only have to type the unit if you want to use a different one, such as *pt* (points) or *in* (inches).

Spacing within a Paragraph. The line spacing default is single spacing, but you can specify double, triple, or whatever you want; you can even use fractional line spacing if your printer can handle it. Line spacing affects the amount of space that appears between lines within the paragraph. It also affects space above formatted paragraphs. That is, if you type 2 to create double spacing when several paragraphs are selected, an extra space appears before each paragraph as well as between the lines. Try it out.

1. Make sure the cursor is in a paragraph that contains at least two lines.
2. Choose the Format Paragraph command.
3. Move the cursor to the **Line** field in the **Spacing** group, then type **2**.
4. Choose <OK>, then examine the effect.
5. Move the cursor to the adjacent paragraph.
6. Choose the Format Paragraph command.
7. Move the cursor to the **Line** field in the **Spacing** group, then type **3**.
8. Choose <OK>, then examine the effect on screen. Print it if you want.

You can use Ctrl+1 and Ctrl+2 to speedily format the spacing of paragraphs. No other spacings have speed formatting keys, however.

1. With the cursor in the triple-spaced paragraph, press Ctrl+2.
2. Now press Ctrl+1 to restore single spacing.

Spacing around Paragraphs. Sometimes you'll need extra space before or after paragraphs. You may want to add a blank line after each heading, or put a blank line before a list of items. While you can achieve this by pressing ↵, paragraph formatting lets you attach the spacing to the paragraph to make sure it doesn't get removed accidentally. The remaining options in the **Spacing** group box of the Format Paragraph dialog box help you do this.

If you want extra space before the paragraph, type the number of lines of space in the **Before** field. If you want extra space following the paragraph, type the number of lines in the **After** field. If necessary, you can type values in both fields.

If you need a space that isn't in lines, and your printer can handle it, you can type the value. Typing **10 pt** requests 10 points of space. If you type a value that can be converted to lines easily, Word will do it. For example, if you type **6 pt** while using a 12-point font, it gets automatically converted to 0.5 li.

1. Make sure you have a document open that contains several pages.
2. Make sure the ruler is displayed.

3. Change the first paragraph to be indented one-half inch from each margin with an additional one-half-inch indentation on the first line.
4. Change the second paragraph to be justified and indented one inch from the left margin.
5. Change the third paragraph to be double spaced.
6. Change the second paragraph to have one line space before it.
7. Save this file if you like.

Use the View menu or the ribbon/ruler icon to display the ruler. The Format Paragraph command gives you access to the dialog box for making all the changes required by this exercise.

Tip Be sure to use the letter O in the following speed formatting key. You might get a beep if you use the zero key, or it might call up some other effect.

The Ctrl+O speed formatting key provides one line space before the paragraph. Try it out.

1. Press Ctrl+O.
2. Press Ctrl+X to remove the blank line.

Section Page Formatting

Much of the document formatting affects an entire section. In this chapter, we'll deal with margins and page numbers. A section is often an entire document (you'll learn in Chapter 10 how to include more sections in a document). A section is indicated by the double line of dots across the screen. This section indicator may not appear in your documents yet; Word doesn't insert it until you make some change that affects a section. Once the section mark appears, be sure you add text to your file in front of the section mark. If you type after it, you'll be creating another section. Formatting in one section doesn't carry over to another.

Tip You can delete a section mark just like any other character. If you get a second double row of dots in your document, just move the cursor to it (it will highlight) and press the delete key. This removes all the section formatting.

All section formatting codes are stored in the section mark, so don't delete it by mistake. If you cut it, you can use Edit Undo to replace it, but remember that pressing the Delete key means you have to use Edit Undo immediately or it's gone forever.

When you make a change to the section formatting, it immediately applies to the entire section. When you change the margins, for example, you see the effect on the screen immediately for the entire section.

Setting Page Margins

Margins are set by section. If you want to change margins briefly within a file, you can use paragraph formatting to change the indents. But that means you have to make sure to affect every paragraph. To cause a change in margins to affect the entire file, you have to work at the section level. To change margins permanently for different parts of a file, you can start a new section; that's covered later in the book. In most cases, you'll set margins for the entire file.

To change margins, use the Format Margins command (Alt,T,M). If you choose Format Section (Alt,T,S), you can select the <Margins> button to take you to the same dialog box, which is shown in Figure 5.5.

If you happen to be using a nonstandard size paper, you would change the paper size in this box. Just change the height and width values in the upper

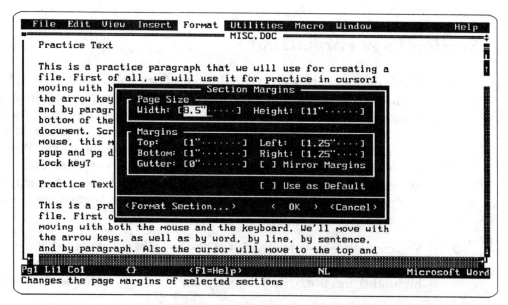

Figure 5.5. The Format Section Margins Dialog Box

part of the dialog box. If you aren't using inches, be sure to type the unit indicator as well.

You can set margins for the left, right, top, and bottom of a page. The default margins are one inch on top and bottom and 1.25 inches on left and right. These result in a six-inch line length (8.5 minus 2.5) and nine inches of vertical text (11 minus 2). To change the top, bottom, left, or right margin, type the new value in the appropriate field. If you don't use inches, be sure to use the unit indicator. You can change any or all of these margins. Try it out. First scroll through your file so a page break (single row of dots) appears on the screen.

1. Choose the Format Margins (Alt,T,M) command.
2. Move the cursor to the **Top** field and type **2**.
3. Move the cursor to the **Bottom** field and type **1.5**.
4. Choose <OK> and notice that the page break in your file is at a different location.
5. Choose the Format Margins command again.
6. Move the cursor to the **Left** field and type **2**.
7. Move the cursor to the **Right** field and type **2**.
8. Choose <OK>. Then notice that the line length has changed, resulting in a still different page break location.
9. If you want, preview or print the document to see how it looks.

Setting a Gutter Margin

If the document you are creating will be bound, you might want to specify a gutter margin. This causes an additional margin to be placed on the inside, the binding edge; the gutter margin appears on the left edge of odd-numbered pages and the right edge of even-numbered pages. If you want an extra half inch for binding, type .5 in the **Gutter Margin** field. If you make no other margin changes, this results in a line length of 5.5 inches, since the gutter margin is used in addition to the right and left margins.

Setting Mirror Margins

If the document will be eventually printed on two sides, you might want different margins for the even (left) and odd (right) pages. For example, you might want a two-inch margin on the outside edges but a one-inch margin on the inside (binding) edge. You can ask Word to use a mirror image on the right and left. Specify the right and left margins for the odd-numbered pages and turn on the **Mirror Margins** field. The margins will then be reversed for even pages. If you use both mirror and gutter margins, the gutter margin is added to the inside edge of each page.

Changing the Default Margins

If you don't like Word's default margins, you can change them. Just type the values you want to use in the appropriate fields and check the **Use as Default** field. The new values will take effect instead of the old ones.

Later in this book (Chapter 9), you'll see how to change the default style; that will override any change you make here.

Using Page Numbers

By default, Word does not number pages. It keeps track, of course, since you see the page number in the status line, but that number doesn't appear when you print the file. You can turn on page numbers to appear on all printed pages in any of several formats. You can even select the starting number.

Word lets you turn on page numbers through the Format Section command. Choose the Format Section command to bring up the Format Section dialog box, shown in Figure 5.6. Notice the buttons at the bottom of the dialog

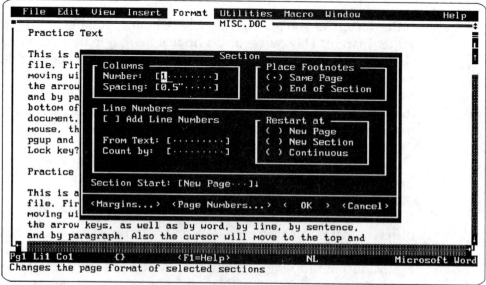

Figure 5.6. The Format Section Dialog Box

box. The <Margins> button brings up the Section Margins dialog box you've already seen.

1. Choose the Format Section command.
2. Press the <Page Numbers> button.

You'll see the dialog box shown in Figure 5.7. In it, you must tell Word the vertical position of the page number; that is, you must specify whether you want the page number to appear in the top or bottom margin. By default, it appears half an inch from the top or bottom edge of the paper, whichever you select. You needn't work in inches; remember that you can use a different unit of measurement by including the unit indicator shown in Table 5.1.

You must also specify the alignment of the page number. It can be at the left margin, at the right margin, or centered in the text area of the page. To place it at a different position, type the distance from the left edge in the field.

Normally, Word uses standard Arabic numerals for page numbers, as you see in the **Format** field. As you can see by opening the field menu, however, there are four alternate formats you can use: uppercase letters starting with A, B, C; lowercase letters starting with a, b, c; uppercase roman numerals starting with I, II, III; lowercase roman numerals starting with i, ii, iii. Just select the format you want to use.

Finally, you can start where you want. The default, Auto, starts with page number 1 when you print the file by itself. If you print several files as a group,

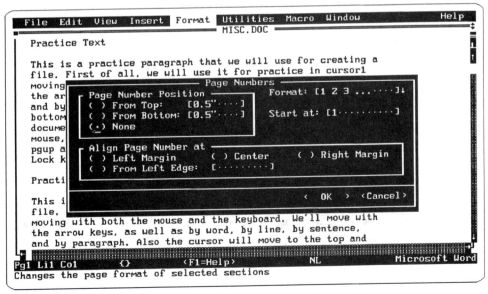

Figure 5.7. The Page Numbers Dialog Box

Auto lets Word number the pages in sequence; you'll see how to use that feature later in the book. To start with a different number, just type it in the field. If the file containing Chapter 1 of your novel ends with page 21, type 22 as the starting number for the file containing Chapter 2. The value Auto is valid here; it comes in handy later on when you learn to print several documents at once. For now, type 1 to make sure it starts with 1. Try printing page numbers for your file. First notice in the status line what page number is current. (The Insert Page Numbers command gets the same dialog box.)

3. Turn on the **From Top** field; leave the default position.
4. In the **Start At** field, type **5**.
5. Choose <OK>.
6. Notice that the page number is now four higher than it was previously.
7. Choose the Format Section command.
8. Choose the <Page Numbers> button.
9. In the **Start At** field, type **1**, then choose <OK>.

1. Make sure your current document has several pages. Use README.DOC if you don't have a long document available.
2. Change the top margin to 1.5 inches and the bottom margin to 2 inches.
3. Change the right margin to 1.5 inches and the left margin to 1 inch.
4. Add a one-half inch gutter margin and mirror the margins on the right.
5. Put a page number centered at the top of the page in standard Arabic numerals starting with 3.
6. Print the document to see how it looks.
7. Change the page number to the left edge of the bottom margin, using lowercase Roman Numerals starting with 1 (or i).
8. Print the document again, or at least preview it to see the difference your formatting has made.
9. Close this file without the changes if you opened a different one and open your practice file again.

Use Format Margins commands to change the margins. Use Format Section and choose the <Page Numbers> button to insert and position the page numbers. Use the standard printing method to see the results.

Pagination in Word

Word can do pagination automatically in the background, or you can have it ignore pagination until you request it or print the document. So far, you've let it handle this automatically, and most of us keep it that way. As you type or remove or format the document, Word inserts and adjusts the page breaks so they show where one printed page ends and another begins. These are called "soft" page breaks, and you can't delete them. The current page number (the page that contains the cursor) is shown at the very left of the status bar.

If you want to turn off automatic pagination, use the Utilities Customize command and turn off the **Background Pagination** field. Then paging isn't done until you request it. If you want to worry about exact paging and exact line breaks all the time, you might turn on the line break display through the View Preferences command. In the resulting dialog box, turn on the **Line Breaks** field.

Suppose you want a certain paragraph to always start at the top of a page. Or you want to leave a blank page to insert a separate item after printing. You can insert a page break manually whether or not Word is handling pagination. To insert a page break manually, follow these steps:

1. Put the cursor just below where you want the page to break.
2. Press Ctrl+⏎.

This creates a manual or "hard" page break that won't be changed, even if you add text in front of it. It looks much like an automatic or soft page break, but a dot appears in every position instead of every other one. You can delete a hard page break, but you can't delete an automatically placed or soft break.

Tip You can use a Replace command to search for all the hard page breaks (use ^p as the **Text to Search for**) and replace them with nothing. If you turn off **Confirm Changes**, they are all removed automatically and Word repaginates the document.

Reviewing Pagination

A special utility lets you check out the pagination and see where page breaks occur. It even lets you modify exactly where they occur before you print a document. You'll find this especially useful if you have just prepared a long file and want to make sure the page breaks are at reasonable places. If you've been typing without background pagination, you'll have to use it before you can print the file.

To paginate an unpaginated file, choose the Utilities Repaginate Now command (Alt,U,P). The resulting dialog box gives you only one field. If you want to visually confirm each page break, check the field. If you just want paging done, leave it unchecked. Then press the <OK> or <Cancel> button and Word gets to work. It turns on the line break display, if it was turned off before, so you will see the exact characters on each side of the page break location. If the page breaks aren't confirmed, it is done quickly and control returns to you with no further effort.

Confirming Page Breaks

If you asked to confirm page breaks, Word stops at each page break, rests the cursor on it, and displays a prompt in the message line to tell you what to do. The message differs depending on whether the page break is a hard or a soft one. If it's hard, the message is "Press Enter to confirm the page break or Del to remove it." Those are your only choices. If you like the page break there, press ↵. If not, press the delete key and it is removed. Word will continue repagination and you'll see the next page break.

When repagination encounters a soft page break, the message is "Press Enter to confirm page break or use direction keys to reposition it." Again, if you like the page break where it is, you can just press ↵ and repagination shows you the next page break. When you see a soft page break, however, you can move it; actually what you can do is put it in a different place and make it into a hard page break. Just press ↑ to move the page break a few lines up on the page. When it is where you want it, press ↵. Word inserts a hard page break at that point and continues to the next page break for you to confirm. Word won't let you move the cursor below the automatic page break, but you can use ↓ to reposition the page break location once you've moved it up. Try it out:

1. Choose the Utilities Repaginate Now command.
2. Turn on the **Confirm Page Breaks** field.
3. When you see the message at the first page break, press ↓. The beep indicates that you can't adjust it that way. Press ↑ six or seven times, then press ↵.
4. Whenever the message appears again, just press ↵ until you reach the end of the file.

5. Press Ctrl+Home to see the beginning of the file, then press PgDown until you see the first page break. Notice that it has a dot in each position, indicating a hard page break.

To cancel the repagination process at any time, just press Escape.

Page Break Application

In most cases, it's better to leave soft page breaks in your document. If you insert hard page breaks, any later insertion or deletion of text may result in a strange looking document. Later in this book (Chapter 8), you'll learn to specify that paragraphs be kept on a single page, which helps you control page layout. If you really need hard page breaks, put them in when the document itself is ready for final printing.

Line Number in the Status Line

Reviewing the location of page breaks is all well and good, but it is more useful if you know how many lines appear on the page. When a hard page break occurs, for example, you don't know if 15, 25, 45, or what number of lines appear before it on the page. When a soft page break occurs, you know the page is filled, but you still might want to know how many lines there are.

To turn on the line number display in the status line, choose the View Preferences command. Turn on the **Show Line Numbers** field. The number of the line containing the cursor will appear in the status bar. Only lines actually containing text will be counted. If you want to count blank lines in the top margin and between text, as well as text lines, turn on **Count Blank Space** to get an absolute line count. If you are using double spaced paragraphs, you might want to do this to find out where the final page will end. The line number display appears between the page number and column number in the left portion of the status bar.

1. Choose the View Preferences command.
2. Turn on the **Show Line Numbers** field.
3. Choose <OK>, then notice the line number display in the status line.
4. Move the cursor up to a soft page break and notice how many lines appear on a page.
5. Choose the Utilities Repaginate Now command.
6. Turn on the **Confirm Page Breaks** field.

7. Choose <OK>.
8. At the first message, notice the line number display.
9. Delete the hard page break since it isn't near the bottom of the page.
10. Press ↵ at all other page breaks, after noticing the line number.

You'll find the line number display very useful when you are formatting documents for printing. If you didn't choose **Count Blank Space**, the line number display gives the number of the current text line (the one containing the cursor), starting with 1 and extending through the number of text lines that fit on the page. If you turned **Count Blank Space** on, the display gives the absolute line number from the top of the page. If you have the default one-inch top margin, the display will show *Li7* when the cursor is in the first line of text. If your bottom margin is also one inch (and you are using 11-inch paper), the display will show *Li60* when the cursor is on the last line of text for a page.

1. Make sure you have an open document containing several pages. Use README.DOC if you don't have a different one available.
2. Select all the paragraphs and set them at double spacing.
3. Change the top margin to 1.5 inches with a centered, Arabic page number.
4. Put a hard page break at the end of the first paragraph and somewhere on the last page.
5. Repaginate and confirm the page breaks. If any hard page break occurs more than 10 lines before the end of the page, delete it.
6. Print or preview the document to see the effect.
7. Exit Word without saving any changes.

*Use Ctrl+↵ to insert a hard page break. Use the Utilities Repaginate Now command to scan and adjust the page breaks. If the current line number does not appear in the status line, use the View Preferences command and turn on the **Show Line Numbers** field.*

Exercise

This chapter has covered the fundamentals of character, paragraph, and section formatting. You can now make words, paragraphs, and pages look the way you want in your documents. You can practice using these features in this exercise.

1. Close any open files, and exit Word.
2. Start Word and type a few paragraphs to create a new file. Repeat the paragraphs until you have more than a page of text.
3. Format four words in the first paragraph as bold, four others as underlined, and four more as small caps. Add a sentence at the end applying italics as you type.
4. Change the case of one sentence to all caps using Shift+F3.
5. Restore two of the bold words to normal text. Put one of them in superscript.
6. Set the first three paragaphs at double space. Give the fourth paragraph a hanging indent.
7. Set the margins for the entire document at 2 inches on each side, then turn on page numbers at the bottom and print the document.
8. Save it as PRAC5.

To apply character formatting after text is typed, select the text, then use the speed formatting key, the ribbon, or the Format Character command. To apply formatting as you type, use the speed formatting key (Ctrl+I for italics), type the text, then use the speed formatting key again. Ctrl+Spacebar resets selected characters to normal.

Use Format Paragraph or speed formatting keys to change the spacing or indentation of selected paragraphs. Use Format Margins to change the page margins and Format Section or Insert Page Numbers to insert and position page numbers.

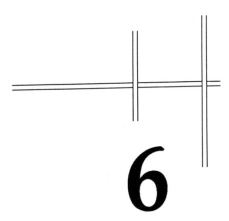

6

Using Word's Windows

So far in this book, you've been working with one document window at a time. Word actually lets you have up to nine windows open at once, including a help window. When you have several windows open, you can arrange them in whatever way you want, switch from one window to the next, copy and move text between windows, and even split a single window into two panes. In this chapter, you'll learn to manipulate multiple windows on the Word screen. In particular, you'll learn to:

- Open multiple files and documents
- Switch between open windows
- Close all open documents at once
- Save all open documents at once
- Move and copy text from one window to another
- Change the size or position of an open window
- Arrange windows on the screen
- Split a window into two panes
- Use the same document in more than one window
- Conserve screen space when several windows are open

Microsoft Word 5.5

Windows within Word

The document window you've been using and the help window are both typical of windows within Word. All have borders, a title bar, scroll bars, and icons. The active window is always the one containing the cursor; only one window is ever active at a time. But you can switch between open windows quickly using either the mouse or the keyboard.

Using Multiple Documents

When you start up Word, a blank window with Document1 in the title bar is on the screen. If you immediately open a file, that file fills the document window and the file name replaces Document1 in the title bar. You still have just one window open.

Suppose you start up Word and type into the blank document window. Then, a few minutes later, you open a file. Now Word opens a new document window and places the newly opened file in it. You have two windows open. The screen will look something like the one in Figure 6.1. Notice that the window just opened almost completely overlaps the Document1 window and contains the cursor. It is the active window. The top border of the active window is double, as you can see in the figure.

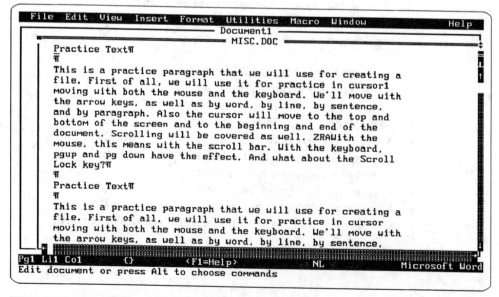

Figure 6.1. Two Windows Open

When windows overlap on the screen, the active window is always fully shown. If you open another file, it overlays the active window and immediately becomes active.

1. Start up Word.
2. Type your name and address into the Document1 window.
3. Open one of your other documents. Use README.DOC if you don't have any others.

When the Word screen contains more than one window, the title bar of the active window is highlighted as you can see on the screen. The cursor is in that window. Other window features such as the scroll bars and the ruler appear only in the active window. If the ribbon is displayed, it remains above any windows.

Switching between Windows

Once more than one window is open, you will probably want to switch between them. Before you can make changes or scroll in a window, you have to get the cursor there, to make the window active.

Using a Mouse. With a mouse, you can just click on any part of any window that is visible, and the clicked-on window becomes active. It comes to the front of the screen if part of it was hidden before. That works with the current layout, as you can see the top and left edges of the Document1 window.

1. Click on any part of the Document1 window that you can see.

Now the Document1 window is active, but you can't see the other window. You'll have to use another technique to switch to it.

Using the Window Menu. The Window menu, shown in Figure 6.2, lists all the open windows; they are numbered starting with 1. A dot indicates the currently active window. You can change to a different window by selecting it just like any other menu option. You can use the cursor to highlight the window name and press ↵ or click on it with the mouse. You can even just press the number.

All the commands on this menu help you manipulate windows on your screen. We'll cover all of them in this chapter.

Microsoft Word 5.5

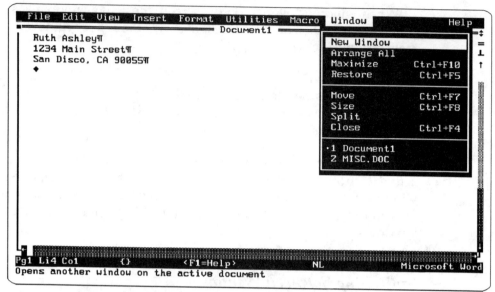

Figure 6.2. The Window Menu

2. Drop down the Window menu (Click or Alt,W) and notice the numbered list of open windows at the bottom.
3. Click on the name of the inactive window or type its number. Notice on the screen that the other window is now active.
4. Choose the command to make the Document1 window active (Alt,W,1).

The menu is effective and useful whether or not you use a mouse. It gives you a quick listing of what windows are open and lets you switch among them by name. It also shows you the sequence of the windows.

Using Shortcut Keys. A third way of changing windows is to use shortcut keys. Use Ctrl+F6 to switch to the next document window in the order they are numbered in the Window menu. Use Shift+Ctrl+F6 to switch to the previous document window; this moves through the open windows in reverse order. If only two windows are open, these two key combinations have the same effect.

1. Use the File Open command to open another file. Notice that it becomes the active window.
2. Drop down the Window menu (Click or Alt,W) and notice the order in which the windows are numbered.

3. Click outside the menu or press the Escape key to release the menu.
4. Press Ctrl+F6. Notice that the next window is active.
5. Press Ctrl+F6 again twice. Notice that you are back at the new file you opened.
6. Press Shift+Ctrl+F6 several times. Notice that the sequence of windows is the reverse of pressing Ctrl+F6.
7. Restore Document1 as the open window.

Opening a New Document

You can already open existing files by selecting their names. You can even create a new file by typing a new file name after selecting File Open. Either method causes Word to open a new window on the screen. Sometimes you may not want to provide a file name right away. You may just want a new window to hold temporary notes or to start a file. You can open a new document window by choosing the File New command. The resulting dialog box lets you specify the type of window you want; for now, leave the default **Document** chosen. If you want to send the document to a different directory, you can select a nondefault path here. Usually, however, you can provide the directory information when and if you save the document as a file.

1. Choose the File New command (Alt,F,N). Notice the **Document** field is selected.
2. Choose <OK>.

The new, empty document window appears on the screen and is active. The name Document2 appears in the title bar. Every time you open another unnamed document window with File New, another number is added to the name Document$n$.

3. Drop down the Window menu. Notice that four windows are now listed.
4. Switch back to the Document1 window.

Opening a New Window for the Same Document

Sometimes you may want more than one window for the same document. You might want to work with the last part of the file, for example, but refer frequently to the introductory paragraphs. You might want to make sure the headings are parallel in different parts of a report. Or you might want to use a different view in each window. You might want all the hidden characters displayed in one, for example, and none in the other. Word lets you have the same document in several windows. Any changes you make to the document in one window affect it in all windows. The overall limit of nine windows applies, of course. If a document is in four windows, you can have only five additional windows open.

You use the Window New Window (Alt,W,N) command. Word opens a window and copies the current document into it. The title bar shows the document or file name followed by a colon and the number 2. If the window containing PRAC2.DOC was active when you chose Window New Window, the window with PRAC2.DOC:2 in the title bar is opened. The cursor is at the beginning of the file. Both windows appear at the bottom of the Window menu. You get the same effect if you choose File Open to reopen a file that is already on the screen. Word assumes you just want another window for it.

1. Choose the Window New Window command (Alt,W,N). Notice that the new active window has Document1:2 in the title bar.
2. Drop down the Window menu. Notice that Document1:1 and Document1:2 are both listed. Release the menu.
3. Type a sentence in either Document1 window. Press ↵, then type another sentence.
4. Change the view so that the non-printing characters are all shown or none are shown (whichever was not true before).
5. Examine the other Document1 window. Notice that the views are not identical.

When you have multiple windows for a document open, you can switch between them just as between other windows. When you close a window, just that window is affected. To go from three windows containing a file to one, you'll have to close two of them. When you save a file, it affects all windows containing the file, since there is only one file.

Saving Changes

You can already save changes to a single open document by choosing File Save, File Save As, File Close, or File Exit Word. It's a little different when you have more than one document open. You can still save or close each window individually using the menu command or close box when the window is active. If autosave is turned on, it saves all open files automatically.

The File menu also includes the File Save All and File Close All commands. You can choose either to process all the open documents at once.

The File Save All Command

When you choose File Save All, any open windows containing files that have been saved before are saved as usual. Any open windows that haven't been saved yet result in the standard File Save As procedure. When the cursor returns to the Word screen, all windows will contain saved files. The Window menu and title bars reflect any name changes that occurred.

Saving files doesn't change the number of windows that are open. If you save the Document1:2 window as JANREPT, for example, the title bar will contain JANREPT.DOC:2. The Window menu will contain JANREPT.DOC:1 and JANREPT.DOC:2; if the document is in more windows, they'll be shown as well.

The File Close All Command

When you choose File Close All, any open windows containing files that have had no changes since the last time you saved them or opened them are quietly closed and removed from the screen. If necessary, you'll see a File Save As dialog box for previously unsaved files. Any open windows containing files that have had changes result in dialog boxes that ask if you want to save each file. You'll have a choice of <Yes>, <No>, or <Cancel> for each one.

When you choose <Yes>, the changes are saved; you'll be prompted for new file information if necessary. When you choose <No>, the changes are abandoned. When you choose <Cancel>, the File Close All operation is stopped. Previous documents may have been saved, but none of them will be closed.

Exiting Word with Windows Open

If you choose the File Exit Word command, the effect is the same as choosing File Close All, then exiting. The open windows will be treated individually.

Using Multiple Documents

Once you have several windows open and can switch between them at will, you can edit, format, and print the documents just as if the active window were the only one. The active window has the full borders, the distinctive title bar, the scroll bars and mouse icons. You won't really have any question about which window is active.

If you want to copy or move text between windows, first make the window containing the text active. Then select the text and choose the Edit Cut or Edit Copy command. Then switch to the window that will receive the text. Position the cursor and choose Edit Paste. If you have a mouse you can use speed copying and moving between windows, just as within a single document.

Tip ‖ Remember that you can press Shift+Delete for Edit Cut, Ctrl+Insert for Edit Copy, and Shift+Insert for Edit Paste.

1. Choose the File Save All command (Alt,F,E).
2. When prompted, provide a name like PRAC6 for Document1.
3. Add a few words to the active window.
4. Switch to a different window and add a few words.
5. Choose the File Exit Word command.
6. Save changes to one window, but not to another.

1. Start up Word and add a few lines to Document1.
2. Open two files, PRAC2 and another one.
3. Add two more windows containing PRAC2. Then add a line at the beginning of one PRAC2 window.
4. Save Document1 as SELF6. Then add another line to it.
5. Make the other document (not PRAC2 or SELF6) active.
6. Close all the windows, saving all the changes.

Use the File Open command to open files and Window New Window to add more windows of the active file. Use File Save when any window containing a document is active to save just one file. Use the mouse, the menu, or the shortcut keys to switch from one window to the next. Use File Close All to close all files, and choose <Yes> to save all the changes.

Using Help Windows

As you know, you can show a help window overlaying a document window. One way to remove help windows is to click elsewhere on the screen; this actually keeps the help window on the screen but puts the other window in front of it. If you remove help windows by clicking in the close box or pressing the escape key, you've been closing the window.

At times, you may want to keep a help window on screen while you work in a document. When a help window is displayed, the menu bar is still active. The Window menu lists the open help window along with the document windows; it receives the letter H instead of a number.

1. If you don't have any files open, open one.
2. Press F1 or click on the help reminder in the status bar. Notice that the Help Index window appears.
3. Drop down the Window menu. Notice that the Help window is listed and given the letter H.
4. Release the menu.

Arranging Open Windows

So far, you've seen that each window you open is a bit smaller than the last, so they overlap on the screen. Of course, when you make the original window active again, it completely overlays smaller windows. Word provides several ways you can arrange windows on the screen. And you already know how to remove certain window elements to save space on the screen and let you display more lines of data. In this section, you'll learn to let Word arrange the windows automatically so they don't overlap. Then you'll see how to make the active window fill the entire screen and return to its previous size. Finally, you'll learn to change the size and position of a window individually.

Automatic Window Arrangement

Word can arrange your windows automatically so you see them all at once. If you have two windows open, choosing the Window Arrange All command divides the screen horizontally, putting one at the top and one at the bottom. If you have three windows, Word creates three horizontal slices.

1. Choose the Window Arrange All command (Alt,W,A). Notice that the help window is at the bottom.
2. Choose the File New command, then choose <OK>. Notice that the new document overlays the arrangement.
3. Choose Window Arrange All again. Notice that the new window is at the top of the screen.

When you add a fourth window to the arrangement, Word splits the bottom window area vertically, so the screen has room for four. The next two windows you add to the arrangement cause the center and top window areas to be split. The seventh window you add causes the bottom third of the screen to contain three windows, as shown in Figure 6.3. You can see that nine windows is a practical limitation!

Notice that only the active window has a double top border; in this view, it also has scroll bars, icons, and the cursor. You can still use any method to switch between windows; the menu, clicking, or Ctrl+F6 and Shift+Ctrl+F6.

1. Make a different window active. Notice how the window changes.

If you close a window after using Window Arrange All, the remaining windows don't rearrange automatically. You'll see the blank screen in the area. You'll have to use Window Arrange All again to rearrange the screen.

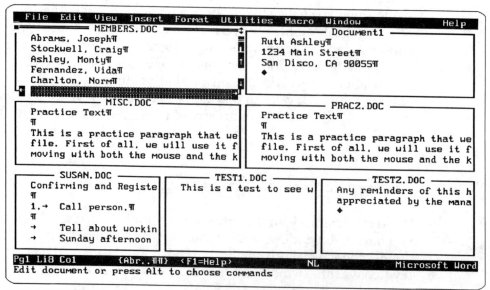

Figure 6.3. Arranging Seven Windows Automatically

2. Make the help window active, using any method.
3. Close the window using any method. Notice the screen appearance.
4. Choose Window Arrange All again.

Conserving Space on the Screen

If you are working with several windows, you might feel that the screen is too small. The display includes just one ribbon and one ruler; they reflect the active window. The menu bar also appears just once on the screen, as do the message bar and the status bar. You can turn off any or all of these elements using the View menu and the View Preferences dialog box. Each line that isn't displayed gives you one more line to show window data on the screen.

Only the active window includes scroll bars; when you change the active window, the scroll bars go to it. But you can turn these off too. You may find the scroll bars very useful in small windows, since not much of the text shows at a time. Even the horizontal scroll bar at the bottom can be well used in windows that don't extend across the screen. If you don't use a mouse, however, you'll want to turn the scroll bars off.

You can also turn the window borders off, but they don't make any difference on the multiple window display. You'll still see the borders and the icons. Removing borders is useful only when you maximize the window, which is covered next.

1. Drop down the View menu and turn off the status bar. Turn off the ruler and ribbon if they are on.
2. Choose the View Preferences command and turn off the menu bar, the message bar, and both scroll bars. Then choose <OK>.

Now your screen has more lines, so the individual windows can be larger.

Tip || Remember that pressing Alt brings the menu bar back temporarily.

3. Restore any elements you want to keep on screen.

Maximizing the Window Size

Usually, most of your work is in a single window. You may want to arrange the windows so you can see them all, but then enlarge the one you are working with. Maximizing a window makes it occupy as much of the screen as possible.

You can maximize the active window by choosing the Window Maximize command or by clicking on the maximize icon (↕) in the upper-right corner. The MX indicator appears in the status bar. The active window then takes over the screen, much as the first document you open in a Word session. If you switch to a different window, it will be maximized as well.

If borders are turned off, the largest display is possible, but then you won't see the close or maximize icons. You also need the borders to do some moving and sizing, which are covered later in this chapter. If you use a mouse, you'll probably want to leave the borders displayed.

A maximized window overlays all other open windows; you can still access them using the menu or the shortcut keys. Once a window is maximized, switching to another window causes it to be maximized as well. In fact, if you exit Word with maximize turned on, the next time you enter Word and open a file, it will be maximized as well.

1. Use any method to make a window containing a lot of text active.
2. Choose Window Arrange All.
3. Choose Window Maximize or click on the maximize icon. The maximized window occupies the entire screen.
4. Choose the View Preferences command and turn off the window borders. Notice the difference.
5. Choose View Preferences again and turn off the scroll bars and the message bar. Notice that more lines are visible.
6. Choose View Preferences again and restore the scroll bars, the border, and the message bar.
7. Switch to a different window, using any method. Notice that it is maximized too.

To "unmaximize" a window, you can choose the Window Restore command. This restores the active window to the size, shape, and position it was in before you maximized it. If you have a mouse, you can click on the maximize icon again to restore it; it is a toggle. If your window doesn't have borders, you won't see the maximize icon, so you'll have to use the menu.

1. Choose the Window Restore command.
2. If you have a mouse, click on the maximize icon. Then click on it again to restore the former window.

Many people like to work with several windows open and arranged on the screen. The primary window can be maximized while you are doing data entry or editing, then restored when you check information in other windows.

1. Make sure at least three document windows are open, then have Word arrange them automatically.
2. Open a help window, then have Word include it in the arrangement.
3. Make one document window active, then maximize it.
4. Remove at least two standard components of the screen and see how it looks. Then restore them.
5. Make a different window active. Then restore it to its former size.

Use Window Arrange All to arrange your windows. Click on the maximize icon or use Window Maximize to maximize a window. Click again or choose Window Restore to restore it. Use View menu commands to control the screen appearance.

Changing Window Size, Shape, and Location

Many times you won't want to use Word's default window arrangement. You might want to work with two windows side by side, for example, as shown in Figure 6.4. Or you might want a short help window at the bottom and a much larger document window above it. Word lets you change the size and shape of an individual window or move it to a different location on the screen.

Changing the Window Size

You change a window's size from the lower-right corner. The upper-left corner remains where it is. If the window is currently maximized, you can only make it smaller. If it's smaller than the maximum size, you can make the window larger or smaller. There is a minimum size that you can make a window: about four lines of text and 16 characters across. If you also want to move the window, you have to do that separately.

When you are ready to change a window's size, choose the Window Size command. The border of the active window turns black, the word SIZE appears at the right end of the status bar, and the message "Use direction keys to resize window, and press Enter. Press Esc to cancel." appears in the message bar. You must use the arrow keys at this point to change the size; you can't use the mouse. As you press the arrow keys, the black border moves to show you the current size.

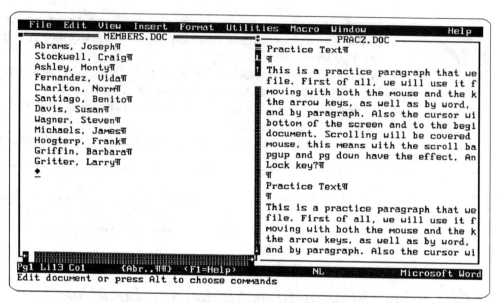

Figure 6.4. Side-by-Side Windows

1. Make a document window active.
2. Choose the Window Size command (Alt,W,S).
3. Press ↑ about eight times and ← about ten times. Then press ↵.

The window now has a new, smaller size. If you maximize it, the window fills the entire screen. If you then choose to restore it, it will return to this size.

4. Maximize the window.
5. Restore the former size.

Using the Mouse. If you have a mouse, you can size any window that has its borders displayed. Click on the size icon in the lower-right corner of the window and drag that corner to where you want it to be. When you release the button, the window is resized. To cancel it, just drag the icon back.

Moving a Window

You can move a window using the Window menu. Choose the Window Move command (Alt,W,M). A black shadow appears around the edge of the window, the word MOVE appears on the right end of the status bar, and "Use direction keys to move window, and press Enter. Press Esc to cancel." appears in the message bar. You use any arrow keys to move the window within the screen limits; you won't be able to overlay the menu bar or status bar.

Once the window is in the position you want, press ↵ to fix the position. You can change the size or shape some more if you wish.

Using the Mouse. If you have a mouse, you can move the window very easily. Just position the pointer on the top or left border of the window and drag the whole thing to wherever you want it. You can't do this if the borders aren't displayed.

1. Choose the Window Move command (Alt,W,M).
2. Use any arrow keys to reposition the window on the screen. When you are ready, press ↵.
3. If you have a mouse, place the pointer on the left border and drag the window to another location on the screen. Then release the button.

Arranging the Screen

Suppose you want to display your main document window in the upper two-thirds of the screen and have a help window in the bottom third, as shown in Figure 6.5. Here's how you might accomplish it.

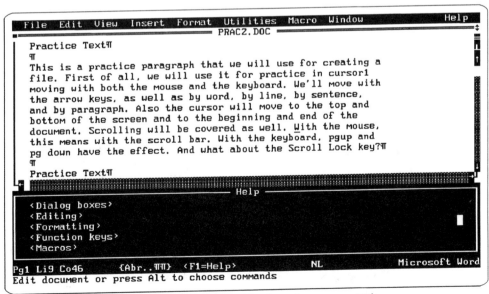

Figure 6.5. Manual Window Arrangement

First resize your document window so that it occupies about the top two-thirds. Then get the help window you want. Resize it so that it is about one-third screen high and the full width of the screen. Finally, move the help window to the bottom of your screen.

1. Suppose you want to have two document windows shown side by side. Make sure you have two document windows open.
2. Resize and locate one window on the left side of the screen.
3. Resize and locate the other window on the right side of the screen.
4. Activate both windows in turn to make sure there isn't any overlap. If there is, correct it.
5. Maximize one window, then return it to the manually arranged location and size.
6. If you have a mouse, resize one of the windows using the other method.
7. Arrange the windows in the default arrangement.

If you use the menu commands, you must use the arrow keys to do the sizing and moving. If you use the icons, you must use the mouse for all of it.

Window Panes

Sometimes you don't want two separate windows for the same document, but you do want to be able to see two parts of it at once. If you are just referring to the beginning, for example, while entering text at the end, you can split the window into panes instead of using up another document window. In window panes, you have full access to the document in both windows. Figure 6.6 shows an example. Notice that a double line divides the panes. A separate vertical scroll bar is provided for each pane, but there is only one full window.

If the ruler is on when you split a window into two panes, or if you turn it on while the panes are present, a separate ruler appears for each pane; in that case, the double line doesn't appear. You can do the same editing and scrolling in both panes. You can move and copy between panes just as within a single window or between windows.

When you scroll vertically in one pane, the other doesn't change. This lets you leave data for reference in one window while scrolling or typing in the

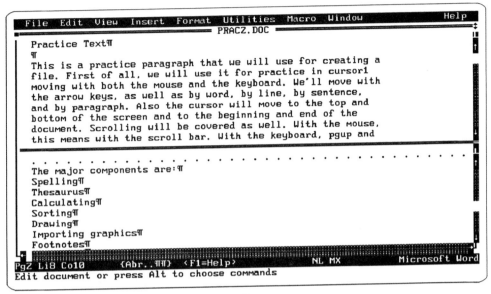

Figure 6.6. Window Panes

other. When you scroll horizontally, both panes scroll. This would be useful with wide columns of data, for example. Panes not only save a window, but they also keep you in a single window so you can see both at once all the time, even when the window is maximized.

Splitting a Window

To split a window into two panes, choose the Window Split command. A double line appears at the top of the window, opposite the split icon (=) at the top of the vertical scroll bar. The message "Use direction keys to move split, and press Enter. Press Esc to cancel." appears in the message bar. You can use ↓ to move the split line. If you overshoot, use ↑ to help you position the split where you want it. The document splits and part of it shows in each pane. After you press ↵ to end the command control, you can scroll and edit separately in each window pane.

1. Choose the Window Split command (Alt,W,T).
2. Press ↓ to move the split line to about midscreen. Then press ↵.
3. Press PgUp or PgDown to see which pane is active.

With the mouse, you can place the pointer on the split icon (=) and drag it down to the location you want. When you release the button, the panes are set.

4. If you have a mouse, drag the split icon a few lines in one direction, then release it.

Switching Panes

As with windows, only one pane can be active at a time. With the mouse, just click on the other pane to activate it. With the keyboard, use F6 to move to the next pane or Shift+F6 to move to the previous pane. Since you'll only have two panes at a time, these keys really have the same effect.

1. If you have a mouse, click in the inactive pane.
2. Press F6. Notice the cursor moves to the other pane.

Ending the Split

To remove the split, you have to get the split icon back to the top of the vertical scroll bar. With the mouse, you can just drag it back up, and the split and panes are gone. Or you can double-click on the split icon with the left mouse button. With the keyboard, you can choose Window Split and use ↑ to return it to the top of the screen. When you press Enter, the window is again a standard document window.

3. Choose the Window Split command.
4. Use ↑ to put the split line as far up as it will go. Then press ⏎.
5. If you have a mouse, drag the split icon down about half way.
6. If you have a mouse, drag the split icon back to the top of the window.

Panes in Arrangement

If a window is resized while it is split into panes, you may not be able to see the split. The absolute position of the split from the top of the window remains constant. If you create two approximately equal panes on a maximized screen, the split line may be at about line 10. If you then arrange three windows with Window Arrange All, each window has only about seven lines, so the bottom pane won't show. And you won't even be able to get at the icon without enlarging the window.

In most cases, you won't want to combine multiple window arrangements with window panes in one of the windows. But if you do, don't panic if your split line disappears. It is still there, and will be visible when you enlarge the window.

1. Make sure you have a fairly long document in the active window.
2. Split the window into two approximately equal panes.
3. In the top pane, move the cursor to the top of the document.
4. In the lower pane, move the cursor to the bottom of the document.
5. Cancel the split.
6. Close all files, abandoning all changes.

If you have a mouse, drag the split icon to set up or cancel the split, and just click to activate a pane. Otherwise, use the Window Split command to set up and eliminate the split. Move the cursor using standard methods.

Exercise

This chapter has covered various ways you can use Word with more than one window; you can have one document in multiple windows, several documents open, or even keep help open on the screen. You can also split a window into panes that scroll independently. This exercise lets you practice using these features.

1. Start up Word, open three files, and have Word arrange them automatically on the screen.
2. Open another window for the second or third file you opened. Then open a new document and type a few lines into it.
3. Have Word arrange all the files automatically.
4. Move to the first file you opened, and maximize it on the screen. Hide the borders. Activate a different window. Then restore the borders and return the current window to the previous size.

5. Make a document containing several pages active, then split the window into two panes, at about the middle of the screen. Scroll in the top pane.
6. Resize this file so it occupies the left half of the screen.
7. Size and move the windows that contain the same document so they fill the upper and lower portions of the right half of the screen.
8. Change the paragraph and tab mark display in one of the right windows so that it is different from the other.
9. Practice moving and switching among all the windows. Then put all these files away and exit Word.

Use Window Arrange All for automatic window arrangement. Maximize a window with the Window Maximize command or with the maximize icon. Use the View Preferences command to turn the window borders on and off.

To create and manipulate window panes, use the Window Split command or drag the icon. To change the size or location or windows manually, drag them with the mouse or use the Window Move and Size commands. Remember that windows are sized at the lower left. To change the active window, click in the one you want or use the Window menu.

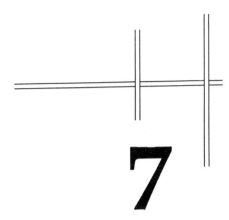

7

Managing Files through Word

S o far in this book, you have been using files in the current directory on the current drive. You have also seen how to change to a different directory using the **Directories** list box in the File Open and File Save As dialog boxes. In real life, you may want to be able to access or list files in any directory, and on any drive. Word's File Management feature makes this easy. It lets you edit or view summary information for any file. Through this feature, you can also print, copy, rename, or delete files. In this chapter, you'll learn to:

- View or edit summary information for a file
- Specify a search path for locating files
- Specify the extensions of files to be located
- Search for files that contain specified text
- Search for files based on summary information
- Determine the order in which files are listed
- Mark files to be affected by an operation
- Print files from disk
- Rename files
- Open a file from File Management
- Copy or move files
- Delete files from disk

File Management Concepts

If you have a hard disk, it is most likely set up with a directory tree. You may want to have files for each project in a different directory. You'll also want to be able to place a file on the A: drive occasionally. If you don't have a hard drive, you'll have to be able to access them both. High-density diskettes can also be structured with directories. You'll want to be able to access files no matter where they are stored on any available drive.

If you don't know how to create and manage directories under DOS, refer to Appendix C for an introduction. You'll have to use the DOS commands MKDIR to create a new directory and RMDIR to remove a directory, but changing directories and managing files can be done from within Word.

The File Management Window

Many file management features of Word can be reached through the File File Management command.

1. Choose the File File Management command (Alt,F,F).

The resulting dialog box is shown in Figure 7.1. The buttons are used for choosing the action you want. The <Close> button removes the dialog box; it doesn't close any files. Pressing Escape also removes the dialog box.

The bulk of this dialog box contains the **Files** list, which includes all the files indicated by the **Path(s)** field above. The path C:\WORD\BOOK shown in the figure includes all files in the directory that have the DOC extension.

You'll see how to modify the path and determine which files are listed shortly. The top line of the dialog box shows how the list is sorted, the type of view in effect, and whether the files can be edited. You'll see how to change all these values in this chapter.

Examining the File List

The **Files** box contains names of files in the specified directory path. Each file name includes its path. Two columns of names are displayed at a time; if the path is too long to fit in the column, directories in the middle of the path may be represented by three dots between two backslashes. For example, if the file D:\PAYROLL\MANFACT\REGULAR\LABOR\WEEK1.DOC were listed, it might appear as D:\PAYROLL\...\LABOR\WEEK1.DOC.

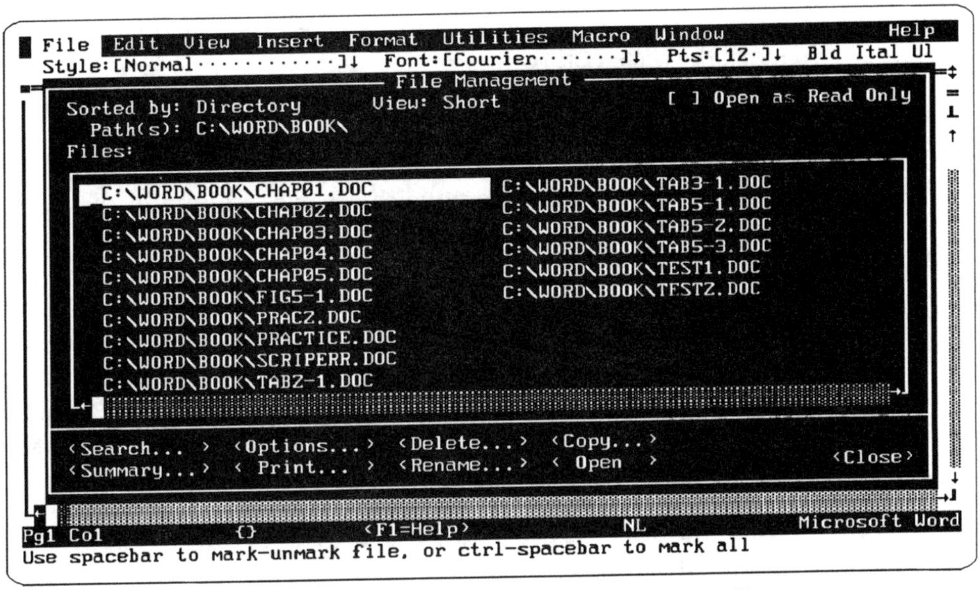

```
■ File  Edit  View  Insert  Format  Utilities  Macro  Window          Help
  Style:[Normal··········]↓  Font:[Courier·······]↓  Pts:[12·]↓  Bld Ital Ul
  ┌──────────────────── File Management ────────────────────┐
  │ Sorted by: Directory     View: Short        [ ] Open as Read Only │
  │   Path(s): C:\WORD\BOOK\                                          │
  │ Files:                                                           │
  │ ┌─────────────────────────────────┐                             │
  │ │ C:\WORD\BOOK\CHAP01.DOC          │  C:\WORD\BOOK\TAB3-1.DOC    │
  │ │ C:\WORD\BOOK\CHAP02.DOC          │  C:\WORD\BOOK\TAB5-1.DOC    │
  │ │ C:\WORD\BOOK\CHAP03.DOC          │  C:\WORD\BOOK\TAB5-2.DOC    │
  │ │ C:\WORD\BOOK\CHAP04.DOC          │  C:\WORD\BOOK\TAB5--3.DOC   │
  │ │ C:\WORD\BOOK\CHAP05.DOC          │  C:\WORD\BOOK\TEST1.DOC     │
  │ │ C:\WORD\BOOK\FIG5-1.DOC          │  C:\WORD\BOOK\TEST2.DOC     │
  │ │ C:\WORD\BOOK\PRAC2.DOC           │                             │
  │ │ C:\WORD\BOOK\PRACTICE.DOC        │                             │
  │ │ C:\WORD\BOOK\SCRIPERR.DOC        │                             │
  │ │ C:\WORD\BOOK\TAB2-1.DOC          │                             │
  │ └─────────────────────────────────┘                             │
  │                                                                  │
  │  <Search...  >  <Options...>  <Delete...>  <Copy...>            │
  │  <Summary...>  < Print...  >  <Rename...>  < Open  >   <Close>  │
  └──────────────────────────────────────────────────────────────┘
 Pg1 Col           {}         <F1=Help>           NL       Microsoft Word
 Use spacebar to mark-unmark file, or ctrl-spacebar to mark all
```

Figure 7.1. The File Management Dialog Box

If the box contains more file names than can be displayed at a time, you can scroll through them all by using the arrow keys or the horizontal scroll bar.

Selecting a File

A file in the list is selected when it is highlighted; only one file is highlighted at a time as the cursor moves through the list. You can use the arrow keys to move the highlight with the keyboard. With the mouse, just click (left button) on the file name you want to be selected when it is visible in the box.

2. Select a different file with an arrow key or by clicking on it.

Once a file is selected, you can examine its summary information, print it, delete it, copy it, rename it, or open it. You'll see how to perform all these operations in this chapter.

Marking Files

Some operations can be performed on multiple files at a time. You can delete or copy many files at once. You can also identify a group of files to be printed from disk. To do this, you have to go a step beyond selecting a file; you have to mark the ones you want.

When a file is marked, an asterisk appears just to the left of the file name. You can mark as many files at a time as you wish. If the marks are present when you close the File Management dialog box, they'll still be there if you return. Some operations remove the marks automatically. The files are all unmarked when you leave Word.

The standard File Management message in the message bar (shown in Figure 7.1) tells you one way to mark files. To mark a file, first select it by moving the highlight to it with the arrow keys. Then press the Spacebar. With the mouse, you can mark a file by pointing to the file name and clicking the right button. If you want to mark all the files, just press Ctrl+Spacebar. If no files are marked or if some are, this marks them all. You can't mark all the files at once with the mouse.

3. Mark the selected file by clicking the right button or pressing the spacebar.
4. Press ↑ and the Spacebar to mark the previous file, or point to it and click the right button.

The marking process is a toggle; to unmark a file or remove the asterisk, just select the marked file and press the spacebar again or point to it and click the right button again. If several files are marked, you can press Ctrl+Spacebar to mark them all, then immediately press Ctrl+Spacebar again to unmark them. Although some operations unmark processed files, others leave them marked.

5. Press Ctrl+Spacebar to mark all the files.
6. Press Ctrl+Spacebar again to unmark them all.
7. Choose <Cancel> to close the dialog box.

Managing Summary Information

If Word is set up to ask for summary information when you save a file for the first time, you can use this information to locate files. If you haven't been asked for summary information, you can turn this feature on:

1. Choose the Utilities Customize command.
2. Turn on the **Prompt for Summary Info** field.
3. Choose <OK>.

Once a file has been given a name, however, you won't be asked for summary information even if you later turn the feature on. You can add the information, or modify previously supplied information, through the File Management dialog box.

Tip | If you use your Word files through other software, it may result in loss of summary information. For example, Ventura Publisher seems to lose this information. If you stick with Word, however, the information is retained.

Editing Summary Information

Summary information is displayed for only one file at a time, so Word ignores any marked files. You select a file and choose the button.

1. Choose the File File Management command.
2. Select the file using the arrow keys or by clicking the left button.
3. Choose the <Summary> button.

You'll see the Summary dialog box, just as when you first saved the file. Any information you entered earlier is still there. If you didn't enter any, you'll see the file name and size, along with the date the file was created and the date it was last saved. You can't change the file name or size, but you can modify any other information. You can even add new information from scratch. All of the fields have size limits, however.

Field Limitations

The **Title, Author,** and **Operator** fields can hold up to 40 characters each. The **Keywords** field can hold up to 80 Characters. The **Comments** field can hold up to 220 characters. The **Version Number, Date Created,** and **Date Saved** fields can each hold up to 10 characters. Word keeps the two date fields updated, so you won't have to change them unless you want to save a date that is different from the one Word recorded.

Once you see the Summary dialog box, you can make any changes you want. Just move the cursor to the field and make your changes; you can insert, delete, and change information. Then choose <OK> to process your changes or <Cancel> to get rid of them. You'll be returned to the File Management dialog box.

4. Move the cursor to the **Keywords** field.

5. Type **Summary,** then choose <OK>.
6. Choose <Close> to remove the File Management dialog box.

Choosing <OK> or <Cancel> returns you to the File Management dialog box. From there, you can select another file and examine its summary information if you wish. Later in this chapter, you'll see how you can search for information in most of the summary fields--all except for **Title, Comments,** and **Version.**

1. Start up Word if necessary.
2. Examine the files listed in the File Management dialog box. Mark four files, then unmark them.
3. Add a version number to the summary information for one file.
4. Add the word **practice** to the keyword list for two other files.
5. Save the changes and exit File Management.

The File File Management command gets you to the File Management dialog box. To mark a file with the mouse, point to it and click the right button. With the keyboard, highlight the file name and press the spacebar. To unmark all the files at once, press Ctrl+Spacebar twice. To edit summary information, highlight the file name and choose <Summary>. To exit File Management, choose <Close>.

Managing the File List

The files listed in the **Files** list box are all taken from the directory or directories listed in the **Path(s)** field above it. You can change the contents of that field in the Search dialog box. You can also limit the files in the list to only those in the directory paths that meet conditions you specify.

1. Choose the File File Management command.
2. Choose the <Search> button.

Figure 7.2 shows the resulting dialog box. This dialog box has two almost separate functions. One is the specification of the search path, done with the **Search Paths** field and the **Directories** list box. This function specifies which directories and which files in them shall be considered for the file list. The other function is the limitation of the search based on the contents of the file or its summary. This is done using the fields on the left. We'll cover the functions separately, then you'll see how they can work together.

Defining a Search Path

Each search path identifies a specific directory on a disk; it can limit the directory to certain files by use of wildcards in the specification. The path in Figure 7.2 is C:\WORD\BOOK\, which means that all files on drive C: in the \WORD\BOOK\ directory that have the DOC extension will be listed. The first part of the path gives the drive (C:), the second part gives the directory (\WORD\BOOK\). You can also include a third part to limit the file names, but if you omit it, the specification lists all files with the DOC extension. The third part uses a global file name; *.* refers to all files in the directory.

The **Search Paths** field can be empty; if it is, the current directory on the current drive is the default. This is indicated by the directory name just below the right end of the text field. All DOC files in that directory will be listed in the **Files** box if you choose <OK> while the **Search Paths** field is empty.

1. If the **Search Paths** field isn't highlighted, move the cursor to it.
2. Type any character. The field is cleared.
3. Press Backspace to remove the character.

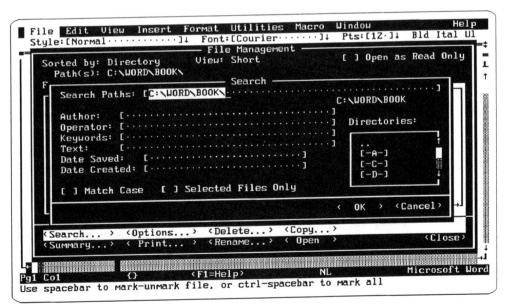

Figure 7.2. File Search Dialog Box

Tip || You can just press Backspace to clear a highlighted text field if you want.

You can type a search path into the field. When you type any character while the **Search Paths** field is highlighted, it immediately erases anything that is in the field; you can't get it back with Undo. If you want to restore the previous value, choose the <Cancel> button, then choose <Search> again on the File Management dialog box.

Tip || When you type or modify a path, be sure to use the backslash (\) rather than the forward slash (/) key.

You can edit an existing search path if you like. Just press ← or click in the field first. The highlight disappears and the cursor moves to the beginning of the field or where you click. You can then continue to do your typing without accidentally clearing the field.

Typing Search Paths

Suppose you want the search path to be the root directory. If you clear the value in the **Search Paths** field, you can just type **C:** or **A:** and choose <OK>. All files with extension DOC in the root directory are listed in the File Management dialog box. Similarly, you can type the full name of any directory you want to see. The symbol .. represents the parent of the current directory. If you clear the **Search Paths** field, then type .. and choose <OK>, you'll see the DOC files from that directory.

Omitting a file specification in a path results in a list of all the files in the directory that have extension DOC. If you would prefer to have all files listed, use *.*. The path C:\WORD*.* causes all the files in the Word directory to be listed, regardless of the extension. Of course, if there is no WORD directory on drive C:, you'll get an error message instead.

You can use the standard DOS wildcard characters (* and ?) as needed. The specification *.OUT means all files with extension OUT. The specification T*.* means all files with any extension if the file name begins with T. The specification STATUS?.RP? means any seven-letter file name beginning with STATUS with an extension beginning with RP.

1. Choose the File File Management command if necessary.
2. Choose the <Search> button, if necessary.
3. In the **Search Paths** field, type **C:\DOS** if you have a hard disk, or **A:** if you don't.

4. Choose <OK>.

Now all the DOC files in the directory path you chose are shown. You may not see any.

5. Choose the <Search> button.
6. In the **Search Paths** field, press ← or click in the field.
7. Position the cursor if necessary, then insert ***.*** at the end.
8. Choose <OK>.

Now all the files in that directory are listed.

Specifying Multiple Paths. You can tell File Management to locate files in more than one directory. Just type a comma at the end of the first path, then type another path. You can use a space following the comma if you like; actually, Word accepts a semicolon as well as a comma.

Tip | | Remember that typing when the field is highlighted erases the contents. Press ← or click in the existing path before starting to type.

The specification C:\WORD,A: sets up two search paths, the WORD directory on drive C: and the current directory on drive A:. The specification C:\DOS,C:\CONFER*.ASC,D:\123\NEW*.* sets up three search paths. The first includes all DOC files in the C:\DOS directory, the second includes only files with extension ASC in the C:\CONFER directory, and the third includes all the files in the D:\123\NEW directory.

Once you enter one or more search paths, you can choose <OK> and files from all those paths will be listed in the File Management **Files** box.

1. Choose the <Search> button.
2. In the **Search Paths** field, type **C:\DOS*.COM,C:\WORD** if you have a hard disk, or **A:*.COM,B:** if you don't.
3. Choose <OK>.

Now all the COM files in the first directory path and all the DOC files in the second path are shown.

4. Choose the <Search> button.
5. In the **Search Paths** field, change COM to *****, then add ***.*** to the end of the second path.
6. Choose <OK>.

Now all the files in both directories are listed.

1. Type a search path so that all the files in your WORD directory are listed.
2. Change the search path so that it lists all the files in your root directory. Check the listing.
3. Add the directory that contains any Word files you have created to the **Search Paths** field. Verify it by checking the listing.
4. Modify the search path so that it lists only the DOC files from each directory. Verify it.
5. Change the search path so that it lists all DOC files from the WORD directory as well as any directory to which you have added Word files. Then return to the main Word screen.

Use the <Search> button of the File Management dialog box for this exercise. To check the listing after typing the search paths, choose <OK>. To terminate File Management, choose the <Close> button.

Selecting Paths using the Directories List Box

The **Directories** list box is located below the name of the current directory. If the root directory is not current, it shows the parent of the current directory first as two dots (..). Then it includes any directories subordinate to the current one. Finally, it lists any other drives. You can activate this box by pressing Alt+D and using arrow keys to highlight directories or by clicking once in the box. You can select a listed directory or drive by highlighting it and pressing ⏎ or by double-clicking on it. This changes the directory listed just above the box. It also causes the list in the **Directories** list box to be updated relative to the new current directory.

Choosing the Current Directory. To list the files in the new current directory, return the highlight to the **Search Paths** field and clear it by pressing Backspace. Then choose <OK>. The resulting listing in the File Management dialog box reflects that path.

1. Choose the File File Management command, if necessary.
2. Choose <Search>.

3. In the **Directories** list box, choose a different directory.
4. Move the highlight back to the **Search Paths** field and press Backspace to clear it.
5. Choose <OK>.

The directory name appears in the **Path(s)** field. And any DOC files from that directory are listed in the **Files** box.

Adding Paths. When you return to the File Search dialog box, the directory that is now current appears in the **Search Paths** field. You can enter the first path in the **Search Paths** field this way, or you can type it. You can then add paths from the **Directories** list box or by typing them. To add a path from the list box, first select the directory you want by highlighting it, then press the comma key. The new path is added. You can modify the file specifications by typing.
    When the **Search Paths** field contains the directories and file specifications you want, you are ready to choose <OK>. The files in the directories you specified will be listed in the File Management dialog box.

1. Choose the <Search> button in the File Management dialog box.
2. Highlight a directory in the **Directories** list box by clicking once or by pressing Alt+D and using the arrow keys.
3. Press the comma key (,).

Notice that the directory you selected is added to the **Search Paths** field.

4. Choose <OK> and examine the resulting list.

1. Clear the search path for the File Management **Files** list box.
2. Use the **Directories** list box to set the WORD directory as the first path in the list.
3. Use the **Directories** list box to add the root directory to the **Search Paths** field.
4. Modify the paths to specify all the files in both directories.
5. Verify the result.

*After using the <Search> button from the File Management dialog box, pressing Backspace clears the **Search Paths** field. To choose the \WORD directory, highlight it, then press ↵ or double-click on it. To add the root directory, highlight* *it then press the comma. To modify the paths, move the cursor to the* **Search Paths** *field, remove the highlight with ← or clicking if necessary, then edit as in normal text. Choose <OK> to see the listed result.*

Limiting the Search

You have seen how to add paths to expand or limit the files to include in the file management listing. At that level, you do your specification based on paths and file names. Sometimes you want to limit the search to files based on what is in the files or their summaries. You do this using the other fields in the File Search dialog box, shown in Figure 7.2.

You can ask Word to search the files specified by the search paths and list the ones that contain a specific string of text or that contain certain summary information. This feature lets you search for a file containing a string of text in several directories at once; just put all directories to be searched in the **Search Paths** field. Or it lets you find all files with a particular author, all files created on a certain date, or all that include a specific keyword. You'll learn to use these features in this section.

When Word locates files for the File Management list, its first search is based on the search paths you specified. Then it looks at the fields you enter. If you ask for files with author RA, for example, only those files, out of all the ones covered by the search paths, will be listed.

Performing the Search

From the Search dialog box, you create the list of files for the File Management dialog box. Once the search paths are set up, you can specify additional strings to search for in the other fields on the screen. When the screen is ready, choose <OK>. Word performs the search and the files that meet your conditions are listed in the File Management dialog box.

To search for a file containing a single string in any of the fields, just type it in the field. You can use a single string in as many fields as appropriate. The search finds only files that contain all of the strings you enter.

1. Choose the File File Management command if necessary.
2. Choose the <Search> button.
3. In the **Text** field, type **practice**.
4. Choose <OK>.

Now only any files that contain the word **practice** are listed. The word can have any case, however.

Searching in the File Text

If you type a string in the **Text** field, Word searches in the text of files indicated by the search paths. It will not look at summary information associated with those files. Use double quotation marks around the entire string if it includes any of these characters: , & ~ < > or space. To search for the string <OK>, type **"<OK>"**. To search for the string Michael Wilson, type **"Michael Wilson"**. To search for the word individual, however, just type **individual**. If the string includes a double quotation mark, double it; to search for 8", type **8""**.

Searching in Summary Information

To locate files that have certain information in the **Author, Operator,** and **Keywords** summary fields, just type the string in the appropriate field. To locate files by the date last created or saved, type the date in the *mm/dd/yy* format as shown in the summary field contents; you can omit leading zeros.

As with the **Text** field, use double quotation marks if the string contains the special characters.

1. Return to the File Search dialog box and make sure the search path in-cludes the WORD directory and any directory you have placed files in. It should specify only the DOC files.
2. Move the cursor to the **Text** field and remove any value that is there.
3. Move the cursor to the **Date Created** field.
4. Type a date on which you know you created a file.
5. Choose <OK>.
6. Examine the listing, then choose <Search> and remove any value you entered.
7. Try a few more simple searches if you like.

Using Multiple Strings

If you want to use multiple strings in any field, you can. You have to connect them with logical operators, however. The logical operators are not complex at all.

OR—Find One String. If you want a file listed if Word finds just one of the specified strings in that field, you want to use the OR logical operator. Word uses a comma for this feature. So if you want to list files with either Ashley or Fernandez as the author, you would type **Ashley,Fernandez** or **Fernandez,Ashley** in the **Author** field. If you want to list files in which the text mentions California, San Diego, or Poway, you would type **California,"San Diego",Poway** (in any order) in the **Text** field. Notice that the quotation marks are required around one string because it contains a space.

When you use a comma to separate strings, only files that contain at least one of those strings in the field are listed. So if any string contains a comma, that string must be enclosed in double quotation marks so as not to mislead Word into thinking you specified two separate strings.

AND—Find All Strings. If you want the file listed only if Word finds all the strings in that field, you want to use the AND logical operator. Word uses the ampersand or a space for this feature. If you want to list files with Ashley and Fernandez specified in the **Author** field, you would type **Ashley&Fernandez** or **Fernandez Ashley** in the field. You can use either order and either the ampersand or the space in each combined string. If you want to list files in which the text mentions California, San Diego, and Poway, you would type **California&"San Diego"&Poway** (in any order) in the **Text** field; you could use a space instead of the ampersand.

When you use a space or an ampersand to separate strings, only files that contain all of the connected strings in the field you use are listed. So if a string contains a space or an ampersand, it must be enclosed in double quotation marks so as not to mislead Word about what you want it to do.

NOT—Find Files Without String. If you want to find files that don't contain a particular string, you want to use the NOT logical operator. Word uses the tilde (~) for this feature. Most times, you'll want this to limit a string. For example, suppose you want to find files that have Judi as the author, but you don't want files with Judith as the author. You could type **Judi~Judith** in the **Author** field. If you just want listed all files that don't include the word California, you could type **~California** in the **Text** field. The NOT operator is often used in connection with other operators. To specify files that contain the word "book" but not the word "summary", you would type **book&~summary**. You could use a space instead of ampersand, of course.

Less Than and Greater Than. For the date fields, you can use the less-than operator (<) to specify a date earlier than the one you specify. You can use the greater-than operator (>) to specify a date later than the one you specify. To list files created earlier than June 1, 1991, you would type **<6/1/91** in the **Date Created** field. To list files saved since November 21, 1991, you would type **>11/21/91** in the **Date Saved** field.

You can specify a range of dates by combining the AND operator with the greater-than and less-than operators. For example, to list files created in August 1991, you could type **>7/31/91&<9/1/91** in the **Date Created** field. Only files with a creation date later than July 31, 1991 and a creation date earlier than September 1, 1991 will be listed.

1. Get to the File Search dialog box.
2. Specify a search for files containing your name as author as well as the text string **the**.
3. Choose <OK> to see the result.
4. Choose the <Search> button.
5. Specify a search for files created after a date about a month ago. (Use the greater-than operator.)
6. Choose <OK> to see the result.

Matching the Case

Once the fields you want the search based on are specified, you can turn on the **Match Case** field if you want only exact case matches to the strings you entered. This field applies to all strings, if you entered more than one. If you leave it turned off, any string in which the characters match, regardless of case, will cause the specified effect. If you turn this field on, a file that includes "ruth ashley" in the **Author** field will not be located if the search string was typed as **Ashley**.

1. Get to the File Search dialog box.
2. Clear the current search string fields.
3. Type **The** in the **Text** field.
4. Turn on the **Match Case** field.
5. Choose <OK> to see the effect.

All the files listed contain the three characters in the specified cases; it might be the word *The*, the word *Therefore*, or any similar string.

6. Choose the <Search> button.
7. Turn off the **Match Case** field.
8. Choose <OK>.

More files are probably listed this time. If not, the string doesn't occur in any other form.

Secondary Search

Suppose you have a list of files in the File Management dialog box. You can specify that a search involve only those files. This is easy. Do a normal search, but don't change the current search paths. Specify the field information only.

If you want to check just one file, select it and choose the <Search> button. Don't change the search paths, but enter the strings. Then turn on the **Selected Files Only** field. If the search conditions aren't found in that file, no file will be listed. If the conditions are found, only that file will be listed.

If you want to check several of the listed files, mark the ones to be searched by clicking with the right button or by highlighting them and pressing the spacebar. When the files you want searched are all marked, choose the <Search> button. Don't change the search paths, but enter the strings to set the conditions for the search. Then turn on the **Selected Files Only** field. The search will include only the marked files. Only files that meet the conditions will be listed on the next File Management dialog box.

If you don't turn on the **Selected Files Only** field, any file markings will be lost.

1. Choose the <Search> button.
2. Clear the **Text** field and choose <OK>.
3. Mark five or six files by pointing and clicking with the right button or highlighting them and pressing the spacebar.
4. Choose the <Search> button.
5. Type **The** in the **Text** field.
6. Turn on the **Selected Files Only** field, then choose <OK>.

Notice that the listed files are selected from the marked ones; no files that weren't marked are listed now.

7. Choose <Search>.
8. Notice that the **Selected Files Only** field is turned off, then choose <OK>.

Now all files from the paths that contain the string are listed.

Tip | If you haven't enough data in your files, add some summary information to a few first so you know what to expect from your searches.

1. Make sure that the search paths include the WORD directory and the directory into which you have been saving files.
2. Search for all files that contain whatever you have used in the **Author** field. Use AND (&) or OR (,) if you used different values.
3. Search for all files that contain **prac** in the **Comments** field.
4. Mark about ten files, then search for all of those files saved before a week ago.
5. Perform a few more searches based on information you put in the text files that you saved.

*The results of this Self-Check depend on what you placed in your files. Be sure to use the **Selected Files Only** field to search only those. Use the less-than operator to find earlier dates.*

Clearing the Search Fields

The search fields are not cleared automatically until you leave Word. If you leave a value in any of the search fields, it will be used to locate files every time you choose the File File Management command.

Controlling the File Management Display

By default, Word displays files in the File Management dialog box in directory order; that is the directories in the various search paths are put in alphabetical order and those in the first one are displayed first. The files are put in alphabetical order within the directory. For example, suppose the search path looks like this: C:\WORD\,C:\DOS\,C:\WORD\BOOK\. All the DOC files in C:\DOS would be listed first, then the files in C:\WORD\, and finally the files in C:\WORD\BOOK\. If the path is very long, Word may condense it by omitting directory names from the middle of the path.

The listing itself, by default, includes only the file names. You can include additional information, or even the entire summary in the display for each file listed.

Both the display sequence and the amount of information in the display can be controlled with options.

1. Choose the File File Management command if necessary.
2. Choose the <Options> button.

You'll see a dialog box like the one shown in Figure 7.3. The group box on the left lets you specify the order in which the listed files will be sorted. The group box on the right lets you specify how much information you will see about each listed file.

Controlling the Sort Order

You can have the files sorted in various sequences, but you can choose only one. Since the fields in the **Sort Files By** group box are radio buttons, only one field in the group can be turned on.

If you turn on the **Author** or **Operator** field, the files will be sorted alphabetically by the summary information stored in the appropriate field. If these values aren't displayed, this might not help you much. (You'll see how to display them shortly.)

If you turn on the **Date Created** or **Date Saved** field, the files will be sorted by the date field value, from oldest to the most recent. Again, this isn't of very much use if the dates aren't displayed as well.

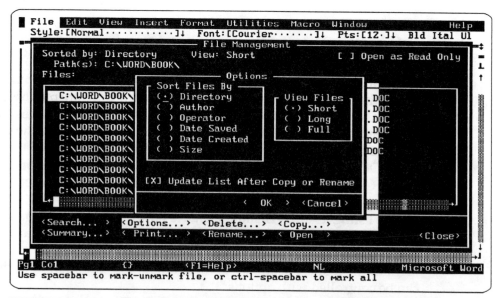

Figure 7.3. The File Management Options Dialog Box

If you turn on the **Size** field, the files will be sorted by the number of characters in the file, starting with the smallest file.

3. Choose the **Date Saved** field.
4. Choose <OK>. The file sequence should be noticeably different.
5. Choose the **Size** field.
6. Choose <OK>. The file sequence should be different.
7. Choose the **Directory** field and choose <OK>.

Controlling the Fields Displayed

By default, you see the most condensed view of the file list, as indicated by **Short** in the **View** field on the top line of the File Management dialog box. As you saw in the Options dialog box, there are actually three choices for the view; only one can be on at a time. The **Short** view includes the path and file name only. If the path is very long, Word may even exclude part of it. You scroll through the short list horizontally; use the scroll bar at the bottom or the arrow keys to see the rest of the list.

The **Long** view includes the path and file name, and also the contents of the **Author** and the **Title** fields. The **Title** field is always displayed in the long view, but the other field changes if you sort by a different field. If you sort by **Date Created**, for example, that field appears along with the **Title** field.

1. Choose the File File Management command, if necessary.
2. Choose the <Options> button.
3. Turn on the **Long** view.
4. Choose <OK>.

The display now shows the path and file name as before, along with the **Author** and **Title** fields. The sort order has not changed.

5. Choose the <Options> button.
6. Turn on the **Date Saved** button.
7. Choose <OK>.

The display is still in the long view. But now it shows the **Date Saved** field instead of **Author**. You can see that the dates are in order from the oldest to the most recent.

The **Full** view shows even more information, as shown in Figure 7.4. The upper part of the screen shows the short file list information. Summary information, or at least the start of each field, is shown in detail for the selected

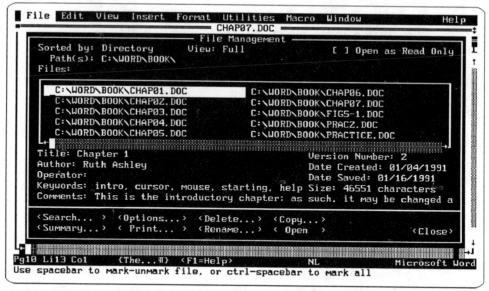

Figure 7.4. The File Management Full View

file. As you scroll through the listed file names, the summary information scrolls to keep up.

If you want to see more of the summary information, you can choose the <Summary> button; then you'll be able to scroll through it all.

1. Choose the File File Management command, if necessary.
2. Choose the <Options> button.
3. Turn on the **Date Created** button.
4. Turn on the **Full** view, then choose <OK>.

Now the files are in order by the date in which they were created. The top part of the file list is in the standard path and file name form. Below it is the summary information for the highlighted file name.

5. Press ↓ repeatedly to see summary information on several more files.
6. Highlight the PRAC2.DOC file or another one you created.
7. Choose the <Summary> button.
8. Add some comments to the beginning of the **Comments** field.
9. Choose <OK>. The comments you entered should be apparent in the dialog box.

To restore the File Management dialog box to its default state, you have to reset the sort order and the view.

1. Choose <Options>.
2. Turn on the **Directory** sort button.
3. Turn on the **Short** view button.
4. Choose <OK>.

The File Management dialog box should be back the way it was before.

1. Arrange the File Management file list display to be sorted by the creation date and listed with the dates.
2. Change the list display so that it is listed from smallest to largest and listed with the size.
3. Change the list display so that it is sorted by the value in the **Author** field and listed with full summary information displayed.
4. Change the list so that it is sorted and listed in default form.

For item 1, turn on the **Creation Date** *sort field and the* **Long** *view. For item 2, turn on the* **Size** *sort field. For item 3, turn on the* **Author** *sort field and the* **Full** *view. For item 4, turn on the* **Directory** *sort field and the* **Short** *view. Be sure to choose <OK> after each to see the effect.*

Opening Files from File Management

You already know how to open a file from the File Open command. If you select a file in the File Management dialog box and choose the <Open> button, it is opened immediately. Even if you have several files marked, the file name with the highlight will be opened.

The <Open> button is the default on this dialog box; if you press ↵, the highlighted file will always be opened. You may already have done this accidentally if you tried to use ↵ instead of the spacebar to mark a file.

Tip | If you press ↵ and open a file by mistake, just close it and choose the File File Management command again. Any files you had marked will still be marked.

1. Choose the File File Management command, if necessary.

2. Highlight a file that you created, such as PRAC2.DOC.
3. Choose the <Open> button.

The file is opened on your screen, just as if you used the File Open command. The File Management dialog box disappears.

4. Choose the File File Management command.
5. Highlight another file you created, or else README.DOC.
6. Choose the <Open> button.

Now you have two files open. You can't close files from the File Management dialog box; the <Close> button there just closes the dialog box. To close files, use the usual techniques—either the File Close command or clicking on the close box.

7. Close both files before continuing.

1. Open a file you created from File Management.
2. Open another file.
3. Close them both.

Highlight one file to be opened, then choose <Open>. The File Management dialog box disappears. To close files, use standard techniques.

You can't create a new file or open an untitled document window from the File Management dialog box. You can only open a file whose name already is listed. If you turn on the **Open as Read Only** field, you'll be able to examine the file but not edit it. This may be useful if you work on a Network.

Printing Files from Disk

You can print one or more files from the File Management dialog box. If no files are marked, the selected (highlighted) file is chosen. If any are marked, all of them are chosen; they are printed in the sequence in which they are listed in the dialog box. Each one starts with the page number it would start with if printed individually. You can select as many to be printed as you need.

Available Features

When you choose the <Print> button in the File Management dialog box, you get the same dialog box as when you choose the File Print command. Most of the print features are available. The <Printer Setup> button, however, is dimmed. If you need to change your printer setup, you must do it through the File Printer Setup command or through the button in the normal File Print dialog box.

When several documents are selected, you can still specify which pages to print. However, any specification applies to all the files. For example, if you have marked three files for printing and you want the first three pages of each, you can type **1-3** in the **Pages** field. If you want different pages printed from each file, you'll have to request the print operation separately for each file.

1. Choose the File File Management command, if necessary.
2. Mark two files you created to print.
3. Choose the <Print> button.
4. To print the complete documents, choose <OK>.
5. To print the same page or pages from all marked files, type the pages in the **Pages** field, then choose <OK>.

Renaming Files

The File Management dialog box lets you select one file to rename. Renaming a file involves only changing its name; the file itself isn't moved or changed in any other way. Since you have to supply a new name for each file, Word assumes you want to rename the selected file. No matter how many files are marked, the one that contains the highlight, whether it is marked or not, is considered to be the one you want when you choose the <Rename> button.

Selecting the Feature

When you want to change the name of a file, move the highlight to it by using the arrow keys or by clicking on it. Then choose the <Rename> button.

1. Choose the File File Management command if necessary.
2. Highlight the PRAC2.DOC file.
3. Choose the <Rename> button.

Microsoft Word 5.5

You'll see a dialog box like the one shown in Figure 7.5 and you can now provide the new name.

Completing the Rename

The full path and name of the selected file appears at the top of the box. You enter the desired new name in the text box. The **Files** and **Directories** list boxes are available for reference, but you can't choose a name that is already in use in the current directory.

You must type the name you want in the dialog box. Word supplies the extension DOC automatically; if you want a different extension, however, you must type it. As soon as you type a character, the highlighted value in the field disappears.

4. Type **PRAC7**.
5. Choose <OK>.

The Rename dialog box is closed and you are back at the File Management dialog box. You can tell immediately that the file was renamed.

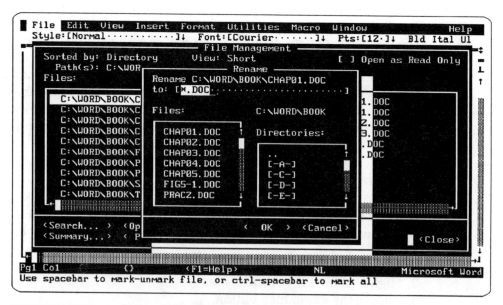

Figure 7.5. File Rename Dialog Box

1. Change the name of a file you created to CHECK7.DOC.
2. Print the first page of the file through File Management.
3. Mark two or three short files and print the entire documents through File Management.

Choose the <Rename> button to rename the highlighted file. To print files from disk, highlight one file name or mark more than one to be printed. The Print dialog box works just as from File Print.

Copying Files

You can copy files from one directory or drive to another through File Management. You can't change the file name, however, so you can't put a new copy of a file in the same directory. If no files are marked, Word assumes you want to copy the selected (highlighted) file. If any files are marked, Word assumes you want to copy them all to the same drive or directory. If you want to copy several files to different locations, you'll need to use several different operations.

How Copy Works

When Word copies a file, it makes a duplicate in the directory you specify. If you ask it to, Word will then delete the original file; this results in a move operation. You can also ask Word to copy associated style sheets with the file; you'll learn what these are in Chapter 9. When you choose <OK>, Word will copy all your marked files to the same target directory.

Selecting the Feature

You must arrange your search paths so that any directory you want to copy files from is listed in the File Management dialog box. Then highlight the file (if you only want to copy one) or mark the ones you want copied. Then choose the <Copy> button.

1. Choose the File File Management command, if necessary.

2. If the WORD directory and the directory containing files you created aren't listed, choose the <Search> button and change the path.
3. Highlight or mark the files to be copied. Mark three files that you have created.
4. Choose the <Copy> button.

At this point, you will see a dialog box like the one shown in Figure 7.6. Notice that the marked or selected file names are not shown.

Completing the Copy Operation

The path shown in the **Path Name** field is the path of the first file you marked; that's where at least one of the files is being copied from. You have to type or select a different path here; if you don't change it, you'll see an error message box telling you that you can't copy files onto themselves. You can just type the path you want or use the **Directories** list box in the usual way until the path you want is displayed in the **Path Name** field. For example, if you want to copy the files to the root directory on drive A:, you would type **A:** in the field. You could type **D:\SAVE\ASHLEY** to copy the files to that directory. The directory must already exist, however.

Tip || To create a directory, you use the DOS MKDIR command.

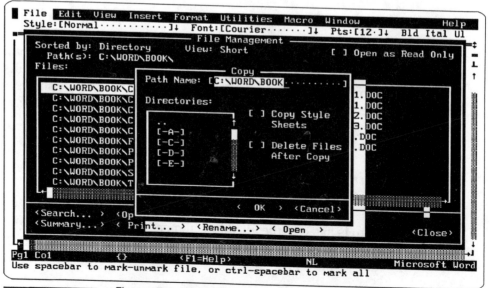

Figure 7.6. The File Copy Dialog Box

If the files have associated style sheets, you'll want to turn on the **Copy Style Sheets** check box; you'll learn to use style sheets later in this book.

If you want the files removed from their original location after they are copied to the new directory, turn on the **Delete Files After Copy** check box. After they are successfully duplicated in the target directory, the files will all be removed from their original location. Notice that you can't pick and choose; you can have the files all left in their original locations or all removed.

5. Type or select a different directory. (Use your root directory or a different drive.)
6. Choose <OK>.

You'll be returned to the File Management dialog box. If any files were marked, the marks are turned off. You can check up on the copy by changing the Search Path and viewing the list of files in the target directory.

Moving Files

When files are copied, then removed from the original directory, the process is often called moving files to a different directory. It works just like the regular copy operation, except that you must turn on the **Delete Files After Copy** field before choosing <OK> in the Copy dialog box.

1. Choose the File File Management command, if necessary.
2. Select one file or mark several files to be moved to another location.
3. Choose the <Copy> button.
4. Select or type the target directory path.
5. Choose <OK>.

The files that were selected or marked are not listed when you return to the File Management dialog box.

1. Copy two files you created from their current directory to the root directory of the hard disk or to the root directory of A: or B:. (Be sure to insert a formatted diskette.)
2. Rename the files in the new location. (You'll have to change the search path first.)
3. Copy one of the files under the new name back to the directory it originally came from.

4. Copy the other file to any other directory or disk drive, removing it from its current location.

To copy several files, mark them before choosing <Copy>. To copy a single file, highlight it before choosing <Copy>. To cause the source file to be removed, turn on the **Delete Files After Copy** *field.*

Deleting Files

You can remove files from your disks through File Management as well. If no files are marked, Word assumes you want to delete the selected (highlighted) file. If any files are marked, Word assumes you want to delete them all.

Selecting the Feature

To delete files, they must be listed on the File Management dialog box. If you want to delete files from several directories, include them all in the search path so they are all listed. To delete one or more files, mark them in the **Files** list box. If no files are marked, Word assumes you want to delete the selected (highlighted) file.

When the file(s) you want to delete are marked or highlighted, choose the <Delete> button.

1. Choose the File File Management command, if necessary.
2. Modify the search path if necessary to list the files you want to delete.
3. To delete a single file, highlight it. To delete several files, mark them all.
4. Choose the <Delete> button.

Completing the Operation

A dialog box lets you confirm the action. It doesn't list the files by name, but just asks if you want to delete the marked (or selected) files. Choose <OK> and they are gone. Choose <Cancel> and they aren't affected.

5. To delete the file(s), choose <OK>.

You are returned to the File Management dialog box, and the files are gone. You can't recreate them from within Word.

Tip || Some utility programs let you "unerase" files. If you delete files in error, look into these before you do anything else with your system.

1. Remove the file you copied to the root directory.
2. Create a new short file and save it as TEMPORY.DOC. Then delete the file through File Management.

Deleting files is permanent, so be careful. If no files are marked, the highlighted one is deleted. If any are marked, they are all deleted.

Inserting a File

Occasionally, you may want to copy an entire file into the current document. You can do this by using the Insert File command. The resulting dialog box is much like the File Open dialog box. You can change the directory if necessary and select the file. If you want to insert a Word or ASCII document file, that's all you have to do.

1. Position the cursor at the beginning of a paragraph.
2. Choose the Insert File command.
3. Select a short file you created, then choose <OK>.

The entire file is inserted into the current document before the cursor. No change is made to the file that remains on disk.

Other File Inserts

You can use this dialog box to insert files in other formats as well. For example, you can import data from a Microsoft Works, Multiplan, Microsoft Excel, or Lotus 1-2-3 spreadsheet. If you don't want the entire file, use the **Range** field to supply a name for an area defined within the spreadsheet or provide a range using its format. If you check the **Link** field, Word inserts codes in hidden text into the document. You can choose the <Update Links> button at any time to import the same area in its current form. Leave the **Link** field turned off if you won't want to update the data.

1. Copy a file into the current document.
2. Print the document to see the effect.
3. Terminate Word.

*Use Insert File to get the file into the document. Don't turn on the **Link** field.*

Exercise

This chapter has covered various ways you can manage and locate files through Word's file management features, saving you the hassle of exiting to DOS when you want to work with your files. You can practice many of these commands in this exercise.

1. Start up Word and use File Management to rename a file you created.
2. Change the summary information for this and another file to show a new keyword and different operator information. Use the same keyword for both files.
3. Change the search paths so that files from at least three directories are listed. You may want to use all extensions.
4. Sort the files in date saved order and display the most informative view with the most information.
5. Copy two files from the current listing into another directory included in the current listing.
6. Delete one of the copied files from its new location.
7. Rename the remaining copied file as TOGO.DOC.
8. Move TOGO.DOC back to its original directory location, deleting it from the current location in the same command.
9. Modify the current list of files to include only those containing the keyword you placed in two summaries.

Use the File File Management command for most of these items. Mark files with the spacebar or by clicking with the right button. Choose the <Search> button to specify a different path; remember that *.* means to list all files in that directory. Choose the <Sort> button to sort the listed files. Use <Summary> to access summary information for the highlighted file. Use <Delete> to remove the highlighted file and <Rename> to change its name.

To copy a file, you'll be prompted to specify the target directory. To limit the list to specific files, enter the text you want to search for in the **Keyword** *field of the search dialog box.*

8

Advanced Formatting

$\overline{\hspace{3cm}}$ Word provides many formatting commands and options that you haven't seen yet. You'll want to be able to use the fonts and sizes your printer has available. Some documents will benefit from elements such as paragraph borders, shading, and positioning. Others need headers, footers, and footnotes. Word also supports multiple column formats, even documents containing several different column structures. In this chapter, you'll learn to:

- Locate and manage formatting codes
- Use all available character fonts
- Change the point size of fonts
- Add complete or partial borders to paragraphs
- Add shading to paragraphs
- Define headers and footers
- Include page numbers in headers and footers
- Define and manage footnotes
- Define multiple columns
- Use multiple sections in a document

Managing Formatting

When you format characters, paragraphs, or a section, Word places codes in the document that you can't see on the screen. You have to know where the codes are located so that you can manipulate them.

Format Code Storage

Character formatting codes, such as those for bold or subscripts, are stored before and after the formatted string of characters. All of these formats have one code to turn on the feature and another to turn it off. If you insert characters in the middle of a formatted string, the inserted characters will have the same formatting. Deleting the first or last character of the string doesn't affect the formatting. The code has its own position in the document.

Paragraph formatting codes, such as those for spacing, alignment, and indentation, are stored in the paragraph mark at the end of the paragraph. Although you can see the paragraph marks if they are turned on (through View Preferences), you can't actually see the formatting codes.

If you press ↵ at the end of a formatted paragraph, the format carries on to the new paragraph. So if you format the first paragraph while you are creating a new document, the format will be duplicated every time you press ↵. If you split a paragraph into two by pressing ↵ in the middle of it, both parts have the same format. If you join two paragraphs with different formats by deleting the paragraph mark at the end of the first, the combined paragraph takes on the formatting of the second.

Section formatting codes, such as those for margins and page numbers, are stored in the section mark at the end of the section. The section mark is inserted the first time you do any section formatting. If you accidentally delete the double row of dots, any section formatting is lost. However, you can use Edit Undo immediately to replace it.

Locating Formatting Codes

In a normal search operation, you can't include formatting codes; you can't search for a particular bold string, for example. To locate formatting codes in a document, you must choose the <Search for Formatting Only> button in the Search dialog box. In the resulting dialog box, you choose the <Character>, <Paragraph>, or <Style> button. (Styles are covered in Chapter 9.)

1. Start up Word if necessary.
2. Open a document containing several paragraphs and more than one page.
3. Choose the Edit Search command.
4. Choose the <Search for Formatting Only> button.

The <Character> button brings you a dialog box just like the standard Character Format dialog box; you can choose from any combination of font and size, appearance features such as bold, and position features such as superscript. When you have selected the ones you want to search for, just choose <OK>. If the combination you selected is found, the string of characters in that format is selected. You can press Shift+F4 to repeat the search if necessary.

5. Choose the <Character> button.
6. Turn on the **Bold** field.
7. Respond to any message boxes you see.

If no bold strings are found, set three separate words to have bold formatting by selecting them and pressing Ctrl+B. Then repeat steps 3 through 7.

8. After the first bold string is found, press Shift+F4 to find the next one.

You might want to search for paragraph formats as well. You might locate figure captions in a document by searching for centered paragraphs, for example. The <Paragraph> button brings you a dialog box just like the Format Paragraph dialog box. You can choose from any combination of features in the box, from indentation to line spacing to alignment. If the format feature or combination is found, the paragraph containing it is selected.

1. Place the cursor in a paragraph and choose Format Paragraph.
2. Type **2** in the **Line** field to set up double spacing, then choose <OK>.
3. Move to the beginning of the document, then choose Edit Search.
4. Choose the <Paragraph> button.
5. Type **2** in the **Line** field, then choose <OK>.

The double-spaced paragraph is selected.

Replacing Formatting Codes

Word lets you replace formatting codes in much the same way as you locate them. You choose the Edit Replace command instead of Edit Search. You choose the <Replace Formatting Only> button, and again choose between <Character>, <Paragraph>, and <Style>.

When you choose <Character> or <Paragraph> this time, you'll see first the Replace Character Formatting or Replace Paragraph Formatting dialog box. These are much like the corresponding Search dialog boxes, except that each includes a <Replace With> button. When you have selected the character or paragraph formatting codes to search for, select the <Replace With> button.

You'll see next the Replace With Character Formatting or Replace With Paragraph Formatting dialog box; these have the same format fields within the box as in the corresponding Search or Replace dialog boxes. Here you select the format you want to use instead. Then choose <OK>.

Word prompts you to confirm the first replacement with a dialog box like the one shown in Figure 8.1. If you choose <Yes>, the format of the string or paragraph is replaced. If you choose <No>, it isn't.

If you turn off the **Confirm** field, the text above it (Do you want to replace the selection) changes to Replace All; if you then choose <Yes>, all formats will be replaced as you requested.

You can't remove formats this way; if you don't choose a replacement format, the string or paragraph will be located, but no replacement is done. You'll be asked if the next occurrence should be located.

1. Choose the Edit Replace command.

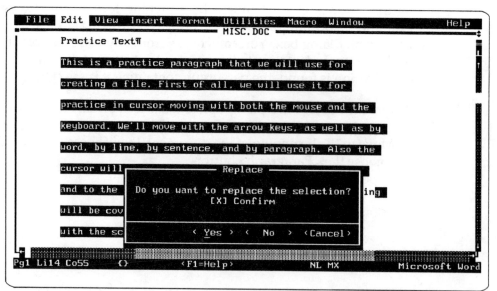

Figure 8.1. The Replace Formatting Dialog Box

2. Choose the <Character> button.
3. In the Replace Character Formatting dialog box, turn on the **Bold** field, then choose <Replace With>.
4. In the Replace With Character Formatting dialog box, turn on the **Italic** field, then choose <OK>.
5. When you see the dialog box, choose <Yes>.
6. When you see the dialog box again, turn off the **Confirm** field and choose <Yes>.

The remaining two bold fields will be changed to italics.

1. If a document is open, change all italic text to all caps. If the document doesn't contain any italic text, format several separate words as italic first.
2. Locate an all caps field. Format one first if necessary.
3. Locate a double-spaced paragraph. If necessary, format it first so it can be located.
4. Change the formatting of the double-spaced paragraph to single spaced.

*Use the Edit Search command with the <Character> button for item 2 and the <Paragraph> button for item 3. Use Edit Replace with the <Character> button for item 1; turn on the **Italic** field in the first dialog box and the **All Caps** field in the second. Use Edit Replace with the <Paragraph> button for item 4; type **2** in the **Line** field in the first dialog box and **1** in the same field in the second.*

Using Fonts

So far, you've been using the default font for your printer. Depending on which printer is installed, you can probably use different fonts and different type sizes. A font is the type style used to form the characters. Most of Word's fonts affect only printed characters. A few fonts, such as the Symbol and Zapf Dingbats fonts, produce characters that differ from the standard printable characters. These may be displayed on the screen. The size, usually specified in points, indicates the height of the printed characters; it also reflects the width. A point is 1/72 of an inch.

Most printers default to a 12-point fixed-pitch font. This size font usually requires ten characters to make up an inch and prints six lines to the inch. Fixed pitch means the font uses the same amount of linear space for each character; the letters m and i take up the same space. A proportional font uses different widths for these two characters.

Specifying Fonts

You can specify fonts from the Format Character command or by using the formatting ribbon. In either case, the text to be affected must be selected first.

1. Choose the Format Character command.
2. Drop down the **Font** field menu or use ↓ to cycle through the choices, then restore the default.
3. Choose <Cancel>.

You can use the formatting ribbon even if it isn't displayed. Just select the text, then press Ctrl+F and the ribbon appears, with the current font value highlighted.

To choose a font from the field menu in the ribbon or the dialog box, select it normally. Double-click on it with a mouse or highlight it and press ↵ from the keyboard. Unless the character produced is changed, you won't see the font change displayed on the screen; you'll see it when you print the document, however.

1. Select an entire paragraph.
2. Press Ctrl+F or choose the Format Character command.
3. Select a different font from the default.
4. Choose <OK>.
5. Print the document (or at least the page).

You will see the effect of the different font in the printed pages, but probably not on the editing screen. Preview mode may show the difference if you have a VGA screen.

To change the font in an entire document, first select the entire document with Shift+F10 or with Ctrl+Double-click in the selection bar (left edge of the window). Then change the font. Once the entire document is changed, inserted characters will be in the new font as well.

Specifying Font Size

Changing the font size, too, can be done through the ruler or through the Format Character command. In this case, you use the **Point Size** field in the dialog box or the **Pts** field on the ribbon. Pressing Ctrl+P brings up the ribbon automatically.

The field menu shows the point sizes that your printer can handle; some printers can handle more than are shown. Your printer may be able to handle only a few discrete sizes or it may be able to handle every size from 1 to 127 points. If you know what point sizes are available, you can just type it in the field instead of selecting a size. A smaller point size means a smaller character.

To change the point size for existing text, first select the text to be affected. To change the size for the entire document, select the entire document first. For a paragraph or several words, just select text to be changed.

1. Select a sentence in a paragraph.
2. Press Ctrl+P or choose the Format Character command.
3. Select a larger point size than the default.
4. Choose <OK>.
5. Print the document (or at least the page).

The letters in the formatted sentence are in a different size, but you won't see this on the screen unless you are in layout view. If you format an entire paragraph in a different font size, the ruler and screen line length change to reflect the new size in layout view.

Your printed document may not look quite right. If the paragraph is set for single spacing with the value 1 in the **Line** field of the Format Paragraph dialog box, the lines are still set at six per inch. If you are going to use a nondefault font size, you'll want to change this field to **Auto**.

1. Choose the Format Paragraph command.
2. Change the value in the **Line** field to **Auto**, if it isn't set that way already.
3. Print the document again.

If you use several different fonts on a line, automatic line spacing will adjust to fit the largest font. You can specify line spacing exactly in inches or points if you prefer.

1. Restore a complete formatted document to normal paragraph formatting.
2. Set up three paragraphs so that each has a different font and/or size, then print it.
3. Change the font for the entire document. Make the last paragraph a smaller size.
4. Add a title line in a very large font to the beginning of the file.

Use Shift+F10 followed by Ctrl+X to restore all paragraphs to normal. The fonts and point sizes you use depend on your printer, but you can use either the Format Character command or the ribbon. Be sure your normal paragraph line spacing is set to Auto.

Arranging Paragraphs

A few additional commands and options are available to help you tailor paragraphs to meet the needs of your document. You can specify that a paragraph is not to be split over a page, for example. Or you can specify a border or shading to set off the paragraph.

In order to handle some of these features, you may sometimes want to use Shift+⏎ instead of ⏎. The result is a new-line character that starts a new line without starting a new paragraph. If you have the paragraph marks display turned on, the new-line character appears as a ↓. You'll want to work with paragraph marks on whenever you are formatting paragraphs.

Keeping a Paragraph on One Page

Sometimes you want to make sure a paragraph isn't split over a page break. One way to do this is to turn on the **Keep Paragraph Together** field in the Paragraph Formatting dialog box. Then whenever the entire paragraph won't fit on the page it starts on, Word moves it all to the next page. While this leaves space on the first page, the paragraph is kept together.

1. Place the cursor in a paragraph that spans two pages. If necessary, insert text ahead of it to make it span.
2. Choose the Format Paragraph command.

3. Turn on the **Keep Paragraph Together** field.
4. Choose <OK>.

The paragraph now starts at the top of a page. No matter how much text you insert before it, the paragraph will not be split over a page.

The **With Next** field keeps two paragraphs together; it keeps the end of the current paragraph and the beginning of the next from being divided by a page break. This is especially useful to keep a heading on the same page as the following text.

Paragraph Borders

If your printer can draw lines, you may want to individualize a paragraph with a border. Word considers each paragraph as a rectangular space or frame on the page, so the border always makes a regular shape.

A border places an actual line around the paragraph or paragraphs you choose. You can create a complete box around each paragraph or specify which sides (top, bottom, left, and right) are to be drawn. The line style can be normal line, bold, double, or thick. Figure 8.2 shows the effects on screen. You may have additional choices that let you use a medium or light line. You can check to find the effects on your printer.

```
 File  Edit  View  Insert  Format  Utilities  Macro  Window          Help
============================== MISC.DOC ====================================
 ¶
 ┌──────────────────────────────────────────────────────────────────┐
 │Abrams, Joseph¶                                                     │
 └──────────────────────────────────────────────────────────────────┘
 Stockwell, Craig¶
 ════════════════════════════════════════════════════════════════════
 Ashley, Monty¶
 ────────────────────────────────────────────────────────────────────
 Fernandez, Vida¶
 █ Charlton, Norm¶                                                  █
 Santiago, Benito¶
 ┌──────────────────────────────────────────────────────────────────┐
 │Davis, Susan¶                                                      │
 └──────────────────────────────────────────────────────────────────
 Wagner, Steven¶
 ══════════════════════════════════════════════════════════════════
 █ Michaels, James¶
 Hoogterp, Frank¶
 Griffin, Barbara¶
 Gritter, Larry¶
 Pg1 Li45 Co15      {}         <F1=Help>         NL MX    Microsoft Word
 Edit document or press Alt to choose commands
```

Figure 8.2. Examples of Boxes

Boxing Paragraphs. If your printer can handle this, it is easy. Just place the cursor in the paragraph and choose the Format Borders command; you can choose the <Borders> button from within the Format Paragraph dialog box as well. Both routes result in the dialog box shown in Figure 8.3.

You must choose to create the border as a box around each paragraph or as a set of lines. If several paragraphs are selected, a box results in setting off each paragraph, even a paragraph mark alone on a line. Here's how you can box a paragraph:

1. Place the cursor in the paragraph or on its paragraph mark.
2. Choose the Format Borders command.
3. Turn on the **Box Each Paragraph** field.
4. Turn on the desired **Line Style**; try **Normal** first.
5. Choose <OK>.

You'll see the effect on the screen immediately. If you print the page, you'll see the effect there.

Suppose you want to box several paragraphs. Just select text that extends into all of them, then use the same procedure. You'll see that each paragraph is boxed separately. The bottom line of one paragraph's box and the top line of the next are actually the same line. This dividing line is always in normal line style. Try it with another line style and see what happens:

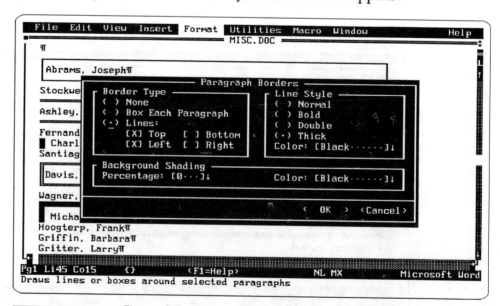

Figure 8.3. The Paragraph Borders Dialog Box

1. Select three paragraphs.
2. Choose the Format Borders command.
3. Turn on the **Box Each Paragraph** field.
4. Turn on the **Double** or **Thick Line Style**.
5. Choose <OK>.

Notice the difference in the lines. To remove them, just press Ctrl+X before unselecting the paragraphs.

Removing Borders. Border formatting can be removed like other paragraph formatting. Just put the cursor in the paragraph and press Ctrl+X to remove all the paragraph formatting. If you want to remove just border formatting, choose the Format Borders command again and set the **Border Type** field to **None**.

Using Lines. Suppose you want a box around the outside of all three paragraphs. There are a few ways to accomplish this. One way is to use Shift+⏎ to end each of the first two. That way, it really is only one paragraph and the box will work just fine. Another way is to use the **Lines** option.

First select all paragraphs in the set to be bordered as one, and apply the right and left lines to all of them. Then select the first paragraph and add the top border. Finally, select the last paragraph and add the bottom border.

1. Select three paragraphs.
2. Choose the Format Borders command. Leave the **Line Style** at **Normal**.
3. Turn on the **Lines** field, then turn on **Left** and **Right**.
4. Choose <OK>.

At this point, lines appear on both sides of the three-paragraph selection.

1. Place the cursor in the first paragraph.
2. Choose the Format Borders command.
3. Turn on the **Lines** field, then turn on **Top**.
4. Choose <OK>.

Now the top of the box has been drawn.

5. Place the cursor in the last paragraph.
6. Choose the Format Borders command.
7. Turn on the **Lines** field, then turn on **Bottom**.
8 Choose <OK>.

At this point the group of paragraphs is enclosed in a single border. If you want a different line style, you have to choose it each time. Your printer may support additional styles in the **Color** field. Actual colors may be listed for a color printer, but others may include such choices as dark, medium, and light. These result in broken or gray lines, depending on the printer.

Shading a Paragraph

Sometimes you may want to shade a paragraph, either to bring attention to it or to make it unreadable. You can do this through the Format Borders command, either in addition to a border or instead of one. The same dialog box lets you specify the shading.

The shading is specified as a percentage, where 0 is no shading and 100 is fully black. (If you have a color printer, you'll be able to choose additional colors for background shading.) If your printer doesn't support unlimited shading variations, the **Percentage** field menu will list the valid ones. Shading isn't shown in the document window, but it shows up nicely in Print Preview screens, so you'll be able to check it out before you print a document.

1. Put the cursor in a paragraph.
2. Choose the Format Borders command.
3. In the **Percentage** field, choose any percentage except 0 or 100.
4. Choose <OK>.

You won't be able to see the effect on the screen, even in layout view.

5. Choose File Print Preview. Notice the shaded area, then press Escape.

With some printers you can accomplish additional levels of shading by selecting colors, even if the printer is a standard black-on-white type. For example, choosing yellow produces a lighter shade of gray than does the 10% shading option.

Tip ||| The degree of shading is best seen on your printer, so you may want to print several different shadings to see the effect.

1. Add a normal border and light shading to one paragraph.
2. Add a thick top and bottom border and no shading to another paragraph.

3. Add dark shading and a double border to a third paragraph.
4. Print the page or the document.
5. Restore all the paragraphs to normal formatting.

You can use the Format Borders command for the first three items. Be sure to place the cursor in the paragraph first. To restore the paragraphs, select the entire document and press Ctrl+X.

Positioning a Paragraph

Ordinarily, Word controls the position of paragraphs on the page, moving them up or down as needed as you insert and delete material. Word keeps them in order and inside the defined margins. Sometimes, you want to fix a paragraph in a particular position on a page. For example, you might want to make sure a table is always at the top or bottom of a particular page, letting the other paragraphs flow around it. Or you might want to position a label starting in the left margin. You can accomplish these with the Format Position command. We aren't covering the details of positioning paragraphs in this book, but you might want to try it out in your practice documents.

Headers and Footers

When you create a document, you may want to have the same text at the top or bottom of each page. Word lets you include several paragraphs in a header or footer if you want, but most headers are just one or two lines. Each can contain a page number. You can define different headers and footers for even and odd pages if you like.

When you define a header or footer, it affects the next page top or bottom. To cause a header or footer to affect the entire document, define it at the very beginning of the file. If you want the header to change, insert a new one between the top of the page preceding it and the first text line on the new page. If you want a footer to change, insert a new one on the page in which it is to appear.

Headers and footers do not appear in their printed positions in the document window. When layout view is off, you can see the paragraph that defines the header or footer. You can't even see that when layout view is on. You can see the headers or footers in place in preview mode or in printed pages.

Creating Headers and Footers

The first step in creating a header or footer is to type its text. Then select the paragraph (it is often a single line) and choose the Format Header/Footer command. If this command isn't available, you are probably in layout view.

1. Move to the beginning of the document (Ctrl+Home), press ↵, then ↑.
2. Type **This is a sample header**.
3. Leave the cursor in the just-typed paragraph.
4. Choose the Format Header/Footer command.

Tip || If your Header/Footer command is not available on the Format menu, check the View menu. Layout must be turned off to work with headers and footers.

The resulting dialog box is shown in Figure 8.4. Notice that you can format the paragraph as **Header, Footer,** or **None**; normal text is formatted as none. You can specify that the header will appear on any or all of the **First Page, Odd Pages,** or **Even Pages**. If you want the header or footer to appear on every page, make sure all three are turned on. The **First Page** field refers only to a header or footer defined at the beginning of the document. If you leave this field turned off, the header or footer will not be printed on the first page.

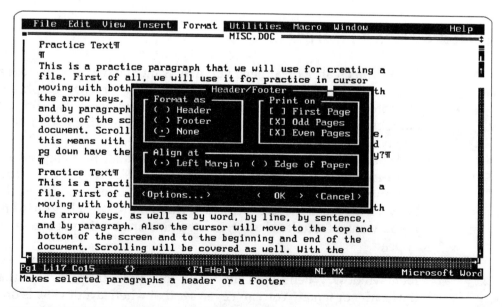

Figure 8.4. The Header/Footer Dialog Box

If you choose **Odd Pages**, you can define a different header or footer to appear on the even pages. They will both be in effect when the document is printed. If you define another header or footer for the same pages, however, the new one is printed instead of the one defined earlier.

The header is aligned at the **Left Margin** by default; you can have it start at the left **Edge of Paper** instead. You might do this to have the header or footer extend beyond the standard text in the document for easier reference. It also gives you more space on the line. Notice that both of these start at the left side of the page. If you want your header or footer aligned differently, use the Format Paragraph command to change the paragraph alignment.

5. Turn on the **Header** button.
6. Turn on all the **Print on** fields, then choose <OK>.

On the screen, the caret (^) symbol appears in the style bar (the blank column) just to the left of the first line of the paragraph. This reminds you that the paragraph will not print in the inline text position, but it will be used as a header or footer starting at the next opportunity.

7. Choose the File Print Preview command and examine the result.

You can use a longer paragraph as a header or footer. Just type it, select it, and tell Word what it is and where to put it. If you want to use several separate lines, use Ctrl+⌐ at the end of each so they form a single paragraph.

Positioning a Header or Footer

By default, headers start one-half inch down from the top of the page and footers end one-half inch up from the bottom of the page. If the header or footer is longer than two lines, the top or bottom margin will be extended so the complete header or footer is printed, with at least one blank line between it and the adjacent text.

You can modify the Header or Footer position by choosing the <Options> button in the Header/Footer dialog box. When you do, you'll see the **Header Position from Top** and **Footer Position from Bottom** fields, each with the default value of 0.5" in the field. You can change this to whatever you want.

1. Make sure the cursor is in the header paragraph.
2. Choose the Format Header/Footer command.
3. Choose the <Options> button.
4. Type 1 in the **Header Position from Top** field.

5. Choose <OK>.
6. Choose the File Print Preview command to see the effect.

Removing a Header or Footer

You can remove a header or footer by deleting or cutting the paragraph, just like any other paragraph. If you want to keep the paragraph as normal text, turn on the **None** button in the dialog box.

1. Make sure the cursor is in the header paragraph.
2. Choose the Format Header/Footer command.
3. Turn on the **None** button.
4. Choose <OK>.
5. Choose the File Print Preview command to see the effect.

Inserting Page Numbers

You may want to place page numbers in a header or footer. If you do this, do not use the Insert Page Numbers command or the <Page Numbers> button from the Format Section dialog box to print the page numbers. These page numbers are separate from headers and footers, and may result in your having two page numbers on a page. If you want to start numbering pages with a number other than 1 or use a different page numbering style, you can set those values through the Insert Page Numbers command. Just leave the **Page Number Position** set at **None**.

Suppose you want a page to have a running foot that says - *n* -, where *n* is the page number of the document. To do this, you would type - **page** and immediately press F3. What you typed is changed to - **(page)** and you then press the spacebar and type -. When you print the document, Word replaces **(page)** with the actual page number. Once you get it typed, you format the paragraph as a footer. On page 17, the footer will show - **17** - in the position you specified.

The string **(page)** acts as a placeholder; you use it as what Word calls a glossary. In Chapter 10 you'll learn to use other supplied glossaries as well as to create your own.

1. Move to the top of your document, and type **Footer line page page** then immediately press F3. Notice the insert of the new string.
2. Choose the Format Header/Footer command.

3. Turn on the **Footer** button.
4. Check all pages for printing.
5. Turn on the **Edge of Page** button.
6. Choose <OK>.
7. Print the document.

Notice that the pages are numbered starting with 1. Suppose you want to start with number 120.

1. Choose the Insert Page Numbers command.
2. Move the cursor to the **Start At** field and type **120**.
3. Choose <OK>, then print the document again.

When you include the page number in a header or footer, use the Insert Page Numbers command only to set the starting point or the number style.

1. Remove any headers and footers from your current file or open a different multipage document.
2. Add a header to appear on all odd pages that includes your name followed by a dash and the page number.
3. Add a header to appear on all even pages that includes the page number, followed by a dash and your name.
4. Modify the spacing or format of each header so the right header starts on the right and the left header starts on the left.
5. Add a footer in the center of each page that shows CONFIDENTIAL.
6. Print the document and correct the codes if necessary.
7. Make the document start at page 12 and use Roman numerals instead of Arabic numbers.
8. Print it again to see the full effect.

To insert the page number, type **page** *then press F3. For item 2, turn on the* **Odd Pages** *and* **First Page** *fields. For item 3, turn on the* **Even Pages** *field. For item 4, turn on the* **Edge of Page** *field for each header; use the Format Paragraph command to align the header for even pages on the right. For item 5, create the footer, then use the Format Paragraph command to center it. For item 7, use the Insert Page Numbers command to change the number style and starting point.*

Using Footnotes

Footnotes are generally references or comments that are treated separately from the body of the text. Word can number them automatically or use reference marks that you supply. It can place them at the bottom of each page, in which case it rearranges text to fit, or at the end of the document.

If you use automatic numbering, Word inserts a number, starting with 1, into the text. This number looks on the screen like you typed it; it isn't flagged in any way that you can see, but Word knows it is actually a footnote reference. Whether or not you are in layout view will affect what you see next.

If you aren't in layout view, Word immediately moves to the end of the file (following the section mark) and inserts the same number there for you to enter the text of the footnote. You can move to the end of the document at any time to edit or change your footnotes.

If you are working in layout view, you'll see a footnote pane instead. It displays any footnotes referenced on the current page. You can edit any of these. You can't turn off layout view while the footnote pane is displayed.

No matter which view you are in, the reference character appears as a normal character in the footnote text. It has no following space, no different position, font, or size. You can format it like any other character.

Creating a Footnote

When you reach the position in the text where you want a footnote to appear, you choose the Insert Footnote command. The resulting dialog box is shown in Figure 8.5. To accept automatic numbering, just choose <OK>.

To use a reference mark other than sequential numbers, enter it in the **Footnote Reference Mark** field. You can use up to 28 characters, but you'll probably want to use an asterisk or some other short reference mark. If you use automatic numbering, Word will renumber your footnotes if you insert or renumber notes, or if you cut and paste text containing them. If you specify individual reference marks, even letters in sequence, you'll have to maintain the sequence yourself.

With Layout View Off. If you aren't in layout view, Word transfers you to the end of the document to enter your footnote text.

1. Turn layout view off if it is on.
2. Move the cursor into a paragraph.
3. Choose the Insert Footnote command.

4. Choose <OK> to use automatic numbering.

At this point, Word positions the cursor at the end of the document following the section mark. You'll see the footnote number before the cursor.

5. Type a line or two explaining that this is the first footnote.
6. Choose Edit Go To (F5).

At this point, the Edit Go To dialog box is set to return you to the point in the text where you entered the reference mark. The **Footnote** button is turned on and **F1** appears selected in the **Go To** field.

7. Choose <OK>.

The cursor is back at the reference mark just inserted in the document.

With Layout View On. When layout is turned on, Word gives you a special footnote pane to work with. If your document is already displayed in two panes, the one that did not contain the reference number disappears.

1. Turn layout view on.
2. Move the cursor into a later paragraph.

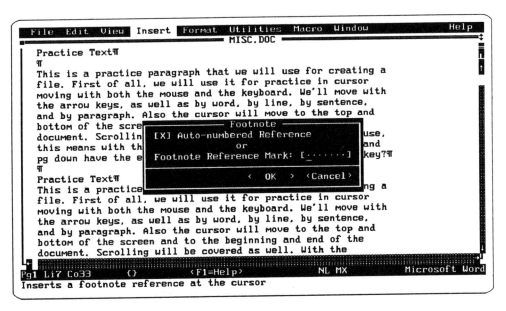

Figure 8.5. The Footnote Dialog Box

3. Choose the Insert Footnote command.
4. Choose <OK> to use automatic numbering.

At this point, the window splits into two panes. You'll see the reference mark and can type the text. You won't see any previous footnotes, however, unless the reference marks are contained in the current page of the document.

5. Type a line explaining that this is the second footnote.

If you have a mouse, you can return to the insertion point easily; just click on it in the upper pane. But you can continue to work with the footnote pane displayed in any case by pressing F6 to make the other pane active. As you enter text or scroll in the text pane, any footnotes referenced on the page that is displayed appear in the footnote pane. You can adjust the pane size in the usual way, by dragging the split icon or by choosing the Window Split command and using the directional arrows.

To get rid of the footnote pane, drag the split icon to the top or bottom of the screen with the mouse or by using the Window Split command.

6. Remove the footnote pane.
7. Turn off layout view.
8. At some point in your document, add another footnote.
9. Choose the Edit Go To command, then choose <OK> to return to the document.

Moving to a Footnote

To move to the next footnote reference mark in the text, choose the Edit Go To command (F5). Turn on the **Footnote** button, then type **f** (for footnote) in the **Go To** field. When you choose <OK>, the cursor moves directly to the next footnote reference mark. You can use Edit Repeat (F4) to move through all the reference marks. To move to a specific footnote, type the number of the footnote in the **Go To** field. When you choose <OK>, you'll be moved directly to the reference number in the text.

To move to the text of a footnote once the cursor is on its reference number, choose the Edit Go To command again. The reference number is preentered as F*n*. When you choose <OK>, you'll be at its text, where you can edit it at will. When not in layout view, Edit Go To lets you toggle between the footnote reference and the text at the end of the document.

If you aren't working in layout view, you can just move to the end of the document and edit any footnote. This is easier if you are going to do much editing. In Layout view, you can display the text of one footnote, then scroll through the text to other footnotes; the text will be displayed whenever the page that contains the footnote reference is in the upper pane. You can edit any text you can see.

1. Turn off layout view.
2. Move to the end of the document (Ctrl+End).
3. Add a few words to the second footnote, then place the cursor on its reference mark.
4. Choose the Edit Go To command.
5. Type **1** in the **Go To** field.
6. If **Footnote** isn't on, turn it on, then choose <OK>.

The cursor is now at the first reference mark inserted in the document.

7. Choose the Edit Go To command.
8. The **Footnote** button is already turned on. Type **f** in the **Go To** field, then choose <OK>.

The cursor is now at the second reference mark in the document.

9. Press F4 to repeat the operation.

The cursor has moved to the next reference mark.

Moving or Deleting a Footnote

You can delete a footnote by moving the cursor to the reference mark and cutting it or deleting it. The text is gone as well. If you cut the reference number, you can paste it somewhere else to move the entire footnote reference and text. If you delete it, you can use Edit Undo to put it back.
 Word renumbers the footnotes if you used automatic numbering.

1. Select reference mark 1.
2. Choose Edit Cut (Shift+Delete).
3. Move the cursor to a location near the end of the document and choose Edit Paste (Shift+Insert).

Notice that Word has automatically renumbered the reference marks in the document. It has also rearranged and renumbered the footnote text.

Using Special Reference Marks

If you want to enter a footnote with an asterisk or some other reference mark, enter it in the **Footnote Reference Mark** field in the Footnote dialog box. When you choose <OK>, that mark appears in the text and in the footnote entry area. If you mix automatically numbered footnotes with special marks in the same document, Word internally numbers them all.

Move to a specially marked footnote with the equivalent footnote number or search for the special mark. Once the special footnote reference is at the cursor, you can move directly to the footnote text by choosing the Edit Go To command and choosing <OK>.

Printing Footnotes

When you print a document containing footnotes, Word prints them, by default, at the bottom of the page. A short solid line (about 2 inches long) separates the footnotes from the text.

1. If your document doesn't have any footnotes, add two or three.
2. Choose the File Print command.
3. Choose <OK>.

To have the footnotes printed at the end of the document, use the Format Section command and specify the location in the **Place Footnotes** section by turning on the **End of Document** button. They will be printed immediately following the last paragraph of text. If you want them to start at the top of a new page, insert a hard page break (with Insert Break) at the end of the text section or at the very beginning of the footnote section.

1. Choose the Format Section command.
2. Turn on the **End of Document** button.
3. Choose <OK>.
4. Choose the File Print command.
5. Choose <OK>.

This time the footnotes are printed at the end of the document.

Formatting Footnotes

By default, Word doesn't format footnotes. Rather, it formats them just as it does every other paragraph. You may want a different format. For example, you may want the footnote reference marks to be superscripted, so they appear a bit above the baseline. You may also want them to be a bit smaller, especially if the document is single spaced. You can format each reference mark in the document and in the footnote text.

Tip

If you want a space to appear between the footnote reference mark and its text, you can insert the space before you type the text or add it later. If you want a blank line between two footnotes on the same page, put ↵ at the end of each.

1. Select the footnote reference mark.
2. Choose the Format Character command.
3. Turn on the **Superscript** button.
4. Change the **Point Size** field to be several sizes smaller, then choose <OK>.

The reference mark is now a small superscript number. You can use Edit Go To to get to the footnote proper and format its reference mark as well. In Chapter 9, you'll learn to format footnotes much more easily.

1. With layout view off, add another footnote anywhere in the document.
2. Turn layout view on, then add another footnote to your document. You may continue to work in layout mode if you wish.
3. Print the document with all the footnotes at the end of the document.
4. Move the paragraph containing the last footnote to a position near the beginning of the document. Print it again to see the numbering effect.
5. Move to the third footnote reference, then to the footnote text. Format its reference numbers to be in bold, then print the document again.

If you work in layout mode, you have the footnote pane always available. Remove it with Window Split or by dragging the split icon to the top or bottom of the window. Create footnotes with Insert Footnote. Format references with Format Character. Use Edit Go To to move to footnote references in the text. When a reference mark is selected, Edit Go To takes you to the text.

Annotations

Annotations work much like footnotes, but they have a different purpose. Annotations are notes included in a document for a special purpose. The annotation references can be individualized and the results can be handled in ways that are different from footnotes. We aren't covering the use of annotations in detail in this book, but you might want to try them out on your own.

Using Columns

Word lets you use multiple columns of text on a page in newspaper style. When one column is filled, text flows automatically into the next column on the page. When the last column on the page is filled, Word starts a new column on the next page. The columns affect how footnotes and annotations print, but they don't affect headers and footers.

If you work in layout view, you see the columns side by side on the screen. If not, they are displayed as one long column, but you see the actual layout in preview mode or when you print the document. Working in layout view may take longer, since Word has to work harder to lay out and rearrange the display whenever you make changes or scroll.

Tip It's often easiest to enter the text without layout view, then switch to layout view for final formatting and editing.

Column definition is done on a section basis; a default section has a single column six inches wide. If you change the right and/or left margin, you change the column width. If you want a document to have two columns, you use the Format Section dialog box. If you want to change the column structure within a document (from one to two columns, for example), you have to start a new section with the Insert Break command. You specify whether the new section is continuous with the old or whether it starts on a new page, so you can have different column structures on the same page.

Setting Up Multiple Columns

To change an existing document so that it appears in several columns, just choose the Format Section command and type the number of columns desired in the **Number** field of the **Columns** box. The **Spacing** field specifies how much space appears between columns; 0.5" is the default but you can change

it if you like. When you set up multiple columns this way, they have equal widths.

1. Choose the Format Section command.
2. In the **Number** field, type **2**.
3. Choose <OK>.

Your document appears as either one narrow column or two side-by-side columns.

4. If it appears as one column, choose the View Layout command.

Now you see both columns and you are in layout view.

1. Choose the Format Section command.
2. Type **3** in the **Number** field.
3. Type **.3** in the **Spacing** field.
4. Choose <OK>.

Now you see three columns in the document.

5. Print the document.

Moving in Column Mode

Moving the cursor in column mode is no problem if you aren't in layout view. Just move as usual. In layout view, however, you might want to move across the page to the adjacent column. If you use a mouse, just click in the column you want. With the keyboard, first make sure NumLock is off, then press Alt+5(keypad) followed by → or ←. The cursor jumps to the indicated column.

1. Turn off NumLock (so that NL doesn't appear in your status bar).
2. Press Alt+5(keypad),→. The cursor moves to the column on the right.
3. Press Alt+5(keypad),←. The cursor moves to the column on the left.

Selecting text with multiple columns is done much as with a single column, since the selected text must all be adjacent. You can select from the bottom of one column into the next, but you can't select just the top part of adjacent columns. If you normally use the selection bar with your mouse, you'll see that it affects only the leftmost column, so you'll need to drag to select text in other columns.

Ending a Column Early

Normally, text fills one column and then flows into the next. When all the columns on a page are filled, the first column on the next page is started. If you want to end a column early, you can use the Insert Break command and turn on the **Column** button. A hard column break appears as a row of closely spaced dots, and the following text will appear at the top of the next column. If you want to make sure the next column starts on a new page, turn on the **Page** button instead.

1. Put the cursor in the leftmost column, about halfway down.
2. Choose the Insert Break command.
3. Turn on the **Column** button.
4. Choose <OK>.
5. Choose File Print Preview to examine the effect.

A hard column break is inserted, leaving a blank space at the bottom of the column. You can remove a hard column break in the same way you remove a hard page break—put the cursor on it and press Delete.

6. Place the cursor on the hard column break and press the Delete key.

Footnotes in Multiple Columns

If you include footnotes in a section with multiple columns, the footnotes are column specific. That is, they appear at the bottom of the appropriate column. If they are printed at the end of the document, they are still one column wide. They appear immediately after the final printed column unless you insert a page or column break at the end of the document. If you insert a page break, the footnotes appear on the next page, still formatted for the same column width. If you insert a column break, they appear at the top of the next column.

Multiple Column Layouts

Suppose you want a document to have several different column structures. You might want a single column for the first few lines or pages, then switch to two columns in the middle of a page, then return to one column, then finally have several pages of three-column text. Or you might want to have two columns of text, but print footnotes at the end of the document extending across the entire page. All these require you to use multiple sections in your document.

Starting a New Section

To start a new section, position the cursor where you want it to start and choose the Insert Break command; turn on the **Section** button. Initially, both sections have the same format. But once you create a new section, you can put the cursor in it, then use the Format Section command to format it as you want.

When you choose Insert Break and turn on the **Section** button, you see the type of section break for the current section. By default, sections start on a new page. If you prefer, a section can start on an odd or even page or be continuous, on the same page as the preceding section. The settings here apply to the current section. After you create a new section, you can specify how it starts.

When you choose <OK>, the section mark (a double row of dots) is inserted. The section mark extends across the current column.

1. Move the cursor to the beginning of your document, just following any header or footer paragraph.
2. Choose the Insert Break command.
3. Turn on the **Section** button.
4. Choose <OK>.

Now a new section has been inserted at the beginning of the document. The section marker is one column wide. Notice that S1 appears next to the page indicator in the status bar. If you move the cursor down into the following text, it will change to S2. This way you always know which section you are in.

To make the second section continue on the same page after the first, you have to format the section.

1. Move the cursor into the second section, so S2 appears in the status bar.
2. Choose the Format Section command.
3. Drop down the **Section Start** field and select Continuous.
4. Choose <OK>.

Deleting a Section Mark. You can delete a section mark just like you delete a paragraph mark. As with a paragraph mark, that removes all the section formatting, since the formatting is stored in the section mark. Choosing Edit Undo (Alt+Backspace) restores the deleted mark if you choose it immediately.

Formatting a Section. To format the new section, you can use the Format Section command to set it up the way you want. Remember that it has the same margins and column structure as the former section. Suppose you want to format the first section as a single column and include a heading.

1. Place the cursor on the leftmost character of the section mark and press ↵.
2. Move the cursor up one line and type **This is a one-column heading**. Make it bold.
3. Choose the Format Section command.
4. In the **Columns** box, type **1** in the **Number** field.
5. Choose <OK>.
6. Examine the page under preview mode or print it to see the effect.

On the screen, the section mark extends across the entire column. As you move the cursor from one section to another, you can see that the page number doesn't change.

1. Add a paragraph explaining that this demonstrates two sections on one page.
2. Print the document or choose File Print Preview to see how it looks.

You can use such a section at the beginning of a document to insert a large heading or banner across the page. This is a useful technique for newsletters or announcement flyers. Just type the heading in the first section and use the Format Character command to change it to a larger point size. You can also change the font and do any other formatting, of course.

1. Delete the paragraph you just added in the first section.
2. Use character formatting to specify a larger font for the heading line.
3. Use paragraph formatting to center it.
4. Press ↵ again, then type the current date and press ↵ again.
5. Format the current date to appear boldface and centered.
6. Print the document to see the effect.

More Complex Breaks

Suppose your document contains several pages of two-column text and must change in the middle of a page to one or three columns. If you insert a section break, then format the new section and turn on the **Continuous** button to make the second section continue on the same page, the columns will be rearranged automatically. If you let the section start on a new page, a soft page break will be inserted and you'll start on the next page.

1. Move the cursor to the first character on page 2 (or the last page of regular text), then insert a new section mark.
2. Format the last section for three columns.
3. Use hard column breaks (Ctrl+↵) to make the three columns end at the same point.
4. If your document contains any footnotes or annotations, insert a new section at the end of the document text and format it for a single column starting on a new page. Print all the footnotes at the end.
5. Print the document, then make any changes needed to polish up the format.

For item 1, use the Insert Break command. Then use Format Section in the last part of the document to specify three columns. In adjusting the columns, use Insert Break. For item 4, insert another section break at the end of the document text, start it at a new page, and format it for one column.

Exercise

This chapter has covered several advanced formatting techniques that enhance Word documents. You can now use fonts, borders, and shading to modify your text and paragraphs. You can also use headers, footers, footnotes, and columns in a document. This exercise lets you practice using these features. Preview or print the document after each item to see the effect.

1. Open or create an unformatted document. To create one, type a one-line title, then a paragraph of about ten lines. Copy the paragraph seven or eight times.
2. Change the entire document to use a font size about two points larger, if available.
3. Make the title bold and even larger in size, if possible.
4. Add a border of some type to the first full paragraph.

5. Shade the first complete paragraph on page 2 lightly.
6. Define a header for all pages to appear at the left edge of each page. It should show *Rough Draft - Do not distribute.*
7. Define a footer showing *Page n,* centered on each page. Define the actual page number to appear in place of *n.*
8. Add two footnotes on the first page and one on the second.
9. Modify the document so that the title is centered across the entire page and the rest of the document is in two columns.
10. Print the document and examine the output.

Use the Format Character command or the ribbon to adjust the font and size. Your printer determines what you can do here. Use Format Borders to place a border around the current paragraph or to shade it.

Use Format Header/Footer to define the **Left** *and* **Right** *headers and the footer. For the footer, type* **Page page** *and immediately press F3 to cause the page number to be inserted. Use the Insert Footnote command to insert the footnotes .*

To insert a new section, move the cursor to the beginning of the line following the title and choose the Insert Break command. In the resulting dialog box, turn on the **Section** *button and choose <OK>. Then move the cursor into the second section and choose the Format Section command. Change the* **Section Start** *field to show* **Continuous,** *then type* **2** *in the* **Columns** *field and choose <OK>. The document should be formatted as you want it.*

9

Styles and Style Sheets

Data entry is the easy part of word processing. Formatting characters, paragraphs, and sections, however, can take up a great deal of time and effort. So far you have learned to do direct formatting of all three. Styles let you do indirect formatting. A style is sort of a blueprint for formatting, containing all the formatting instructions so that you can apply them with just a few keystrokes. A style sheet is a separate file that contains a collection of styles that can be used with a document. In this chapter, you'll learn to:

- View a style sheet
- Attach a style sheet
- Apply styles from an existing style sheet
- Control the appearance of the style bar
- Remove styles from a document or a style sheet
- Create a new style sheet
- Move and copy styles
- Rename styles
- Record and define styles
- Modify existing styles
- Define automatic styles
- Merge style sheets
- Convert file formatting from styles to direct

Formatting Documents

All the formatting you have already learned is called direct formatting. Any direct formatting overrides formatting applied with styles. If you type straight text that doesn't need much formatting other than an occasional indentation or bold characters, direct formatting may be all you need. But if your documents use several different formats of paragraphs, and if you find you use the Format menu commands several times per paragraph, you'll want an easier and quicker way to format documents.

For example, suppose you type a lot of correspondence. You format the return address area in centered, bold type, indent the first line of every body paragraph, and arrange the close separately. You could develop a style sheet containing these styles, one for each type of paragraph. You could even include extra styles to include the date and signature lines.

Or suppose you type mostly reports. Each report has three levels of heading, a specially formatted header, normal paragraphs, some indented and italic paragraphs, and numbered lists that need a hanging indent. Another style sheet could handle this formatting quickly.

What Is a Style?

A style is a set of formatting codes for a character string, a paragraph, or a section. It lets you format with just a few keystrokes. For example, suppose you frequently use headings in your documents. The highest level heading you use is in Bookman type, 16 point, bold; it starts one-half inch into the left margin of the page, and has an extra line space before and after it. If that is defined as a paragraph style, you can apply it to any paragraph you want to treat as a heading. Then you won't have to work with the separate format elements every time, and you know all the headers are formatted the same way. If the rules change—for example, if your boss wants a different font—you can change it in the style and it automatically applies wherever that style is used.

Or suppose you want to use a proportional font and a wide left margin every time you start a new document. You could define a special section style that would take effect every time you start a new document. You can include almost any combination of formatting in a style to apply it with just a few keystrokes whenever you want.

What Is a Style Sheet?

A style sheet is a file that contains a collection of styles. The default style sheet, NORMAL.STY, is automatically attached to every new document you create. It contains no defined styles originally. You can set up your default format by adding styles to this style sheet.

Normally, you create separate style sheets for the various types of documents you type. You might have separate style sheets for letters, memos, reports, manuals, proposals, overhead transparencies, lesson plans, and so forth.

You can open any style sheet file to examine the styles, but you can use the styles in it only when the style sheet is attached to a document. The style sheet file always has extension STY.

The Contents of a Style Sheet

As you've noticed, you can't see formatting codes on the screen in a document window. They are hidden just before the first and after the last character of strings, in the paragraph mark, or in the section mark. In the style sheet, Word translates the formatting codes in every style for you so that you can tell what each does. Each style has five parts, as indicated in Figure 9.1. The parts are explained in detail.

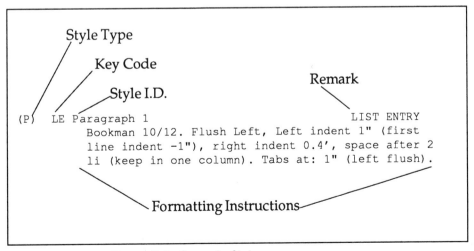

Figure 9.1. Sample Style

Style Type

The style type indicates the type of formatting in the style. It can be (C), (P), or (S) for character, paragraph, or section. If the style type is (C), the style contains character formatting only. If the style is (P) or (S), the style contains paragraph or section formatting; character formatting may be included if it applies to the entire paragraph or section.

Key Code

The key code is an optional one- or two-character code that you can use for quick application of the style. If the code is H1, you apply it by placing the cursor in a paragraph and pressing Ctrl+Shift+H,1. Key codes have a letter or number for the first character; the second can be any printable character. Using a single character limits the number of codes you can have in a style sheet. If you have a style named H, you can't have another named H1.

The key code is usually related to the Style I.D. or to what the style does. You might use H1 for a level-1 heading or BI for a bold indented paragraph.

When a style has been applied to a paragraph, the key code appears in the style bar when it is turned on through View Preferences. You'll see how to do that shortly.

Style I.D.

The style I.D. is the label for a style; it is often called the style name. Table 9.1 lists the style I.D.s that you can use in each style sheet. You can see that plenty of different styles are available. You can use any of these names, or Word will suggest one if appropriate. The style I.D. names with no numbers are called automatic styles, while the ones with numbers are available for whatever use you want. The Normal paragraph and section styles are applied to every paragraph or section that isn't assigned a different style.

The *automatic styles* automatically apply to a specific type of text. For example, any page number you use is formatted with the Page Number style. Any footnote reference is formatted with the Footnote Ref style. The text of a footnote is automatically formatted with the Footnote paragraph style. The Heading styles apply automatically to headings in outlines, but you can use them in text as well.

A general character style, for example one that sets a superscript to italic and small caps, could use the Style I.D. Character 1. A paragraph style could use any of the I.D.s Paragraph 1 through Paragraph 55. The numbers don't have to be used in sequence.

Remark

The remark is a reminder of what the style does. It is limited to 28 characters, and gives you more flexibility than the Style I.D. The remark appears in menus and lists of styles and lets you see the effect of using that style. The style for Paragraph 4 may be indented on both sides and single spaced, for example. The remark might be "Indent and single" or "Quoted material." Some listings show only the first 10 characters, so don't start all your paragraph style remarks with PARAGRAPH, for example.

Tip   If your documents will be transferred to a Macintosh or to Word for Windows, the remark becomes the style name, so be sure to use descriptive remarks. Almost anything is more helpful than "Paragraph 12."

Table 9.1. Available Style I.D.s

Character
  Page Number
  Footnote Ref
  Annotation Ref
  Line Number
  Summary Info
  Line Draw
  Character 1 through Character 23
Paragraph
  Normal
  Footnote
  Annotation
  Header/Footer
  Heading 1 through Heading 7
  Index 1 through Index 4
  Table 1 through Table 4
  Paragraph 1 through Paragraph 55
Section
  Normal
  Section 1 through Section 21

Formatting Instructions

The formatting instructions are generated by Word to tell you in plain (or not-so-plain) English what codes are part of the style. In the example, the formatting instructions give the font, the point size, the spacing, the alignment, the indentation, and the character style. Word doesn't let you edit the formatting instructions directly, but you can modify them with the various Format commands.

The Default Style Sheet

By default, Word attaches a style sheet named NORMAL.STY to each document. If you attach a different style sheet, it stays associated with the file. The attached style sheet, either NORMAL or another one, is available whenever you open that file.

Originally, NORMAL doesn't contain any individual styles. All paragraphs are formatted in the default way that you are used to. You can insert styles into NORMAL.STY if you like; then they will be available for every document that doesn't have a different style sheet attached. For example, if you usually want to use different margins, different font, or first-line indentation, you could add this format to NORMAL.STY. You'll see how to do that later in this chapter.

Existing Style Sheets

Word comes with several style sheets that you can use or modify. You can see the list of style sheets in the Word directory through the File Open command.

1. Choose the File Open command.
2. Turn on the **Style Sheets** button in the **Show Files** group box.

All files in the current directory with extension STY are shown. If you don't see any, or very many, change the directory to the one that contains Word. You should see about eight, including NORMAL.STY and SAMPLE.STY.

Tip If anyone else uses Word on your computer, these files may have been changed. If you don't see exactly what we describe, don't worry about it. The structure of the style file and the procedures for using it will be the same.

At this point, NORMAL.STY is probably empty. You'll learn to add styles to it in a bit. For now, we'll use SAMPLE.STY to show you how to view a style sheet and how to apply styles to paragraphs in a document.

3. Select SAMPLE.STY and choose <OK>.
4. Maximize the window.

Your screen should look something like Figure 9.2. The file name in the top border shows SAMPLE.STY. The first style in the style sheet is highlighted.

Viewing the Style File

In a style file, an entire style is always selected; you can't edit these directly. You can move the highlight and scroll through the file to see them all.

5. Press ↓ or click on an unselected style.
6. Move to the end of the file to select the last style in the file.
7. Move back to the first style.

You can delete, move, and copy styles in a style sheet. You can even move or copy styles from one style sheet to another. The process is the same as for

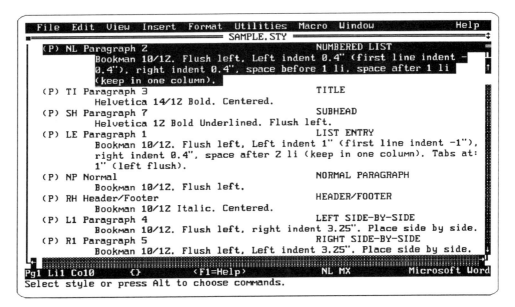

Figure 9.2. The SAMPLE.STY File

handling text in documents. You always deal with an entire style, or multiple styles, however.

The SAMPLE.STY file contains styles for several different kinds of paragraphs. The first one in the figure is a style for a numbered list. By reading the formatting instructions, you can get an idea of how the paragraph will be formatted.

The style type is (P) or paragraph for all of these styles. Every one of them has a key code; it's NL for the first one. The style I.D. is the standard paragraph name; it's Paragraph 2 for the NL style. The remark is shown in all caps; it's NUMBERED LIST for this style.

You can modify an open style file using various menu commands. To edit a specific style, you'll have to select it first. We'll get to that later.

Style Menus

The actions you can take when a style sheet window is active aren't the same as for a document window. The menu bar looks just the same, but the menus themselves are different. They have all the commands you'll need while a style sheet is active.

The Edit menu contains only the Undo, Repeat, Cut, Copy, and Paste commands, as well as the Rename Style command, which you'll learn to use in this chapter. The View menu is limited to the Ribbon, Ruler, Status Bar, and Preferences commands.

The Insert menu contains two new commands only, New Style and Style Sheet, which you'll learn to use in this chapter. The Format menu, however, contains all the standard document commands *except* the ones related specifically to styles; those commands are valid only when a document window is active. The Utilities menu contains only the Customize command, while the Macro, Window, and Help menus are unchanged.

1. Drop down the File menu by clicking on it or pressing Alt,F.
2. Use → or click to see the remaining menus while the style file is active.
3. Release the menus.

Closing a Style File

When you are finished viewing or editing a style file, you close it just like any other file, by clicking on the close box or choosing the File Close command.

4. Close the style sheet window.

If you prefer, you can leave the style window open and treat it just like any other window. If you make any changes to it, you'll be prompted to save it when you close the file or exit Word.

1. Open the file MONTHLY.STY. If this style sheet isn't available, open another one that you haven't looked at before.
2. Scroll through the file, examining all the styles.
3. Examine the Format and Insert menus.
4. Close the style sheet.

*Use the File Open command and turn on the **Style Sheet** button to list the style sheets. You may have to change to the directory containing your Word program to locate the STY files. You can use either the keyboard or the mouse to examine the styles and menus. Use File Close or click on the close box to close the window.*

Using an Existing Style File

So you have seen what is in a style file. Now how do you use it? Well, first you need a document that needs formatting.

1. Open one of your standard unformatted documents; it should have at least six paragraphs.
2. Choose the File Save As command to save it as PRAC9.DOC.

When you create a new file, Word attaches NORMAL.STY. That file contains no styles originally, so all paragraphs are formatted in the same way.

Attaching a Style Sheet

If you want to use an existing style sheet other than NORMAL.STY, you must attach it using the Format menu.

1. Make sure a document is active.

2. Choose the Format Attach Style Sheet command.

You should see a dialog box like the one in Figure 9.3. If the **Files** box is empty, you can change to the directory containing Word with the **Directories** list box. When that directory is current, you should see several style files in the list, just as when you show style sheet files in the File Open dialog box.

3. Select the SAMPLE.STY style by double-clicking on it or by pressing Alt+F and using the arrow keys, then pressing ⏎.

You may not see any immediate effect on the screen, because no individual styles have been applied to paragraphs.

Using the Style Bar

The style bar occupies the leftmost two columns in a document window. When it is turned on, the key code for an applied style appears opposite the first line of every paragraph. If a paragraph doesn't have a specific style assigned, an asterisk or the key code for the Normal paragraph appears in the style bar.

You control whether or not the style bar is displayed with the View Preferences command.

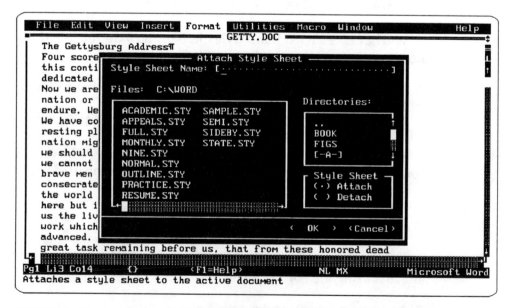

Figure 9.3. The Format Attach Style Sheet Dialog Box

1. Choose the View Preferences command.
2. Turn on the **Style Bar** field.
3. Choose <OK>.

The style sheet you already attached has given the key code NP to the Normal style, so those letters appear in the style bar on the first line of each paragraph. Some style sheets don't have a Normal paragraph definition; in that case, you'd see asterisks. If codes disappeared when you did this exercise, repeat steps 1 through 3 to turn the style bar back on.

Applying a Style

Each paragraph in a document is automatically given the style of the preceding paragraph; that's the normal paragraph formatting if you haven't changed it. You can apply different styles from the current style sheet, either by using the key code or by selecting them from list boxes. You get access to the list of styles through the formatting ribbon or through the Format Apply Style command. The lists show the key codes as well, but the two style listings are laid out in slightly different ways.

The Key Code Approach

To apply a style using a key code, hold down the control and shift keys while you press the first character of the code. If it has two characters, you can release Control and Shift before you type the second character. To use the key code H1, for example, you would press Ctrl+Shift+H,1. When you know the key codes for styles, using them is the easiest way to apply styles from the keyboard.

1. If your document doesn't have a one-line heading as the first line, insert one.
2. Place the cursor in the one-line heading.
3. Press Ctrl+Shift+H,1.

The style has been applied. On the screen, you'll notice a few changes. The key code H1 appears in the ribbon and in the style bar. The appearance of the characters has changed. And a blank line has been inserted following the paragraph.

Viewing the Current Style Sheet

You can open any style sheet with the Open File command, but you can open the current one more quickly through the Format Define Styles (Alt,F,D) command. This command has additional uses that we'll cover later in this chapter. We'll use it now to see what style sheet is attached and what formatting was in the key code just applied.

1. Choose the Format Define Styles command.
2. When the SAMPLE.STY style sheet window appears, scroll through it until you find the style with key code H1.

The style sheet window looks just as it does when you open a style sheet. The name in the window's upper border tells you which style sheet is attached.

The first part of the formatting instructions shows you the font, size, spacing, and character formatting for the paragraph. The font and size are appropriate for your printer. The formatting is bold. Other instructions show that the alignment is flush left, there is one line space after the paragraph, and it will be kept with the beginning of the following paragraph. You already know how to set all these features with direct formatting.

Closing the Current Style Sheet

You can work with the style sheet open if you like. Just switch between windows as needed. You can apply styles whether or not the style sheet window is open, as long as it is attached to the document.

Tip || You can use the Window Arrange All command to display the style sheet window on the screen at the same time as the document window if you like.

To close the style sheet, click on the close box or choose Window Close. The style sheet is not detached from the document, just removed from the screen.

3. Close the style sheet window.

Using the Ribbon

You can select a paragraph style from the style box on the formatting ribbon. If the ribbon isn't displayed, click the ruler/ribbon icon with the right button.

From the keyboard press Ctrl+S; this brings up the formatting ribbon and activates the **Style** field. Using the ribbon is one way to use the mouse to apply paragraph styles.

To see the list of paragraph styles in the style sheet, drop down the field menu. When you do, the style of the current paragraph (the one containing the cursor) is at the top of the box. Since this is a list box, you can scroll through it in either direction.

The style box lists only paragraph styles. It lists all the defined styles in alphabetical order by style I.D. Then it lists the undefined automatic paragraph styles, and finally, the next undefined numbered style I.D. in each category. You can see the key code, if any, for each, as well as the first part of the remarks. In a carefully designed style sheet, the key code and the first part of the remark together give enough information for you to identify the style. To apply a paragraph style using the style box, first place the cursor in the paragraph, or select a number of paragraphs, then choose the style from the ribbon style box.

1. Move the cursor to the beginning of an unformatted paragraph that shows style key code NP. Type **1.** followed by two spaces.
2. Turn on the ribbon if it isn't displayed (Use View Ribbon or the icon).
3. Open the **Style** field menu by clicking on the menu icon or pressing Ctrl+S, followed by Alt+↓.
4. Select the Numbered List (NL) style.

The paragraph is immediately reformatted and the style box closed. Notice the hanging indent and the additional indentation on the right, as well as the extra line space before the paragraph. You could have applied this style just as well with the key code by pressing Ctrl+Shift+N,L.

Using the Format Apply Style Command

You can use the Format Apply Style command in much the same way as you use the ribbon, but it has additional features. And it lets you apply section and character styles as well. This is the only way to apply section or character styles with the mouse.

The major feature is that the dialog box shows you the formatting instructions for the selected style. You can just type the key code or style I.D. to select a style, or you can select a style from the list box. Figure 9.4 shows the Apply Style dialog box. All the parts of the currently selected style are shown in full in the **Style to Apply** field. The key code and style type are shown in the top

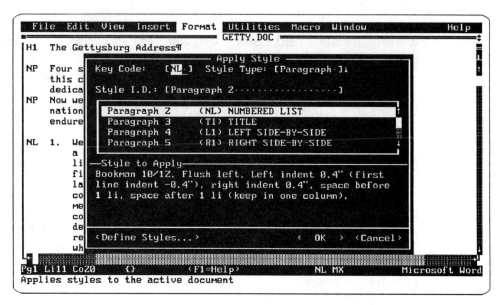

Figure 9.4. The Format Apply Style Dialog Box

line; you can overtype the **Key Code** field or use the **Style Type** menu to select a different style type. The **Style I.D.** field and list box show only styles of the currently style type, either character, paragraph, or section. In the list box, you see the style I.D., the key code in parentheses, and the full remark. If there is no key code for a style, the parentheses are empty. The **Style to Apply** box shows the formatting instructions for the current style.

1. Place the cursor in another paragraph with the NP key code (not the last paragraph in the document).
2. Choose the Format Apply Style command.

The dialog box should have the NP style highlighted in the **Style I.D.** list box. The **Style to Apply** box should show that the normal paragraph style is left aligned with a specific font and point size. You can scroll through the styles in the **Style I.D.** list box just as in any other list box, scanning the formatting instructions as needed. When the style I.D. you want is highlighted, choose <OK>. If you have a mouse, of course, you can just double-click on one to select it as well.

3. Select the L1 style for left side-by-side.
4. Choose <OK>.

The paragraph is arranged so that it is entirely on the left. Using side-by-side paragraphs can get complex if they extend over a page break, but these styles make it fairly simple.

1. Place the cursor in the next paragraph.
2. Choose the Format Apply Style command.
3. Select the R1 style for right side-by-side.
4. Choose <OK>.

What you see on the screen is affected by the current status of layout view. If layout is turned on, the paragraphs appear side by side. If Layout is turned off, the each paragraph occupies one side of the column, but they are sequential. In preview mode, you can see how the text will print.

The styles in the **Style I.D.** list box are listed in alphabetical order by style I.D., just as in the ribbon style box, but here you see only the defined styles for the current **Style Type**. If you change the style type using the drop-down field menu, you can see any defined styles for other style types. The SAMPLE.STY style sheet contains many paragraph styles, one character style for normal characters, and one section style for the normal section formatting. The automatic styles aren't listed in the ribbon style box unless they have been formatted. The Header/Footer style is defined, so you see it in the box. The Footnote style has not been given any special formatting, so you don't see it in this dialog box. You can find it through the ribbon style box, however.

1. Move the cursor to the beginning of the paragraph you formatted with L1. Type **2.** followed by two spaces.
2. Choose the Format Apply Style command.
3. Drop down the **Style Type** field menu and select the **Section** option. Examine the formatting instructions for the Normal section style.
4. Drop down the **Style Type** field menu and change it back to **Paragraph**.
5. Select the Numbered List (NL) style.
6. Choose <OK>.

The paragraph is immediately reformatted to match the other paragraph you formatted as NL.

The automatic styles don't have to be selected. If you use a footnote and have defined a Footnote style, for example, it is applied automatically. The SAMPLE.STY style sheet has a definition for the Header/Footer style.

1. Move the cursor to the beginning of the document and press ↵, then ↑.
2. Type **This is a new header**.
3. Choose the Format Header/Footer command.

4. Turn on the **Header** button and all pages, then choose <OK>.

The header is formatted and centered automatically! This is just a demonstration of an automatic predefined style. We'll cover them in more detail later.

Tip || If the Header/Footer command is dimmed on the menu, use View Layout to turn layout mode off. Then try the Format Header/Footer command again.

1. If they aren't displayed, turn on the style bar and formatting ribbon. If the SAMPLE.STY style sheet is not attached to your current file, attach it.
2. Move the cursor to any one-line paragraph and use the key code to apply the TI style. Then examine the style and see what formatting it contains.
3. Move the cursor to any paragraph formatted as NL and use the formatting ribbon to apply the LE style.
4. Move the cursor to the paragraph formatted as R1 and use the Format Apply Style command to apply the LE style.
5. Add three one-line paragraphs and format them as H1, H2, and H3, using any methods. Then examine the current style sheet to see what formatting was included.

Use Ctrl+Shift+T,I to apply the key code. Click or use Ctrl+S followed by Alt+↓ to pull down the ribbon style field menu. To examine the current style sheet, use the Format Define Styles command.

Removing a Style

You can remove a style from a character string, paragraph, or section in several ways. The most useful way is to just apply a different style of the same type, which removes any effect of the previous one. Applying direct paragraph or section formatting to a styled paragraph or section adds the direct formatting on top of the paragraph or section style.

Speed formatting keys can be used to remove character and paragraph styles, just as they remove direct formatting. You can remove a paragraph style by selecting the paragraph with the cursor, then pressing Ctrl+X; this returns it to the Normal paragraph style.

You can remove a character style by selecting the affected characters and pressing Ctrl+Spacebar to return it to normal. If you want to leave the font and point size unchanged but return any other character formatting to normal, press Ctrl+Z instead.

Creating a New Style Sheet

You probably will want to create new style sheets so that the existing ones remain unchanged. There are two basic ways to create a new style sheet: you can start from an existing one and modify it as you please or you can create one from scratch.

Copying an Existing Style Sheet

A style sheet is a file. As such, you can save it under a new name with the File Save As command. You supply a new file name of up to eight characters, and Word supplies the STY extension.

1. Open the SAMPLE.STY style sheet with Format Define Styles.
2. Choose the File Save As command.
3. Type PRACTICE in the **File Name** field.
4. Choose <OK>.

Voila! Now the window border shows PRACTICE.STY and you can add styles, delete styles, and change what is there at will. The original style sheet is unaltered and you have a start at style definition. Since the two style sheets are identical at this point, you can attach your own style sheet to the PRAC9 document.

1. Open PRAC9.DOC if neccesary.
2. Choose the Format Attach Style Sheet command.
3. Select PRACTICE.STY.
4. Choose <OK>.

Copying an existing style sheet is useful if any of the styles in an existing style sheet are even close to what you want. If you attach a style sheet to a file that already has different styles applied, however, you may have problems. Any styles (by Style I.D.) in the document that aren't in the newly attached style sheet are given normal paragraph formatting for that style sheet.

A New Style Sheet from Scratch

A style sheet is a file. So you can create a new one with the File New command. Just specify that you want a style sheet file, and you'll get an empty style sheet window, just like a new document window.

1. Choose the File New command.
2. Turn on the **Style Sheet** button.
3. Choose <OK>.

The new window shows Style Sheet1 in the top border. If you close the style sheet window without saving it, it will be lost. Since you don't need this one right now, go ahead and close it.

4. Close the Style Sheet1 window.

If you copy styles from another style sheet, then save the new one, you'll be prompted to provide a file name and summary information, just as with document files. Word provides the STY extension automatically.

Modifying a Style Sheet

You modify a style sheet in several ways. You can delete styles. You can copy styles from another style sheet. You can modify existing styles. Or you can add new styles to the sheet. Many times, you'll have to do all these operations.

Deleting Styles

It's easy to delete a style from a style sheet; just select the style you don't want and press the Delete key. You can put it back with Edit Undo (Alt+Backspace), if you try it immediately. Or you can use the Edit Cut command if you might want to put the style somewhere else, either in the same or a different style sheet.

1. Choose the Format Define Styles command to open PRACTICE.STY.
2. Select the last style.
3. Press the delete key. Notice that the style is gone.
4. Choose Edit Undo (Alt+Backspace) to restore the style.

You can delete styles from any style sheet window, whether it was opened with File Open or with Format Define Styles.

Copying or Moving Styles

Styles can be moved to a different position in the same style sheet using Edit Cut and Edit Paste. You might want to make sure certain ones appear together in the list, or you might want to place seldom used ones at the end. The style is pasted in front of the selected style. You can't copy a style within the same style sheet, however, because Word won't let the same Style I.D. appear twice.

You can move (with Edit Cut) or copy (with Edit Copy) styles from one style sheet to another (with Edit Paste). The process is the same as moving and copying selections between document files. Word won't let you duplicate a Style I.D., however.

If you try to duplicate a Style I.D., Word gives you the option of skipping the style, renaming it, or canceling the operation. You can provide a new key code and style I.D.; Word suggests the next available style I.D. if some are still available. You can also change the remark. You can't change the style type or the formatting instructions through this dialog box.

1. Choose the File Open command.
2. Turn on the **Style Sheet** button.
3. Select the NORMAL.STY file and choose <OK>.

The NORMAL.STY style sheet is open. It is probably an empty window, but don't worry if it isn't.

4. Use the Window menu to activate the PRACTICE.STY window.
5. Select the last style and choose Edit Copy.
6. Use the Window menu to activate the NORMAL.STY window.
7. Choose the Edit Paste command.

The style is added to the NORMAL.STY file. Since you don't really want it there, let's delete it.

1. Close the NORMAL.STY file.
2. When asked, do not save any changes.

This has the effect of abandoning any changes to the style sheet since you last opened it. You can also delete a style by selecting it, then pressing the Delete key.

Renaming a Style

You might want to rename a style for several reasons. It might not have a very descriptive key code. You might want to use a different style I.D. or remark. Or you may want to copy it to a style sheet that already uses the same key code or style I.D. When the style sheet window is active, you can choose to rename any style. Choose the Edit Rename Style command. Then type the new key code or remark, or select the style I.D. from the field menu.

1. Make the style sheet window active.
2. Select a style.
3. Choose the Edit Rename Style command.
4. Type AA as the key code.
5. Choose Paragraph 9 as the Style I.D.
6. Choose <OK>.

Now see what happens when you try to copy that style within the same style sheet.

1. Choose Edit Copy.
2. Move the highlight to a different style, then choose Edit Paste.
3. When offered a choice, choose the <Rename Style> button.
4. In the **Key Code** field, type the original key code of the style.
5. In the **Style I.D.** field, choose the original style I.D. from the menu.
6. Choose <OK>.
7. Close the style sheet window or use Window Arrange All to display both windows on the screen.

Creating a Brand New Style

There are two ways to create a brand new style. You can record the style of any paragraph (or character or section) into the current style sheet as a new style. Or you can define all the elements without having a formatted paragraph to start with.

Recording a Style. To record a style from a formatted character, paragraph, or section, just select the character or put the cursor in the paragraph or section, then choose the Format Record Style command (Alt,T,R). Figure 9.5 shows the resulting dialog box. You can provide the key code, choose the style, type the remark, and choose the style I.D.

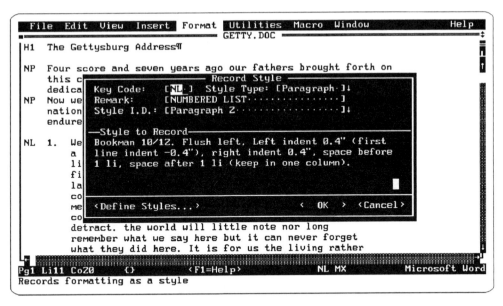

Figure 9.5. The Format Record Style Dialog Box

When you create them, be sure to use mnemonic key codes, specific remarks, and appropriate style I.D.s. In most cases, you'll just use the next style I.D. in numeric sequence.

In the central part of the dialog box, Word shows the formatting instructions for the current selected style type, so you know what you are defining. Notice that you can transfer to the Define Styles dialog box from here.

1. Make your document window active, then place the cursor in an unformatted paragraph (or one with style NP).
2. Choose the Format Paragraph command, and set the paragraph for double spacing, justification, and 1" indent on both sides. Then choose <OK>.
3. Choose the Format Record Style command.
4. Type **DB** in the **Key Code** field.
5. Type **Double+just+indent** in the **Remark** field.
6. Leave the default **Style Type** at **Paragraph**.
7. Leave the suggested **Style I.D.**
8. Choose <OK>.

Now the style is recorded and applied to the model paragraph; the style has replaced the direct formatting. You can examine the style in the style sheet.

1. If your style sheet isn't open, choose the Format Define Styles command.
2. Locate the DB style and notice the formatting instructions.

The style can be applied to any paragraph now that it is a part of the style sheet. Similarly, you can record the format for the selected character string or the character at the cursor to create a character style. If you record a section style, the format of the current section will be used, including such features as margins and page numbers.

Defining a New Style. You may want to define a new style without formatting a paragraph at the time. Of course, you could just format a paragraph and record the style, then apply the original style back to the paragraph. But for the times you want to define a style from scratch, here goes. You use the Format Define Styles command, which, as you know, opens the style sheet window for the current file. To define a style for a noncurrent style sheet, use the Open File command if the style sheet window isn't open.

When a style sheet window is open and active, use the Insert New Style command to set up the style.

1. Choose the Format Define Styles command.
2. Choose the Insert New Style command.

The New Style dialog box appears. At the top it is much like the one in Figure 9.5. You can type a **Key Code** and select the **Style Type**. You can type a specific remark. The **Style I.D.** field has a list box that contains all the available style I.D.s for the current style type; choose the one you want.

3. Type **AA** in the **Key Code** field.
4. Leave the Paragraph value in the **Style Type** field.
5. Type **Hanging Indent** in the **Remark** field.
6. Select Paragraph 9 as the **Style I.D.**
7. Choose <OK>.

Now the style is added to the style sheet in front of the selected style; at this point it uses the default Word format for the character, paragraph, or section. To tailor the style, you have to modify its formatting instructions, which is covered in the next section.

You can also add section styles.

1. Choose the Insert New Style command.
2. Type **SA** in the **Key Code** field to provide a new key code.
3. Change the **Style Type** field value to Section.

4. Type **New Section** in the **Remark** field.
5. Select Normal Section as the **Style I.D.**
6. Choose <OK>.

You can see all the formatting instructions that make up the default Word section. If you want to change any, say for a different set of margins or to place a page number by default, you can modify the style to do so.

 Similarly, you can add a character style. Character styles tend to be simpler, because you are limited to font, point size, format, and position.

Modifying a Style

When you modify a style, you can change any of its formatting through the use of the Format menu commands, much as when you create a new style. Just select the style you wish to modify, and then choose the appropriate commands from the Format menu.

1. In your document format a paragraph to be centered, with a two-inch indent on each side, lightly shaded. Then record the style.
2. Insert a new character style into the style sheet with key code CB and remark "Caps, Bold, Subscript". Then give it these features. Apply this style to four separate words.
3. Modify the L1 and R1 styles so that they use a different font and are justified. Apply them to two adjacent paragraphs in the document.
4. If there is a section style, modify it to use a two-inch top and bottom margin. If there is no section style, define one with these margins and apply it to the document.
5. Print the document to see the effects you have created.

To record a style, first use direct formatting to create it, then choose Format Record Style. To create a new style, use Insert New Style to define it, then the appropriate Format commands to format it. Be sure to choose the appropriate **Style Type** *for each style.*

Defining Automatic Styles

The automatic styles are applied to specific types of characters or paragraphs. In new style sheets, they are formatted just like the normal paragraph. In SAMPLE.STY several of these have been defined and formatted differently. To define an automatic style, choose the Format Define Styles command. Then choose the Insert New Style command. As with other styles, you can type a **Key Code** and a **Remark**, and select a **Style Type**. Then you select a **Style I.D.** from the list box. You'll have all the undefined style I.D.s to choose from, including automatic ones. When you choose <OK>, the new style is inserted into your active style sheet window, using the normal formatting. You can then add whatever formatting you want, using the Format menu commands.

Tip || You never have to use a key code to apply the automatic styles, so you can just bypass that field in the dialog box.

If you select Header/Footer, for example, any formatting you apply becomes part of the Header/Footer style. Any time you designate a paragraph as a header or footer, it takes on that format. If you select Page Number, you might set a particular font or point size. Then any page numbers in your document will appear in the specified style.

Changing the Normal Styles

Many people want to change the normal styles in the NORMAL.STY file so that they don't have to attach a style sheet to every file. For example, suppose you want to use a different font than the default, and indent one-half inch for the first line of a paragraph. And you always want to use a two-inch left margin, with a page number at the bottom by default.

The instructions are given in this section, but don't do them unless you want to modify your NORMAL.STY style sheet. If anyone else uses NOR-MAL.STY on your computer, be sure to discuss any changes you make with the other users. To make any changes to NORMAL.STY, of course, it must be in the active window.

To Change the Normal Paragraph. Changing the font and indentation involve modifying the Normal automatic paragraph style. Here's how:

1. Choose the Insert New Style command.
2. Leave Paragraph selected for the **Style Type** field.

3. Type **Standard Paragraph** in the **Remark** field.
4. In the **Style I.D.** box, choose Normal.
5. Choose <OK>.
6. Choose the Format Character command.
7. Choose the font and size you want, then choose <OK>.
8. Choose the Format Paragraph command.
9. Choose the indentation you want, then choose <OK>.

Every paragraph in a document that uses NORMAL.STY will now be given those characteristics unless you apply a different style. Of course, you can override any formatting with direct commands.

To Change the Normal Section. To change the default margins and page number appearance you have to modify the Normal section style. Here's how:

1. Choose the Insert New Style command.
2. Select Section for the **Style Type** field.
3. Type **Standard Section** in the **Remark** field.
4. In the **Style I.D.** box, choose Normal.
5. Choose <OK>.
6. Choose the Format Margins command.
7. Type the left margin size, or make any other changes, then choose <OK>.
8. Choose the Format Section command, then choose the <Page Numbers> button.
9. Turn on the **From Bottom** button, then choose <OK>.

Every section in a document that uses NORMAL.STY will now be given those characteristics unless you apply a different style. Of course, you can override any formatting with direct commands.

Changing Other Automatic Styles

If your document will include footnotes, you might want the references to be superscripted and a bit smaller than the rest of the paragraph text. And you might want some changes in the footnote text as well. If so, you can format the automatic character style Footnote Ref to change its font and size. Then format the automatic paragraph style Footnote to set the format for the body of the footnote. There are similar automatic styles for annotations.

1. Open your style sheet window, then choose Insert New Style.

2. Select Character from the **Style Type** field menu to define a footnote reference style.
3. Type **Small superscript** in the **Remark** field.
4. Select Footnote Ref from the Style I.D. box.
5. Choose <OK>.
6. Choose the Insert New Style command again.
7. Select Paragraph from the **Style Type** field menu.
8. Type **Indent Times** in the **Remark** field.
9. Select Footnote from the Style I.D. box.
10. Choose <OK>.

Now you have defined two automatic styles. They haven't yet been formatted however.

1. Highlight the Footnote Ref style.
2. Choose the Format Character command.
3. Change the **Point Size** to 8, then turn on the **Superscript** button.
4. Choose <OK>.
5. Highlight the Footnote style.
6. Choose the Format Paragraph command.
7. Change the **Indents From Left** field to 0.3", then choose <OK>.

At this point, both automatic styles have the desired format. If your document already contains footnotes, print it out to see how they look. If not, enter a footnote and text, then print it.

Managing Style Sheets

You have seen how to attach, open, close, and create style sheets. You may want to change the style sheet for another. You may want to combine styles from two or more sheets. You may even want to detach a style sheet completely. Word also lets you print a style sheet to get a printed list of the styles and their formatting instructions.

Changing the Style Sheet

If you attach a style sheet to a document that already has one attached, you replace the previous styles with new ones. Word matches styles by Style I.D. (not by key codes). So all Paragraph 4's in the old style will be reformatted with the new style sheet's Paragraph 4. If a paragraph or section Style I.D. is undefined in the new style sheet, the normal paragraph or section style is used. But the original Style I.D. is remembered and will be used if you switch style sheets again.

If you aren't happy with the effect after you change style sheets, you can just reattach the original style sheet or switch to another.

1. Make your document window active.
2. Choose the Format Attach Style Sheet command.
3. Select the NORMAL.STY style sheet and choose <OK>.

Notice that the formatting seems to have disappeared, but the key codes remain in the style bar.

4. Choose the Format Attach Style Sheet command.
5. Select the PRACTICE.STY style sheet and choose <OK>.

Your formatting has returned. It is a permanent part of that style sheet.

Printing a Style Sheet

You may want to print a style sheet to get a printed list of the formatting instructions for each defined style. This is done much like printing any other file. The printed result is formatted like an open style sheet file.

If the style sheet window is open, choose the File Print command. The **Print** field has the Style Sheet option selected, so just print it as usual.

If the style sheet is not open, you can use the File File Management command. Modify the search path if necessary to display the name of the style sheet file. Highlight the file name and choose the <Print> button. Make sure the **Print** field shows the Style Sheet option, and choose <OK>.

1. Open a style sheet file.
2. Choose the File Print command.
3. Choose <OK>.

Detaching a Style Sheet

Suppose you have a file with a style sheet attached. You might want to remove the entire style sheet to provide a copy of the file to another user without supplying the style file. Removing the style file can have two possible effects. One effect is to remove all style formatting from the document; it returns all paragraphs to the default form, but it has no effect on direct formatting you may have used. The other effect is to convert all the formatting applied through styles to direct formatting. Then the document retains the same format but loses the styles; it is just as if direct formatting was applied. The first step in either type of format conversion is to detach the style sheet.

1. With the document window active, choose the Format Attach Style Sheet command.
2. Turn on the **Detach** button.
3. Choose <OK>.

Losing the Style Formatting

When Word asks if you want to convert style sheet formatting to direct formatting, you can choose to lose it or to convert it to direct formatting. If you choose the <No> button, the style sheet is detached and all the style formatting is lost. Any direct formatting remains.

Converting the Formatting

Suppose you want to provide a colleague with a document on disk, but you don't want to supply your style sheet. You can convert the formatting to direct before detaching the style sheet, then the file can be printed or otherwise processed without the necessity of having a style sheet attached.

To do this choose the Format Attach Style Sheet command and turn on the **Detach** button. When Word asks if you want to convert style sheet formatting to direct formatting, choose the <Yes> button. The formatting is converted, then the style sheet is detached. The style bar will be left completely blank, since no style sheet is attached.

4. Choose the <Yes> button.

Now the style bar is blank and all formatting has been converted to direct formatting. The styles are no longer associated with the document. To remove the direct formatting as well, you can select the entire document and use the speed formatting keys (Ctrl+X and Ctrl+Z) to remove character and paragraph formatting.

1. Remove all formatting, direct and styles, from PRAC9.
2. Attach the PRACTICE.STY style sheet and format three or four paragraphs.
3. Print the style sheet.
4. Define the automatic page number style to print the page number in bold.
5. Define the Normal section style to include the page number at the top of the page.
6. Print the document.
7. Save the document and any style sheet changes to PRACTICE.STY. Don't save any changes to other style sheets.

To remove all the formatting, detach any style sheet and choose the <No> button. Or select the entire document and press Ctrl+X and Ctrl+Z. Use any method to apply styles. Open the style window and use File Print to print it.

To define the page number, first use Insert New Style to define it, then Use the Format Character command to format it. To modify the normal section style, insert it if necessary, then use Format Section and choose the <Page Numbers> button to set the position.

Exercise

This chapter has covered the creation and use of styles and style sheets to make formatting easier and more consistent. You can practice using them in this exercise.

1. Create a new document containing at least three one-line paragraphs for use as headings and four paragraphs of eight to ten lines each.
2. Make a copy of the PRACTICE.STY style sheet named NINE.STY. Then remove styles TI and H3.
3. Format each one-line paragraph as H1 or H2.
4. Modify the normal paragraph (NP) to use a different indentation.
5. Define a new style named B2 that will be just like a normal paragraph but will have a double border around it. Apply this to one of the longer paragraphs.

6. Modify the normal section style to use two columns.
7. Create a character style that will be italic and small caps, as well as superscripted. Apply it to three phrases.
8. Print the document and the style sheet, then save them both if you want to keep them.

Use File Open and turn on the **Style Sheets** *button to select a style sheet to open. Highlight a style and press Delete or choose Edit Cut to remove it. To apply a style, make the paragraph current, then use Format Apply Style, the ribbon, or the key code.*

To modify a style format, select the style in the style window, then use the Format menu to specify additional or different features. To define a new style, you can format the character, paragraph, or section, then choose Format Record Style or start from scratch with Format Define Styles. To print the style sheet, make the style window active and choose File Print. To save the style sheet, choose <Yes> when Word asks if it should save the changes.

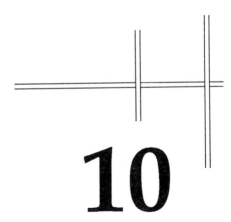

10

Advanced Editing

Word provides several fairly advanced features that you can use to make your editing easier and accomplish more functions. Several of them are covered in this chapter. Using custom tabs and creating columnar tables helps you include nice displays of data in your documents. Glossaries let you insert a string of text with just a few keystrokes. Bookmarks let you move easily between different parts of your document. In this chapter, you'll learn to:

- Set and manipulate custom tab stops
- Control the alignment of custom tabs
- Use the ruler to control custom tabs
- Create columnar tables using tabs
- Select and manipulate columns
- Define and expand glossary entries
- Create and manipulate glossary files
- Insert bookmarks into a document
- Move directly to a bookmark

Custom Tabs

The default tab stops for a document occur every half inch, unless the interval has been changed through the Utilities Customize command. These tab stops affect every paragraph in the document unless you specifically change the tabs for the paragraph. You can create custom tab stops as part of any paragraph format; they can be included in paragraph styles as well.

Custom tab settings appear in the ruler. You can see at a glance what tabs are set. The ruler also indicates other information about the tab settings.

1. Start up Word if necessary and open a practice document.
2. If the ruler isn't displayed, choose the View Ruler command or turn it on with the ruler/ribbon icon.

How They Work

If you set any custom tabs in a paragraph, any default tabs to the left are removed. The tabs can be of several types. The default tab type is left aligned. Custom tabs can be left or right aligned, or centered. The ruler shows L, R, or C at the location of one of these tab stops.

A left tab works like the ones you are used to; you press Tab, the cursor moves to the tab stop, and what you type is left aligned there. A right tab works much the same, but what you type is pushed to the left, so the text is aligned on the right end. When you tab to a centered tab, what you type is centered around the tab stop. For both right and center tabs, the characters are pushed to the left only until they encounter something other than a space. Another character, the left margin, even another tab stop ends the alignment and any additional characters extend to the right of the tab stop.

A custom tab can also be a decimal tab; the character D shows in the ruler. A decimal tab has items aligned at the decimal point. If a decimal tab is set at 3", for example, the value $8,987.67 is aligned so that the decimal point occurs at the three-inch point on the line. A value that doesn't include a decimal point is right aligned one character to the left, so the assumed decimal point appears in the correct position.

You can also specify a vertical bar for a custom tab. The vertical tab is not really a tab stop. It causes a vertical bar to appear in that position on the line, whenever a space would otherwise appear there; a vertical bar also appears in the ruler. You can use the vertical tabs to easily draw lines in tables of data in your documents.

Handling Custom Tabs with Commands

Custom tabs can be set using commands or using the ruler. The Format Tabs command results in the dialog box shown in Figure 10.1. It includes all the information for setting or clearing a custom tab. You can achieve the same effects working with the ruler, as you'll see later in this chapter.

To set a tab, type the position in the **Tab Position** field. Turn on the appropriate button to specify the type of tab. Then choose the <Set> button to set it. The dialog box doesn't disappear until you choose <OK>, so you can set and clear several tabs before returning to the document.

We aren't going to deal with the leader characters; if you want to use a leader other than space, you can select it in this dialog box when you set a tab.

Tip || If you get custom tabs in a paragraph where you don't want them, press Ctrl+X to remove all of the paragraph's formatting.

Using Text Tabs. Normal tabs are aligned at the left. When you tab normally, the cursor moves to the tab position; when you type, characters start at the tab and extend to the right from there. A right-aligned tab starts out the same way. But when you type, characters start at the tab and are pushed to the right, so the result is text aligned right at the tab position. When you type after tabbing to a center-aligned tab, the text is centered character by character as you type.

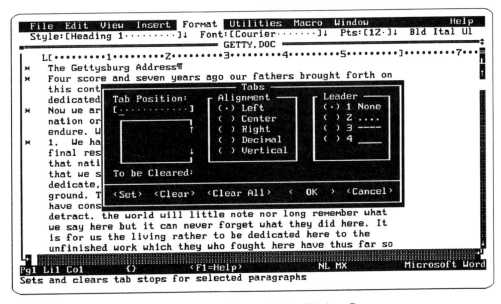

Figure 10.1. The Format Tabs Dialog Box

1. Open one of your practice documents and move the cursor to the end of it. Press ↵ to start a new line.
2. Choose the Format Tabs command.
3. In the **Tab Position** field, type 1 to set a tab at one inch.
4. Turn on the **Left** button.
5. Choose the <Set> button.

At this point, the tab setting appears in the list box as well as in the text field.

6. In the **Tab Position** field, type **2.5** to set a tab at 2.5 inches.
7. Turn on the **Right** button.
8. Choose the <Set> button.

Now two custom tab settings appear in the list box.

9 In the **Tab Position** field, type **4.5** to set a tab at 4.5 inches.
10. Turn on the **Center** button, then choose <Set>.
11. Choose the <OK> button.

You have set three custom tabs. In the ruler, you should see L, R, and C, indicating the location of these tab stops.

1. Press Tab, then type your first name. Notice that the letters extend to the left.
2. Press Tab, then type your middle name or make one up. Notice that the letters are pushed to the left. Pushing stops when they reach the first name.
3. Press Tab, then type your last name. Notice that the letters center around the tab stop position.
4. Press ↵.

The formatting of the current paragraph, including its custom tab stops, carries over to the next paragraph when you press ↵. So you can type another line using the same tabs.

5. Press Tab, then type your last name.
6. Press Tab, then type your middle initial and a period.
7. Press Tab, then type your first name.
8. Press ↵.

If you like, try a few more lines to see how these custom text alignment tabs work.

Using Decimal Tabs. Decimal tabs are specially designed for using with numbers. Suppose you set a tab at the 1" position and set the alignment as Decimal. When you tab to that position and start typing, characters are pushed to the left until a decimal point is typed. The decimal point stays in the tab position, and later characters extend to the right. Here's how a list of figures might appear:

```
456.78
22.3
1234.88
```

Although decimal tabs are designed for use with numbers, they are useful with Roman numeral lists as well. Here's how a decimal tab at the .5" position can be used in such a list:

```
I.      Presidents
II.     Senators
III.    Representatives
IV.     Aides
```

The amount is aligned at the decimal point, normally the period. This is valuable for many types of numeric lists. In some countries, the comma is used instead of the period to indicate a decimal point. The Utilities Customize command lets you change the character in the **Decimal** field to comma; if you do this, the comma causes decimal tab alignment. Word doesn't support any other characters as the decimal tab.

Using Vertical Tabs. A vertical tab inserts a vertical bar on the screen and in corresponding printed output. The vertical bar appears in the position you set if no other character appears there. In most cases, tabbing doesn't stop at a vertical tab stop. If it is at the location of a default tab, however, it might. If you tab to a vertical tab stop, you have to press the spacebar to insert the vertical bar. If you type a character or press Tab again, the vertical bar will not appear.

Suppose you want a list of names and numbers separated by vertical bars. A left-justified name appears, followed by a vertical bar, followed by a salary figure. Here's how it might look.

```
Ruth Ashley        | 45,500.98
Judi Fernandez     | 46,567.50
Michael Sloan      | 21,800.99
```

Try creating a similar set.

1. Move to a new paragraph and choose the Format Tabs command.
2. Type **2** in the **Tab Position** field, then turn on the **Vertical** button and choose <Set>.
3. Type **3** in the **Tab Position** field, then turn on the **Decimal** button and choose <Set>.
4. Choose <OK>. Notice the indicators on the ruler.
5. Type your name, press Tab, then type **555.67**, then press ⏎.
6. Type two more lines in the same format.

Removing or Clearing Tabs

You can remove tabs in several ways. Pressing Ctrl+X removes all the tabs, in fact all the formatting, from the selected paragraph. The <Clear All> button in the Format Tabs dialog box removes all the custom tabs from the selected paragraph, restoring the default tabs. To remove individual custom tabs, select them in the **Tab Position** list box and choose the <Clear> button.

1. Open a new document and set one of each type of tab.
2. Using a word such as **Micro.Soft**, tab to each position and type it.
3. Add three or four lines, using other data on each line.
4. Print the table.

Use the Format Tabs command to set each tab stop. Remember to choose <Set> for each, then choose <OK> when all tabs are set. Each time you press ⏎, the new paragraph has the same formatting as the previous one, including tab stops.

Handling Custom Tabs on the Ruler

The ruler is very helpful in working with custom tabs. It doesn't show the position or alignment of default tabs, but it shows both for custom tabs in the current paragraph. If more than one paragraph is selected, each may include different custom tabs. In that case, the ruler shows only the tab settings that are common to all selected paragraphs.

Two character positions at the left edge of the ruler help to control it. The leftmost one is for leader characters; with the mouse, you can click through these to see the options. With the keyboard, you'll press the character key when the cursor is at the tab stop. The other position always shows one of the tab stop types: L, C, R, D, or |. Which alignment character it is determines the type of tab that is set.

You can use the ruler to change the leader character and the alignment or to set, change, or remove custom tabs with either the keyboard or the mouse.

With the Mouse. The leader character and the alignment indicator can be changed by clicking. The indicators cycle through the possible choices as you click. Here's how to set some tabs using the ruler:

1. Place the cursor on a blank line. Press Ctrl+X to remove any custom tabs from it.
2. Point to the alignment character and click until R is displayed.
3. Point to the position on the ruler where you want a right-aligned tab to appear and click.
4. Point to the alignment character and click until D is displayed.
5. Point to the position on the ruler where you want a decimal tab to appear and click.
6. Type some text using the tabs to see the effect.

Once the alignment character shows the one you want, you can set as many of that type tab as you need. The alignment icon controls the alignment of the next tab set.

To delete tabs, drag them from the ruler bar and release the button. To move a tab, drag it to another location on the ruler.

7. Point to the decimal tab.
8. Click and hold the left mouse button and drag the D from the ruler. Then release the left mouse button.
9 Drag the right tab to a different location on the ruler.

With the Keyboard. Before you can use the keyboard to manipulate the ruler directly, you must turn on ruler mode. Once you press Ctrl+Shift+F10, the cursor moves to the ruler line and you are in ruler mode. To return the cursor to the document window at any time, just press ↵.

To move the cursor along the ruler one position at a time, use the → and ← keys. That's all you really need. You can also use ↓ and ↑ to move to the next or previous tab stop, Home and End to move to the left or right indent marks, or PgDn and PgUp to move the next or previous inch or centimeter mark on the ruler.

To set a tab, position the cursor at the location, then press the letter that indicates the tab alignment: L, C, R, D, or V. The letter or the vertical bar appears in the ruler line.

1. Place the cursor on a blank line. Press Ctrl+X to remove any custom tabs from it.
2. Press Ctrl+Shift+F10 to turn on ruler mode.
3. Move the cursor to a point just past the 2-inch mark and press R.
4. Move the cursor to the 3-inch mark and press D.
5. Move the cursor to the fifth dot past that and press V.
6. Press ↵ to end ruler mode.
7. Type some text on the line to see the effect.

To delete tabs, enter ruler mode and move the cursor to the tab you want to remove. (The ↓ and ↑ keys move by tab stops.) Then press the Delete key. If you want to delete this tab and all custom tabs to its right, press Ctrl+Delete. Then press ↵ to leave ruler mode.

To move a tab in ruler mode, position the cursor at it. Then use Ctrl+→ or Ctrl+ ← to position it at the new location before leaving ruler mode.

1. Press Ctrl+Shift+F10 to start ruler mode.
2. Use any method to move the cursor to the vertical tab.
3. Press the delete key to remove it.
4. Use any method to move the cursor to the right tab.
5. Use Ctrl+← to move the right tab over four places to the left.
6. Press ↵ to leave ruler mode.

1. Return to your new document and add a new unformatted paragraph. (Use Ctrl+X to remove format.)
2. Add a right tab at 3", a left tab at 3.4", a vertical tab at 4", and a decimal tab at 4.5".
3. Type three or four lines in this format, tabbing before each string: (Tab)Ruth Ashley(Tab)COP(Tab)475.98
4. Move the right tab a few positions one way or the other, whichever looks better.
5. Save the document as MYTABS.DOC.

Use the ruler for defining and moving the tabs. Remember to use Ctrl+Shift+F10 first if you don't have a mouse.

Using Tables

Word lets you use custom tabs to set up special tables in your documents. Tables can be almost anything you want. They may be lists of information in various categories. They might be mostly numbers, mostly text, or a mixture. A table often looks somewhat like a portion of a spreadsheet. With Word, you can even perform some of the actions you can do on a spreadsheet. For example, you can add numbers in columns or rows in a table. You can reorganize your table by moving columns or inserting a new column. You can even sort the table.

The custom tab stops help you control placement of data in columns. The real secret of tables, however, is setting up the whole thing as a single paragraph. That simplifies formatting and makes many of the operations possible. Instead of pressing ↵ at the end of each line in a table, you press Shift+↵ to generate a new-line character instead of a standard carriage return.

1. Move the cursor to the end of your document and press ↵.
2. If the paragraph mark doesn't appear, choose the View Preferences command and turn on the **Paragraph Marks** field.
3. Type your name and press Shift+↵. Notice the icon.
4. Type another name and press Shift+↵ again.
5. Type another name and press ↵.

The three lines are now a single paragraph.

6. Place the cursor in one of the three lines and press Ctrl+N.
7. Notice the indentation of all three lines. Press Ctrl+X to remove the paragraph formatting.

Creating a Table

Before creating a table, you need to plan it out. Decide what it will contain, where each tab is needed and what its alignment will be. Figure 10.2 shows a sample table on screen. We'll go through the steps of creating this table. Notice that the custom tab settings are shown in the ruler. The new-line and paragraph marks are displayed on the screen.

1. Move to another position in your document. Make sure the ruler and paragraph marks are displayed.
2. Use any method to set these custom tab stops: Left at 0.9", Vertical at 3.7", Right at 4.2", and Decimal at 5.4".
3. Type the first line of data from the figure. Press Shift+⏎ at the end.
4. Type the next four lines, pressing Shift+⏎ at the end of each.
5. Type the last line, pressing ⏎ at the end.
6. Add a vertical tab at 4.5".

Now you have created a table with four columns. Since it's all one paragraph, you can add a border, change the indentation or alignment, add shading, or whatever you want.

Column headings are often formatted differently from the table, so it helps to make them into a separate paragraph.

1. Place the cursor at the beginning of the first line of the table and press ⏎.
2. Press ↑, then clear any custom tabs with Ctrl+X.
3. Set centered tabs at about the middle of each column after the first.
4. For the headings, type **Number**, then press Tab before each and type **Item Description**, **Quantity**, and **Price**.
5. Make the column headings bold.

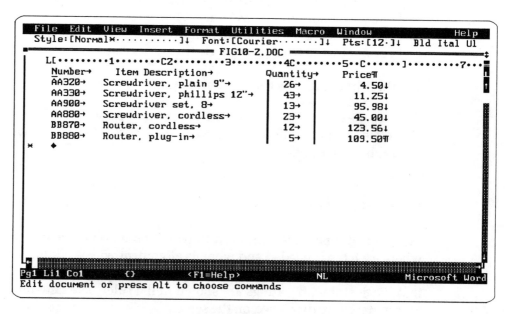

Figure 10.2. Word Table

The table is now ready to work with. One paragraph contains the column heads. The other contains the entire table.

Working with a Table

You can adjust a column position in a table by moving tabs. Don't use spacing for adjustment. Once the cursor is in the paragraph to be adjusted, you can move the tabs on the ruler or by using the Format Tabs command. If you move a tab stop or change its alignment, the table is adjusted immediately.

You can also select a single column, then delete it, move it, or copy it as a unit. You can even sort it or add up the values in it. A column is always a rectangular area of text.

You can select a column with either the keyboard or the mouse. First place the cursor in one corner of the rectangle, either by clicking or with the cursor movement keys. Then press Ctrl+Shift+F8 to turn on column selection; the letters CS appear in the status bar. Finally, click on the opposite corner or extend the selection to include it using the arrow keys. The rectangle will be highlighted on the screen.

Once the rectangle is selected, you can delete, move, or copy it using the usual commands.

Even-Length Lines. If all the lines in a column are the same length, the rectangle is obvious. It can be handled very nicely.

1. Move the cursor to the first character in the table (the first A) by clicking on it or pressing arrow keys.
2. Press Ctrl+Shift+F8. Notice that CS appears in the status bar.
3. Use the mouse or arrow keys to extend the selection to include all the item numbers, but no tab characters.

The rectangle is now highlighted and selected. You can unselect it by pressing the escape key or by pressing Ctrl+Shift+F8 again. Or you can use one of the edit commands. We'll copy the column to follow the table.

1. Choose the Edit Copy command.
2. Move the cursor to the line following the table.
3. Choose the Edit Paste command.

The column is copied. Only the first line added to your document includes the custom tabs, since it was created when you pressed ↵ after typing the table. If you had included the tab characters in the selected column block, the column would advance to the next default tab stop.

Uneven Lines. Many columns don't have all the same length lines because of alignment or the amount of text. To select a column with uneven lines, you have to do a little more work. If you just want to format the characters (or to sort them or do math), you can select the entire column with leading and trailing tab characters. These won't be affected by the operation.

1. Place the cursor on the tab character following the first quantity value (26).
2. Press Ctrl+Shift+F8, then extend the selection to include the complete column of prices.
3. Press Ctrl+B to make it all bold.
4. Select the column again and press Ctrl+Spacebar to restore normal formatting.

If you want to move, delete, or copy the column, you may not want it to include the tab characters. In that case, temporarily change the tab to left aligned, select the column and carry out the operation, then restore the tab alignment.

Column Considerations

Working with columns can get much more involved than shown here. For example, you may want to use a different-sized font that doesn't match the screen display. In that case, you can turn on View Layout and set the Line Break display on (Alt+F7 or in View Preferences).

You might want to add a column. To do that, select the columns to the right of where you want to insert the column and press Tab. A tab character is inserted on each line. You can modify it to allow for your new column.

1. At the end of your MYTABS.DOC document, create a table with five lines that looks something like this:

```
Name              Phone          City            State     Amount
Ruth Ashley       555-1234       San Salvador    CA        540.00
Judi Fernandez    555-9876       El Mirado       CA         98.50
```

2. Format the headings as bold.

3. Copy the phone number column to appear between State and Amount. Then change the Phone headings to Home and Work.
4. Delete the city column.
5. Add a border around the entire table and headings.

The exact positioning of the tabs isn't important. In the headings, you should center each. In the table itself, use all left tabs except the last column, which needs a decimal (or right) tab. To select a column, position the cursor at one corner, press Ctrl+Shift+F8, then extend the selection to the other corner; then do the copy or delete. To add a border, you'll have to work with two paragraphs. Use a top, right, and left border for the heading paragraph, and bottom, right, and left for the table.

Tip ‖ We are going on to another topic, so you can get rid of MYTABS.DOC if you like. We won't ask for it again.

Glossaries

A Word glossary is a special file that contains strings of text for insertion into documents. It may also contain macros, which are covered in more detail in Chapter 13. Each glossary entry is a string of text; it may be as short as a carefully formatted word or as long as a complete document. It may be a sequence of paragraphs, a company name, or a distribution list. In this section, you'll learn to define and use glossary entries and how to create and manage glossary files.

The Default Glossary File

Whenever you start up Word, the default glossary file NORMAL.GLY is open and available. It remains available until you open a different glossary file. You can add entries to NORMAL.GLY just as to any other glossary.

This glossary, and every glossary, contains several supplied entries that you can use at any time. You can't delete them.

While you can use glossary entries to insert text from the keyboard, anything more involved requires the use of the Edit Glossary command. When you use it, you see a dialog box like the one shown in Figure 10.3. Any glossary entries, either supplied or added, are listed in the **Names** box.

The buttons let you do most of the management of glossary files and their entries. While the <Open Glossary> button opens a different glossary file, however, the <Close> button closes the dialog box; it does not close the current glossary file.

1. Choose the Edit Glossary command.
2. Examine the window, then choose the <Close> button.

Supplied Glossary Entries

Most of the supplied glossary entries are concerned with the date, the time, or the page number. Others are used with footnotes or the clipboard. You can use these wherever they are appropriate in your documents.

Dates in the Glossary. Your computer has a system date, which is updated automatically. Word uses this date in the format specified in the Utilities Customize dialog box. The date can be specified as MDY (month-day-year) or DMY (day-month-year). The date 1/13/92 would be inserted as January 13, 1992 or as 13 January, 1992, depending on the format in effect.

The Date glossary entry inserts the current date (as your computer knows it) into the text at the point you specify. The Dateprint glossary entry has the

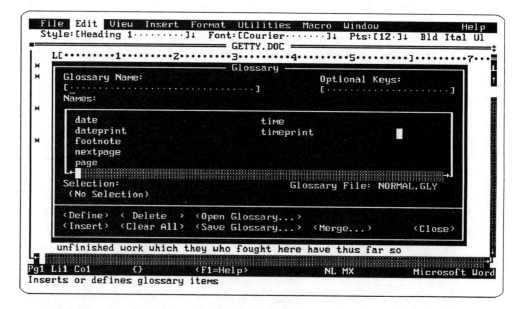

Figure 10.3. The Glossary Dialog Box

effect of printing the current date whenever you print the document; on the screen, you'll see the string (dateprint) where you use this glossary entry. Typing the string with parentheses does not have the same effect.

Times in the Glossary. Your computer also has a system time, which is updated automatically. Word uses this time in the format specified in the Utilities Customize dialog box. The time can be specified in a 12-hour or 24-hour format. When the computer's system time shows 2:45:21:19p, it would be inserted as 2:45 PM or 14:45, depending on the format in effect.

The Time glossary entry inserts the current time (as your computer knows it) into the text at the point you specify. The Timeprint glossary entry has the effect of printing the current time whenever you print the document; on the screen, you'll see the string (timeprint) where you use this glossary entry. Typing the string with parentheses does not have the same effect.

Page Numbers in the Glossary. To include the current page number in the document, you can use the supplied Page glossary entry. It places the string (page) in the text where you specify, and inserts the current page number when the document is printed.

Tip || Chapter 8 showed how to use the Page glossary entry to insert the current page number in a header or footer.

Page numbers inserted this way are always formatted with the Page Number character style. This is the same as the default text formatting unless it has been given special formatting.

Some legal documents must have the number of the next page printed on each page. The Nextpage glossary entry is supplied for this purpose.

Using a Glossary Entry

There are several ways of expanding a glossary entry into the text of a document. You can type its name into the document and press F3 to expand it. You can use the Edit Glossary dialog box and select the one you want or type its name, then choose <OK>. Or you can use its assigned key code. None of the supplied entries have a key code, but you may want to define them with your own glossary entries.

Using F3. Most of the time, you'll be typing text when you need to use a glossary entry, so the easiest way is to type the glossary name, then press F3 to expand it. You did this in Chapter 8 when you typed page then pressed F3 to include the page number in a header or footer.

Suppose you want to insert the current date or time into a document. Here's one way:

1. Place the cursor where you want the current date to appear.
2. Type **date**, then press F3.

The glossary entry is expanded and the date is in the text as regular characters. You can edit them just like normal text, because they are normal text. The results of the Dateprint and Timeprint glossary entries are not normal text, but messages to the printer driver.

3. Place the cursor where you want the print date to appear when the document is printed.
4. Type **dateprint**, then press F3.
5. The string appears enclosed in parentheses. Try to move the cursor into it.
6. Print the page to see the effect.

Selecting a Glossary Entry for Expansion. If you have already typed the text and want to insert glossary entries and expand them, you might find it easier to use the Edit Glossary command and work with the dialog box. This is also handy if you have forgotten the name of the glossary entry. You position the cursor where you want the entry to be expanded, then use the command and dialog box.

1. Place the cursor where you want the time to appear.
2. Choose the Edit Glossary command.
3. Press Alt+N then ↓ or click on it to highlight the **time** entry, then choose the <Insert> button.

The dialog box disappears and the selected glossary entry is expanded at the cursor.

1. Position the cursor at a new line and insert the current time using a glossary entry.
2. On the next line, use a glossary entry to cause the time of printing to be inserted.
3. Add a footer to your document that includes the current page number and the date of printing.

4. Print the document.

---

*Use the **time** entry for the current time, **timeprint** for the time of printing, **page** for the current page number, and **dateprint** for the date of printing. You can select these from the dialog box or press F3 immediately following the string. If the Format Header/Footer command isn't available, choose the View Layout command to turn layout view off.*

Creating a Glossary Entry

You can create new glossary entries very easily. Just type the text (what you will want the entry expanded into) into your document, then select it and choose Edit Glossary. Here you'll supply a name, along with a key code if you like, and tell Word to define it.

Glossary names are like other Word names; you can use letters and numbers, along with the underscore, hyphen, and period characters, but no spaces. The first character must be a letter or number. If you are going to use the name and F3 to expand it, you'll want the names to be fairly short, but Word lets you use up to 31 characters. If you use an optional key code as well, its length is part of those 31 characters.

1. Type your full name into your document and select it.
2. Choose the Edit Glossary command.
3. Type your initials in the **Glossary Name** field.
4. Choose the <Define> button.

Now the glossary entry is defined. You should be able to use your initials to expand it wherever you wish.

5. Place the cursor somewhere else in the document.
6. Type your initials and press F3. Notice that your full name is inserted.
7. Place the cursor at another location in the document.
8. Choose the Edit Glossary command.
9. Select your initials in the **Names** field, then choose <Insert>.

Your name should appear again.

1. Select an entire paragraph or two.
2. Choose the Edit Glossary command.

3. Type **lots** in the **Glossary Name** field, then choose <Define>.
4. Move the cursor to the end of the document.
5. Type **lots**, then press F3. Notice the text is inserted.

Using Optional Key Codes

You've seen how to insert glossary entries by name from the keyboard or by selecting them from the dialog box. If an optional key code has been defined, you can use it to expand the glossary as well. If an entry has an optional key code, it appears in the **Optional Keys** field when that glossary entry is selected. And you type it here when defining a glossary.

The glossary key codes can be one or two characters; in addition, they always start with the control key. If you assign a one-character code, such as Ctrl+C for the company name, you won't be able to use any two-character codes starting with C. And you won't be able to use Ctrl+C as the speed formatting code for centering a paragraph either! You can use any character or two-character combination, but you don't use A as the first character. You'll need Ctrl+A to start the speed formatting keys if you assign any of their letters to glossary entries.

Tip

If a speed formatting key doesn't work because you have redefined that key as part of an optional key code, just use Ctrl+A before the speed formatting key. Ctrl+A,Ctrl+B works for setting characters to bold if Ctrl+B has been used for a glossary entry.

Defining a Key Code. Suppose you want to define a glossary entry that inserts your company name, using key code Ctrl+I,I.

1. Type the company name **Imaginetrics Incorporated** (or whatever) into your document, then select it.
2. Choose the Edit Glossary command. Notice that the selected text is displayed.
3. Type **ImageInc** in the **Glossary Name** field.
4. Move the cursor to the **Optional Keys** field, then hold down the control key and press I. Release the control key and press I again.
5. Choose the <Define> button.

The glossary entry is now defined with the key code, so you have a new way to expand it into the document.

Using a Key Code. When you use the key code, the glossary it represents is inserted into the document at the cursor.

1. Place the cursor in the middle of the last paragraph.
2. Press Ctrl+I,I.

The entry is expanded. You can use any other method to expand it as well. If you intend to use the key code, there is no reason to use a short glossary name.

Deleting a Glossary Entry

Sometimes you may want to get rid of a glossary entry. To do that, just select it in the dialog box and choose the <Delete> button. It's gone unless you use Edit Undo immediately. (Actually, it isn't gone for good until you save the changes; you'll see how to do that, or avoid doing that, a bit later.)

1. Choose the Edit Glossary command.
2. Select the **lots** entry.
3. Choose the <Delete> button.

The <Delete> button leaves you in the dialog box, in case you have more work to do there. The <Close> button returns you to the document.

4. Choose the <Close> button.

Word won't let you delete any of the supplied glossary entries. If you try, you'll be told that it is a reserved glossary name.

1. Choose the Edit Glossary command.
2. Choose the **footnote** entry.
3. Choose the <Delete> button.
4. When the message box appears, choose <OK>, then choose <Close>.

Saving a Glossary File

Once you make changes to a glossary file, they don't become permanent until the file is saved. Generally, you can just wait until the glossary file is saved; Word asks if you want to save any changes. This may occur when you exit Word, for example. Or you can choose the <Save Glossary> button to save the current file at any time.

1. Choose the Edit Glossary command.
2. Choose the <Save Glossary> button.

You'll see a dialog box like the one shown in Figure 10.4. Just choose <OK> to save it as it is.

3. Choose <OK>.

Creating a New Glossary File

To create a new glossary file, you provide a new name while saving an existing one. Any changes you have made then go into the new file. In the **File Name** field, just type the new file name; you can change the directory through the **Directories** list box if necessary. Use any valid DOS file name of up to eight characters; Word supplies the extension GLY.

1. Choose the Edit Glossary command.
2. Choose the <Save Glossary> button.
3. In the **File Name** field, type **myown**.
4. Choose <OK>.

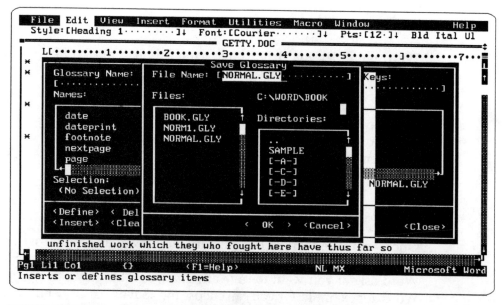

Figure 10.4. The Save Glossary Dialog Box

You now have two glossary files containing the same entries. The new one is current, as you can see in the **Glossary File** field in the Glossary dialog box. You can add entries to it or delete them.

Managing Glossary Files

To open a glossary file, choose the <Open Glossary> button. The resulting dialog box looks much like the Save Glossary dialog box. You select the file you want, and choose <OK>. While you can create as many glossary files as you want, only one can be open at a time. And you have to open it specifically if it isn't NORMAL.GLY. Word doesn't associate a specific glossary with a document, as it does with style sheets.

Changing the Glossary File. To change from one glossary file to another, just open a different one. If you want to use any existing glossary other than NORMAL.STY, you'll have to open it specifically.

1. Choose the Edit Glossary command.
2. Choose the <Open Glossary> button.
3. Select the NORMAL.GLY file and choose <OK>.
4. If you are asked if changes should be saved, choose <Yes>.

The Glossary dialog box is closed and the newly opened file is now active.

Editing Glossary Entries. To change a glossary entry, insert it in the document, make the changes to the displayed text, select it, and choose the Edit Glossary command. This time select the name of the glossary entry you are changing and choose <Define>. You'll be asked if you want to replace the previous entry. Choose <OK> and the glossary entry is modified.

Clearing the Defined Entries. You have seen how to remove a single glossary entry by selecting it, then choosing the <Delete> button. If you have created a new glossary that you intend to use for some specific type of file, such as those dealing with medical topics, you may want to remove all of the formerly defined entries. To do this, use the <Clear All> button.

1. Choose the <Save Glossary> button.
2. Type **NORM1** in the **File Name** field, then choose <OK>.
3. Choose the Edit Glossary command.
4. Notice that the NORM1.GLY file is now open. Choose the <Clear All> button.

Word asks you if you want to delete all the glossary entries now. Choose <OK> to confirm it and remove all except the supplied entries, or choose <Cancel> to stop the operation.

5. Choose <OK>.

The NORM1.GLY file now contains only the supplied glossary entries. If you are the only one who uses your copy of Word, you might want to clear all the added glossary entries from NORMAL.STY as well. They are all stored in MYOWN.STY if you want them again.

Merging Glossary Files. Since only one glossary file can be open at a time, you may occasionally want to combine them. When you merge glossary files, matching names in the merged glossary overlay those in the currently open one. You may want to save the current glossary before merging.

Printing a Glossary File. A glossary file can be printed while it is open. You can't print one from disk using File Management. When the glossary you want is open, use File Print, and make sure the **Print** field has the **Glossary** option selected, then choose <OK>.

1. Choose the File Print command.
2. In the **Print** field, choose the **Glossary** option.
3. Choose <OK>.

Only defined glossary entries are printed; the supplied ones are ignored. If you print the NORM1.GLY style sheet, for example, you'll get a blank page, because you abandoned all definitions there.

Deleting a Glossary File. To delete a glossary file, you have to use the File File Management command. Modify the search path to display the GLY files, then select one or mark several that you want to delete. You can't delete the currently open glossary file. If you try, Word asks you to close it, then try again. The only way to close a glossary file is to open a different one. Let's get rid of NORM1.GLY.

1. Choose the File File Management command.
2. Choose the <Search> button.
3. In the **Search Paths** field, type the full name of the directory that contains your Word files, followed by ***.GLY** to display only files with extension GLY.
4. Choose <OK>.

5. Select the NORM1.GLY file.

6 Choose the <Delete> button.

7. Choose <OK>.

The glossary file is gone. If you try to open a glossary file, NORM1.GLY will not be displayed.

1. Define a glossary entry in the MYOWN.GLY file to insert the string "Intercontinental **Ballistic** Missile" into your document when you type **ICBM** and press F3 or press Ctrl+I,B.
2. Define another glossary entry that will insert your mailing address in three or four-line format when you type **home** or press Ctrl+H,M.
3. Create a new glossary file named TESTING.GLY containing all the entries in MYOWN.GLY.
4. Try out the two new entries in your document.
5. Delete the two new entries from MYOWN.GLY.
6. Merge TESTING.GLY into MYOWN.GLY.
7. Print TESTING.GLY.

Use Edit Glossary for most of these items. To create a new glossary file, use <Save Glossary> and provide the new name. To delete entries, select them and choose <Delete>. To merge two glossaries, the basic glossary must be open. To print a glossary, it must be current; you must select Glossary in the **Print** *field.*

Bookmarks

When you prepare large documents, you may want to move around in them quickly. The Edit Go To command (F5) lets you move to a specific page. But many times, you won't know the exact page and searching takes time. Word lets you embed bookmarks in your document that you can move to quickly. The bookmarks are hidden; you'll never see them on the screen or in a printed copy. Each bookmark has a different name, and you can move among them with Edit Go To.

Bookmarks remain in the file until you remove them. If a document has four main divisions, you might make the heading for each division into a bookmark, naming them **part1**, **part2**, **part3**, and **part4**. Then you can move directly to the beginning of the part you want.

What Is a Bookmark?

A bookmark can be a cursor position or any text selection. If it is a text selection, when you go to that bookmark, the text will be selected. Each bookmark has an *anchor* on each end.

If the bookmark is a cursor position, the character at the cursor serves as both anchors. If you delete this character, the bookmark is deleted. If you delete just one anchor, the bookmark gets smaller, moving in toward the other anchor. If you move text including both anchors, the bookmark moves with the character. If you copy text that includes the character, the text is copied but the bookmark isn't.

If the bookmark is a selection, the first character is the start anchor and the last is the end anchor. If the entire selection is deleted, the bookmark is deleted. If the entire selection is moved, the bookmark moves with it. If the entire selection is copied, the bookmark remains in the original position. If you delete or add characters between the two anchors, the bookmark selection size is adjusted. If you remove characters from the beginning or end of the selection, the bookmark size adjusts as well.

Inserting a Bookmark

Before you insert a bookmark, you must select the text to be included or position the cursor where you want it. Then you choose the Insert Bookmark command and provide the name in a dialog box like the one in Figure 10.5. The key combination Ctrl+Shift+F5 brings you the same dialog box.

Bookmark names, like other Word names, must start with a letter or number and may include dashes, underscores, and periods as well. They are limited to 31 characters.

1. Select a one-line paragraph near the beginning of a document.
2. Choose the Insert Bookmark command.
3. Type **First** in the **Name** field.
4. Choose <OK>.

You won't see any change on the screen. Bookmarks are never displayed.

1. Position the cursor in one of the last few paragraphs of the document.
2. Choose the Insert Bookmark command. Notice that the bookmark you already inserted is listed in the **Name** list box.
3. Type **Last-page** in the **Name** field.
4. Choose <OK>.

Moving to a Bookmark

Once a bookmark has been defined, you can use Edit Go To (F5) to move to it. The dialog box shown in Figure 10.6 is the same one that lets you move to a specific page.

To move to a specific bookmark, turn on the **Bookmark** button and select the bookmark or type its name, then choose <OK>. If you select the bookmark first by pressing Alt+N and ↓ or by clicking on it, the **Bookmark** button is turned on automatically. Double-clicking on the bookmark moves you to it immediately.

1. Choose the Edit Go To command.
2. Highlight the **First** bookmark name.
3. If the **Bookmark** button isn't on, turn it on.

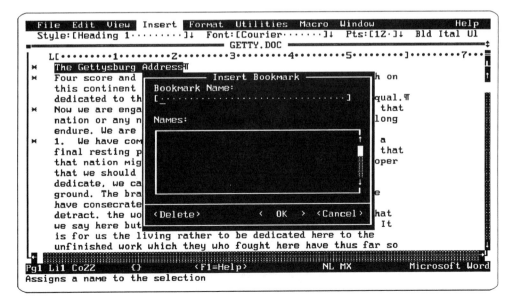

Figure 10.5. The Insert Bookmark Dialog Box

4. Choose <OK>. The heading you selected for the bookmark is now selected again.
5. Press F5.
6. Select the **Last-page** bookmark and choose <OK> or double-click on it.
7. Save the file and exit Word.

Working with Bookmarks

Bookmarks stay in position across Word sessions. If you save the file, the bookmark is saved as well.

1. Start up Word and open your document.
2. Choose the Edit Go To command.
3. Move to the **Last-page** bookmark.

You can move or delete individual bookmarks by moving or deleting the text that includes both anchors.

1. Select text that includes a word on each side of the bookmark position.
2. Choose the Edit Cut command (Shift+Delete).
3. Move the cursor to a position at least a paragraph away.
4. Choose the Edit Paste command (Shift+Insert).

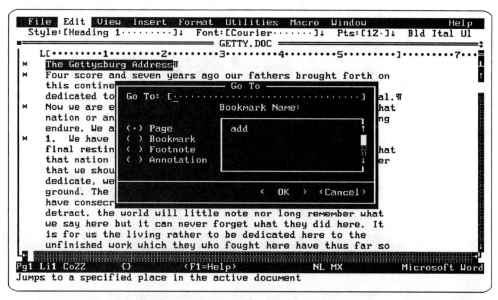

Figure 10.6. The Edit Go To Dialog Box

5. Press the PgUp key.
6. Choose the Edit Go To command.
7. Move to the **Last-page** bookmark.

Notice that the cursor moved to the new location of the bookmark; it was moved along with the text.

You can delete individual bookmarks through the Insert Bookmark command. Just select the one you want to delete and choose the <Delete> button.

1. Choose the Insert Bookmark command.
2. Highlight the **Last-page** bookmark.
3. Choose <Delete> then <OK>. The name is gone from the list box. You can't get it back with Edit Undo.

If you copy text containing bookmarks to another document, the bookmark is copied as well if the document doesn't already have that bookmark name.

1. Delete all bookmarks from the current document.
2. Insert bookmark THREE at the beginning of the third paragraph.
3. Select a complete sentence in one of the last paragraphs and define it as a bookmark named SENT.
4. Make sure you can move to both bookmarks.
5. Delete the first three words in the SENT bookmark.
6. Move the third paragraph to the beginning of the document.
7. Make sure you can still move to each bookmark.

To delete bookmarks, select each in the Insert Bookmark dialog box, then choose <Delete>. Use Insert Bookmark to define them; remember to select any text to include first. When you delete one anchor of a bookmark, the anchor moves up. When you move both anchors, the bookmark moves as well.

Additional Editing Features

Word offers some additional advanced editing features that we aren't covering in this book. The outlining facility is one of them. It lets you enter headings of different levels, manipulate them, and expand the document with text below the headings. You can turn outline view on and off through the View menu. If you notice the characters *T* and *t* in the style bar, you are probably in outline mode. Turn it off via the View menu. When you are more experienced with using Microsoft Word, you might want to check your reference manual and explore outlining in detail.

Exercise

This chapter has covered several advanced techniques that help you create and manipulate documents. Custom tabs and tables help in arrangement of text. Glossaries make it easy to insert boilerplate text. Bookmarks help you move around in documents. This exercise gives you a chance to practice using these features.

1. Define glossary items to print your city, your state and zip code, and your full telephone number with area code. Assign key codes for each.
2. Create a new document to describe a meeting room, using your name, your address, your communications, and your transportation facilities. Use several of the glossary items more than once.
3. Assign three bookmarks in the document, one a single position, one a word, and one a phrase. Practice moving among them.
4. Add a table to the document that shows the facilities available and the cost of each. Use at least one vertical tab and one decimal tab in the table.
5. Print the document.

To define a glossary entry, type the expansion into the text, then choose Edit Glossary and provide the name and key code. To use a glossary, press its key code or type the name and press F3.

Use Insert Bookmark to insert a bookmark, then Edit Go To when you are ready to move to it. Set custom tabs with the Format Tabs command.

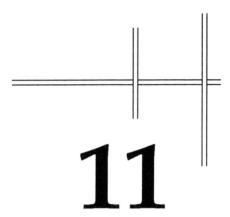

11

Using the Word Utilities

T he Utilities Menu provides access to a variety of functions that can make your life a little easier, your work a little faster, and your documents considerably better. You have already learned to use some of the options on this menu. The spelling utility helps you locate and correct misspelled words and some additional errors. The thesaurus helps you locate synonyms for words. The hyphenation facility will fill up document lines by splitting words at the ends of lines wherever possible. The sort facility will sort a list of items, a table, or even paragraphs. And the calculate facility will perform simple calculations. In this chapter, you will learn to:

- Check the spelling and correct a document or a selected block
- Look up words in the thesaurus
- Hyphenate a document or a selected block
- Insert optional and nonbreak hyphens in a document
- Sort a list of items
- Sort lines in a table
- Rearrange paragraphs in a document
- Perform simple calculations with the calculate facility

The Spelling Utility

Word can help you perfect your document by finding not only mispelled words, but also repeated words (as in "the the dog"), improper capitalization (as in "YOu"), and improper punctuation (as in "that;s"). It doesn't check grammar, so it won't find all instances of improper punctuation or capitalization, but it will find those that occur in the middle of words.

The spelling utility works by comparing every word in a document (or in a selected block) against its dictionaries. If it can't find a matching spelling in its dictionaries, it shows you the word and asks what to do. It will suggest alternate spellings if it can. Figure 11.1 shows an example of the dialog box the spelling checker displays. Notice that the unknown word is shown in the **Not Found** field at the top, a suggested correct spelling is shown in the **Replace With** field, and a list of alternate spellings appears in the **Suggestions** list box.

The buttons provide several possible actions, which fall into three broad categories: you can change the word, leave it as is, or exit.

Starting the Spelling Checker

You start the spelling checker by choosing the Utilities Spelling command (Alt,U,S or F7). To check a specific section of your document, highlight that

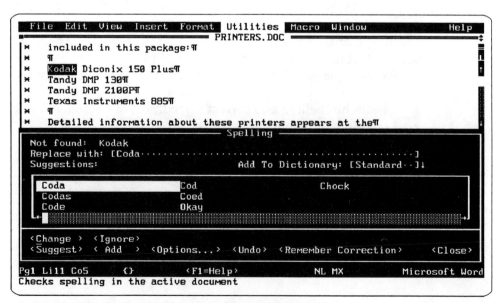

Figure 11.1. The Spelling Dialog Box

part before starting the spelling checker. For example, suppose you have inserted a paragraph into a document that is already checked. You can save time by checking only the new paragraph; highlight it and press F7.

Suppose you don't know how to spell "gastronomic." Type it as best you can—gastranommic, for example—then highlight it and press F7. Chances are, the spelling checker will suggest the correct spelling. The message "No incorrect words found" means you spelled it correctly in the first place.

Tip If you are running Word from diskettes, you'll be prompted to insert the diskette containing the spelling utility. When you are finished, you'll be prompted to restore the standard program diskette.

1. Open any of your practice documents.
2. Position the cursor anywhere in the document and type **occurance** (it is incorrectly spelled).
3. Highlight the word.
4. Choose Utilities Spelling or press F7.
5. Word will suggest the correct spelling of "occurrence." Choose the <Change> button to replace the incorrectly spelled word with the correct one.
6. When the spelling checker terminates itself, press Delete to delete the highlighted word.

If you don't highlight a block before starting the spelling checker, checking starts at the current cursor position and works forward. When it reaches the end of the document, Word asks if you want to continue at the beginning (unless it started at the beginning). If you choose <Yes>, it continues to work forward until it reaches the original cursor position, when it terminates itself.

The spelling checker doesn't display any special dialog box while it is checking words. If it has just started, the document window remains unchanged; if you have just responded to a unknown word dialog box, that box stays on the screen. You might think that nothing is happening, but if you watch the message line, you will see the messages "Loading dictionaries," "Checking document," and "Checking dictionaries." These are your clues that the spelling checker is indeed working.

1. Position the cursor somewhere in the middle of the document.
2. Press F7 or choose Utilities Spelling to start the spelling checker. Watch for messages on the status line.
3. Each time it finds an unknown or incorrect word, choose the <Ignore> button.

4. When it reaches the end of the document, choose <Yes> to continue at the beginning.

Correcting a Word

When the spelling checker displays an unknown or incorrect word in the **Not Found** field, look first at the message on the top line of the dialog box to find out what the problem is. Table 11.1 shows all the possible messages and their meanings. As you can see, the spelling checker not only identifies possible misspellings, but also various types of problems with punctuation and case.

Suppose you decide that the word in your document is wrong, and you want to correct it. You have several ways to do that. Look first at **Replace with** field; if the correct spelling is there, all you have to do is choose <Change>, which you can do by clicking on it, typing **C**, or pressing ↵.

If the correct spelling is not shown in the **Replace with** field, examine the list of alternatives in the **Suggestions** list box. If one of them is correct, move the highlight to that item; it will be shown in the **Replace with** field. Then choose <Change>. If you have a mouse, you can simply double-click on the desired spelling.

If the desired spelling does not appear in the **Suggestions** list box, and you know what it is, just type it in the **Replace with** field yourself. You can edit the default suggestion or completely replace it. (Sometimes you might find this faster than scrolling through the entire list box.) Then choose <Change>.

Table 11.1. Types of Problems Identified by Spelling Checker

Message	Meaning	Example
Not found	The indicated word is not in any of the spelling checker's dictionaries	Elvis bannana
Invalid character	The indicated word contains a digit or other character that is usually invalid	F7 C3PO
Improper punctuation	The indicated word contains punctuation in an unusual position	Hold!it George;s
Improper capitalization	The indicated word contains a mixture of uppercase and lowercase letters (not just an initial capital letter)	DuoTeck THe
Invalid compound word	The indicated word looks like a compound word, but is not made up of known words	Geor/ges Duo-Teck

1. Type these five words in your document: **primt dagget frabich tho kreen**.
2. Highlight all five words and press F7 to start the spelling checker.
3. For the word "primt," the spelling checker will suggest the word "prim." Press ⏎ to accept that suggestion.
4. For the word "dagget," move the highlight to the word "dagger" in the list box and press ⏎. (Or double-click on "dagger.")
5. For the word "frabich," edit the suggested "Francis" to make "France" and press ⏎.
6. For the word "tho," scroll through the entire list box to see all the suggestions. Highlight the word "throe" and press ⏎ (or double-click on it).
7. For the word "kreen," replace the suggested "chron" with "sheen."
8. After the spelling checker terminates, use Edit Undo (or Alt+Backspace) to undo the corrections.

Figure 11.2 shows what the dialog box looks like when the spelling checker can't come up with a suggestion. The text box contains the unknown word, and the default action is <Ignore> instead of <Change>. If you want to correct the word, you have to enter the correct spelling yourself. As soon as you change the text box, the default action changes from <Ignore> to <Change>. Also, the <Suggest> button becomes available so you can ask Word to suggest alternative spellings for the word that is now in the text box.

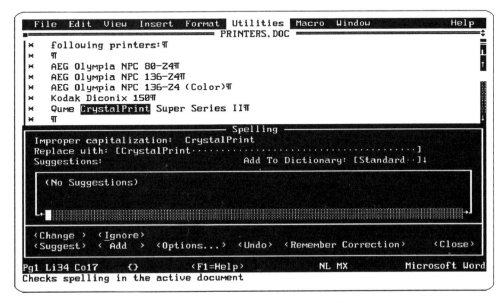

Figure 11.2. Spelling Dialog Box with No Suggestions

1. Type the word **pfirt**.
2. Highlight it and press F7 to start the spelling checker.
3. In the Replace With box, change it to "pirt." Notice that <Change> becomes the default action and <Suggest> becomes available.
4. Choose the <Suggest> button to see spelling suggestions for "pirt."

Sometimes when you replace a word, the spelling checker can't find your new word either. It displays a dialog box asking if you want to accept the new spelling. Choose <Yes> if you're sure the new spelling is correct.

5. Change the text box to "pirt" again and select <Change>.
6. A dialog box warns you that "pirt" is not in the dictionary. Choose <Yes> to accept it.
7. Delete "pirt" after the spelling checker terminates.

Remembering the Correction

Whenever you correct a word with the spelling checker, Word saves the correction and applies it to all future occurrences of the same word during the current spelling check. For example, if you correct "tha" to "the" once, every future "tha" (as a separate word) will be automatically changed to "the" until you exit the spelling checker.

If you would like Word to remember a correction for future spelling checks too, then you should choose the <Remember Correction> button instead of <Change>. Word keeps remembered corrections in a file called REMEM-AM.COR in the Word directory. For example, suppose you frequently type "nad" for "and." Once you choose <Remember Correction>, Word will always correct "nad" in the future without asking you. Use this feature wisely. It's probably safe to remember to correct "hte" to "the," but it wouldn't be so smart to change "tha" to "the," since sometimes "tha" might be a typo for "that" or "than."

Accepting the Unknown Word

Many words unknown to the spelling checker are perfectly good words. The original spelling dictionaries include common, everyday words, not unusual or rarely used words. You can expect the spelling checker to reject many names, foreign phrases, archaic words, technical jargon, abbreviations, slang, and poetic words. In fact, you might find that most of the words unknown to the spelling checker are correctly spelled as far as you are concerned.

There are several ways to tell Word to accept a word as spelled. You can choose <Ignore>, which causes the word to be accepted as correct not just for now, but for the remainder of this spelling check session. Or you can add the word to one of Word's dictionaries so it will be recognized as correct in future spelling checks as well.

Word's Spelling Dictionaries. Word maintains three types of spelling dictionaries: standard, user, and document. The *standard dictionary* is the one that arrives with Word.

The *user dictionary* feature lets you set up a list of words that apply to a particular project (or group of documents), but should not be consulted in other cases. You might have four or five projects going, each with its own user dictionary. The *document dictionary* lets you set up a list of words that are unique to this document.

Why not just put everything in the standard dictionary? The standard dictionary is used for all spelling checks, while a user dictionary is consulted only when you request it. Suppose you use the word "reboot" frequently (the original standard dictionary doesn't recognize this word). You would probably add it to the standard dictionary so that it will always be accepted. But suppose you are writing a book where you need to use the made-up term "monomen." This word might be a typo in another setting. It would be wiser to put it in a user dictionary so it can be used only with the documents that make up this particular book.

A document dictionary is even more limited; it can be used only with the particular document it is created for. Document dictionaries are always named *filename*.CMP, where *filename* is the same as for the document. Word automatically uses a document's dictionary when checking that document; you don't have to request it. Document dictionaries are good places to record words that are highly specific to a particular document. They affect no other document.

But why would you even bother with a document dictionary? Why not just select <Ignore>, which causes Word to ignore the word for the rest of the spell check session? If you were going to check the document only once, there would be no advantage to a document dictionary. But most of us revise documents and recheck the spelling several times. In that case, putting local words in the document dictionary the first time saves a lot of time and trouble in all subsequent spelling checks.

Using the Dictionaries. When you want to add the current unknown word to one of the dictionaries, look at the **Add to Dictionary** field to see which dictionary is targeted. If it's the one you want, choose <Add> to add the current word to it.

If you want to use a different dictionary, put the cursor in the **Add to Dictionary** field and type **S** for Standard, **U** for User, or **D** for Document. (Or you can drop down the field menu and select the desired dictionary.) Then choose the <Add> button.

To create and/or change user dictionaries, choose the <Options> button, which opens a dialog box containing (among other things) a **User Dictionary** field. You can drop down its field menu to select from a list of available user dictionaries. Or you can type the name of a user dictionary in the text box. If it's a new name, a dialog box asks if you want to create the new dictionary. When you choose <Yes>, the new dictionary file is created and made the active user dictionary.

1. Highlight "primt dagget frabich" and press F7 to start the spelling checker.
2. When the word "primt" is displayed, choose <Add> to add it to your standard dictionary.
3. When the word "dagget" is displayed, type **T** to highlight the **Add To Dictionary** field, or click on it.
4. Type **U** to change to the user dictionary, or drop down the field menu and select User.
5. Choose <Add> to add "dagget" to the current user dictionary.
6. When "frabich" appears, type **T** to highlight the **Add To Dictionary** field, or click on it.
7. Type **D** to change to the document dictionary, or drop down the field menu and select Document.
8. Choose <Add> to add "frabich" to the document dictionary.

Undoing Spelling Actions

You can undo an individual spelling change by choosing the <Undo> button the next time the Spelling dialog box appears. Even though another word is now displayed, choosing <Undo> revokes the previous action and returns to that word.

After the spelling check finishes, choosing Edit Undo undoes any changes made during the operation. All words will be returned to their original values. However, remembered corrections and words added to dictionaries are not undone.

1. Change a few words so they are misspelled, then correct them with the spelling checker.
2. Choose Edit Undo (Alt+Backspace) to undo the spelling corrections.

Notice that the words are restored in your document.

3. Press F7 to check the same words again. Correct them for good this time.
4. Press F7 to check them one more time.

The message now shows "No incorrect words found" because all the words encountered were present in a dictionary.

1. Open the file named TYPOS.DOC which was included with your Word software. (This document has many intentional typos in it.)
2. Start the spelling checker for this document.
3. Correct some of the errors, ignore others, and add some to the document dictionary.
4. When the spelling check is done, undo it.

Use Utilities Spelling to start the spelling checker. Choose the <Ignore> button to leave a word unchanged. Select a suggested spelling to place it in the text box or type the correct spelling in the text box yourself. Choose <Change> to replace the unknown word with the contents of the text box. Change the **Add To Dictionary** *field to show Document and choose <Add> to add words to the document dictionary. Use Edit Undo (Alt+Backspace) to undo the entire spell check.*

A Brief Introduction to Advanced Spelling

When you are comfortable with the basics of the spelling utility, you'll probably want to learn some of the advanced features. We'll just briefly describe them here, so that you know what's available when you're ready to enhance your spelling checking skills.

There are several things that you can do in the area of dictionary management. The Utilities Customize command opens a dialog box where you can specify the name of the standard spelling dictionary, which by default is SPELL-AM.LEX. (The AM is for "AMerican.") If you have other dictionaries designed to be used with Word, you can select one here.

You can't edit SPELL-AM.LEX, but you can edit any words that you added to a dictionary. Simply open that dictionary as a document. (Words added to the standard dictionary are stored in UPDAT-AM.CMP.) You can delete words or correct the spelling, but be sure they are in the correct alphabetical order when you're done, or the dictionary won't work. Because the order is so important, don't add words by editing the dictionary. Type them in a separate document, spell check them, and use the <Add> button.

The spelling checker Options dialog box contains several settings you might want to learn to use. You can turn off the suggested spellings feature, which speeds up the whole process greatly, and you can still ask for suggestions by selecting the <Suggest> button whenever you're stuck.

If you don't want to eliminate suggestions completely, you can limit them by selecting the Quick Look Up option. When this option is turned on, Word assumes that the first two letters of the unknown word are correct, which causes a lot less searching for alternative spellings.

You can also set options to eliminate punctuation checking and to ignore words in all caps, which are frequently acronyms, file or directory names, or other words not in Word's dictionaries. These options will also speed up the process considerably.

Word offers another feature that you might want to use in conjunction with the spelling checker: Utilities Revision Marks. This feature marks every correction you make with whatever symbols you specify. You can, for example, insert vertical bars in the margin of every line that contains a change, underline inserted text, and retain but cross out deleted text. This feature can help you review corrections made automatically during a spelling check.

The Thesaurus

Word's thesaurus, just like one in book form, helps you find words from their synonyms. Figure 11.3 shows the dialog box that appears when you look up the word "hardheaded."

1. Type the word **hardheaded**.
2. Position the cursor anywhere in the word and choose the Utilities Thesaurus command (Alt,U,T) or press Shift+F7.

Word automatically selects the word that contains the cursor, or the word that precedes it if the cursor is on a space. In this case, Word selected "hardheaded" in the document.

The Thesaurus dialog box shows that the word "hardheaded" (in the **Synonyms for** field) can have two distinctly different meanings: obstinate and shrewd. At the moment, "obstinate" is selected in the **Definitions** list box, and the words in the **Synonyms** list box are synonyms for that meaning only. To see synonyms for "shrewd," move the highlight to it.

3. Press ↓ to move the highlight to "shrewd." Notice the change in the **Synonyms** box.

To replace the original word with a synonym from either the **Definitions** or **Synonyms** box, highlight the word and choose the <Replace> button. The replacement will match the case, formatting, and punctuation of the replaced word. For example, if you look up *Waterfall* (with initial cap and italics) and select "cascade," Word will insert the word *Cascade*.

4. Highlight "pigheaded" and choose <Replace>.

If you don't see a synonym that satisfies you, the <Synonyms> button lets you look up any of the words in either list box. Sometimes they will produce synonyms the original word didn't have.

5. Press Shift+F7 to look up "pigheaded."
6. Highlight "self-willed" and choose the <Synonyms> button.

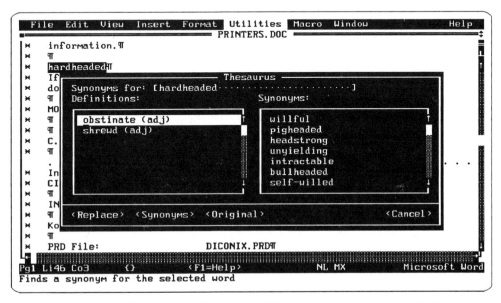

Figure 11.3. Thesaurus Dialog Box for "Hardheaded"

Notice that the **Synonyms for** field at the top changes to "self-willed" and the list boxes change accordingly.

Tip || You can double-click on a word instead of choosing the <Synonyms> button.

If you still can't find the right word, you might want to try a different tack. If you have another idea, you can overtype the word in the **Synonyms for** field and choose <Synonyms>. If you find yourself getting too far away from the original word, choose the <Original> button to return to it.

7. Move the cursor to the **Synonyms for** field.
8. Replace "self-willed" with "independent" and choose <Synonyms>.
9. Choose <Synonyms> to look up "autonomous."
10. Choose <Original> to get back to "pigheaded."
11. Choose <Cancel> to remove the dialog box.

Handling Unrecognized Words

If you try to look up a word the thesaurus doesn't recognize, one of two dialog boxes might appear. If the thesaurus can come close to the word you entered—perhaps the same root but a different ending—it displays the phrase "similar meanings" in the **Definitions** list box and the similar word in the **Synonyms** list box. You can look up the similar word or take some other action. (You can't look up or use "similar meanings" as a replacement.) You might also see "similar meanings" along with other words in a **Definitions** list box.

1. Type the word **placidly** in your document.
2. Place the cursor in the word and press Shift+F7.

The Theasurus dialog box should show "placid" as a similar meaning.

3. Highlight "placid" and choose <Synonyms> or double-click on "placid."
4. Choose <Cancel> to close the dialog box.

If Word cannot recognize the word you entered, it displays a list of words that are alphabetically near it in case you misspelled the word. You can type or select another word to look up, type or select a replacement word, or cancel.

Tip || The thesaurus doesn't do a very good spelling check; you might want to check the word's spelling with F7, then try the thesaurus again if you change it.

1. Type the word "arson" and press Shift+F7.

Notice that the resulting dialog box has a **Not Found** field, and the message "Choose Another Word" appears on the top line.

2. Choose <Cancel> to close the dialog box.

1. Look up a synonym for the word "misfortune."
2. Check the "similar meanings" definition.
3. Look up the word "fortune."
4. Look up synonyms for the definition "luck."
5. Look up synonyms for the synonym "fate."
6. Return to the original word you looked up.
7. Replace the word "misfortune" in your document with "mischance."

You need to type **misfortune** *and choose Utilities Thesaurus (Shift+F7). To examine other words, highlight them and choose <Synonyms> or double-click on them. Choose <Original> to return to the original word. Choose <Replace> to replace "misfortune" with "mischance."*

Hyphenation

A document often looks more professional when the lines are as full as possible, with appropriate hyphenation at the ends of lines. In left-aligned paragraphs, the right margin is smoother, less ragged looking. Justified paragraphs have less space between words and between characters, which can make a big difference in appearance and readability, especially if the document has narrow columns of text. Word can handle hyphenation for you.

With Word, you create the document first, then hyphenate it by choosing the Utilities Hyphenate command (Alt,U,H). Word uses its internal hyphenation rules for deciding where to break a word.

Unless a block is selected, Word hyphenates from the cursor forward to the end of the document, then asks if it should continue at the beginning (unless it started at the beginning).

1. Open a practice document that contains at least three paragraphs.

2. Choose View Preferences and turn on **Show Line Breaks** to make sure you see the actual line endings on your screen. Then choose <OK> to complete the dialog box.
3. Select a paragraph that contains several lines of text.
4. Choose the Utilities Hyphenate command (Alt,U,H).

As you can see, you need to make some initial decisions about what options you want to use.

Hyphenation Options

When you start hyphenation, a dialog box offers two options. You can approve every hyphen individually or you can leave all the decisions to Word. If **Confirm** is checked (the default setting), Word will show you every word to be hyphenated and let you decide what to do. You'll see how this works in a minute. The confirmation process is slow and tedious, especially in a long document, but it probably produces a better result than the automatic method.

You can uncheck **Confirm** to let Word hyphenate automatically. But Word uses a set of rules to decide where to hyphenate, and the result is not always correct (English always has exceptions to any rule). You should inspect the document afterwards and correct any obvious hyphenation errors.

You might also want to uncheck the **Hyphenate Caps** box (it's checked by default) to prevent Word from hyphenating any word starting with a capital letter. This avoids hyphenating proper names, acronyms, key words in titles, captions, headings, and the like.

5. Turn off the **Confirm** and **Hyphenate Caps** fields.
6. Choose <OK>. If prompted, have Word continue hyphenation from the beginning of the file.

Examine the selected paragraph to see if any words were hyphenated. (No hyphens may have been needed.)

7. If no words were hyphenated, add several multisyllable words near the end of lines, then do steps 4 through 6 again.

Tip ||| If you don't like the hyphenation, select Edit Undo to remove it all. This must be done immediately after the hyphenation is finished, before you type anything else or enter any other commands.

Confirming Hyphenation

When the **Confirm** field is turned on, Word prompts you before every possible hyphenation by displaying a dialog box like the one in Figure 11.4. In the document itself, the cursor highlights the intended hyphen. The dialog box shows the whole word, divided at all possible hyphenation points according to Word's rules. The cursor appears on the farthest right hyphenation point that will fit inside the right margin.

If you choose <Yes>, the word will be hyphenated at that point. If you choose <No>, the word will not be hyphenated at all; the entire word will be moved down to the next line. Choosing <Cancel> ends hyphenation for the entire selection or document and returns the cursor to the point where you started hyphenation. It doesn't undo any hyphens inserted. You can also change the **Confirm** and **Hyphenate Caps** fields any time this dialog box is showing.

1. Select another paragraph with several lines of text.
2. Choose Utilites Hyphenate (Alt,U,H) to start hyphenation.
3. In the initial dialog box, **Confirm** is checked and **Hyphenate Caps** is turned off. Choose <OK> to accept these options.
4. If a confirm hyphenation dialog box appears, choose <Yes>.

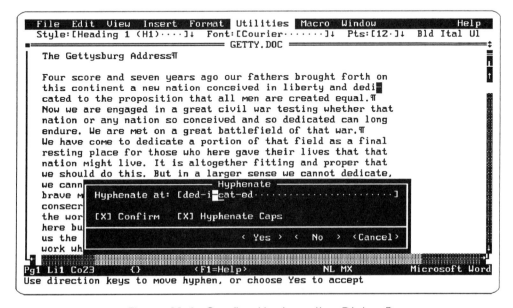

Figure 11.4. Confirm Hyphenation Dialog Box

5. If you get the opportunity to respond to more confirm dialog boxes, try out <No> and <Cancel>.

If the paragraph needed no hyphens, add some long words or select another paragraph and try again.

Moving the Hyphen

When the Hyphenate dialog box is showing, you can change the position of the intended hyphen by clicking on a different location in the word or by using these keys:

↑   Move to next left hyphenation point
↓   Move to next right hyphenation point
←   Move left one character
→   Move right one character

Tip || If you're not sure of correct hyphenation points yourself, book and office supply stores have book showing thousands of correctly hyphenated words.

When you choose <Yes>, the word will be hyphenated at the cursor position. But if it exceeds the right margin, the entire word will be moved down to the next line and the hyphen will be suppressed in print.

1. Select another paragraph with several lines of text. (Alt+F10 selects the next paragraph.)
2. Choose Utilities Hyphenate to start hyphenation.
3. Choose <OK> to accept the initial options.
4. When the Hyphenate dialog box appears, try out all four arrow keys.
5. Choose <OK> to accept the current hyphenation point.
6. Continue hyphenating words until the paragraph is finished.

If no hyphenation was needed in the paragraph, add some words or select another one and try again.

Working with Optional Hyphens

When Word splits a word, it inserts an *optional hyphen*. Optional hyphens appear in print only when they come at the end of a line. If you revise a sentence so that the hyphenated word no longer needs to be split at that point, the optional hyphen is suppressed in print. But it remains in the word and will appear again if a later revision makes it necessary.

Viewing Optional Hyphens. Whether or not you can see optional hyphens on your screen depends on the status of your View Preferences. If **Optional Hyphens** (or **Show All**) is checked, all optional hyphens appear on the screen, even if they don't come at the end of a line. They look just like normal hyphens, but you can usually tell the difference from context.

When **Optional Hyphens** and **Show All** are turned off, the only optional hyphens you see on your screen will be the ones used to split words at the ends of lines. But if **Line Breaks** is also off, the lines are arranged for the convenience of the screen and won't necessarily match the line breaks or hyphenation in print. If you want to see exactly how the optional hyphens will appear in print, turn off **Show All** and **Optional Hyphens** and turn on **Line Breaks**.

1. Choose the View Preferences command.
2. Turn on the **Optional Hyphens** field and turn off the **Line Breaks** field.
3. Choose <OK> and examine the results on your screen.

You should see all the optional hyphens, but they might not come at the ends of lines.

4. Choose View Preferences again.
5. Turn off **Optional Hyphens**, choose <OK>, and examine the results on your screen.

Now the only optional hyphens you see are the ones that fall at the ends of lines. But those aren't necessarily the ones that will appear in print. Let's see how the hyphenation will actually be printed.

6. Choose View Preferences again.
7. Turn on **Line Breaks**, choose <OK>, and examine the results on your screen.

Now you see the line breaks as they'll appear in print. If you have narrow margins or a small font, you might have to scroll sideways to see them.

Inserting and Deleting Optional Hyphens. While typing, you can insert an optional hyphen in a word without going through Utilities Hyphenate. Simply position the cursor and type Ctrl+– (hyphen). The hyphen won't appear unless **Optional Hyphens** or **Show All** is on or the word gets split at that point. You might want to use this feature to hyphenate a particular line (perhaps in a table) when the rest of the document is not hyphenated. Or you can use it to change the position of a hyphen inserted by Word automatically.

To change the position of an existing optional hyphen, turn **Optional Hyphens** on, find the one you want to move, and delete it. Then position the cursor and insert a new one in the correct place. (You could cut and paste the hyphen, but this is just as easy.)

When you're preparing a document, you can mark words that should never be hyphenated by inserting an optional hyphen at the end of the word. When you run Utilities Hyphenate, either in automatic or confirm mode, Word will not hyphenate any word so marked. It's usually not necessary to mark one-syllable words; Word won't hyphenate them anyway. But if you have multisyllable words that you don't want to be hyphenated (such as people's names), it's sometimes easier to mark them in advance than to go back afterwards and remove the hyphens.

You can search and replace optional hyphens using the ^– symbol. You could use this feature to eliminate the hyphenation in a document or selection after it's too late to undo.

1. Select one of your hyphenated paragraphs.
2. Choose Edit Replace.
3. In the **Text to Search for** field, type ^–.
4. Leave the **Replace with** field empty.
5. Turn off **Confirm Changes**.
6. Choose <OK>.

You should see the optional hyphens disappear from the selected text.

Normal and Nonbreak Hyphens

The hyphen that you type by pressing the hyphen key (without Ctrl) is called the *normal hyphen*. It always appears on the screen and in print, no matter what options are selected. Word will use it for a line break if it falls in the right place. But some hyphens should not be used for line breaks. For example, you probably don't want a telephone number (such as 555-1212) or an identification number (such as 153-22-8995) split over two lines. To prevent a hyphen being used for line breaks, use a *nonbreak hyphen* rather than a normal one by pressing Ctrl+Shift+ –.

A nonbreak hyphen acts just like a normal hyphen with one exception: it won't be used to split the hyphenated word over two lines.

1. Open the file named TYPOS.DOC (if it isn't already open).
2. In the third paragraph (not counting the heading), find these words at the beginnings of lines and mark them so they won't be hyphenated: understand really lingo
3. Hyphenate the entire document, using the confirmation feature.
4. Approve some of the hyphens, move some, and reject some.
5. When the hyphenation is finished, undo it all. Then close the file without saving any changes.

Insert an optional hyphen (Ctrl+ –) at the end of words you don't want hyphenated. Start hyphenation by choosing Utilities Hyphenate. Choose <Yes> to accept a hyphen, use the arrow keys or mouse to move it, or choose <No> to reject it. Choose Edit Undo (Alt+Backspace) to undo all the hyphenation.

Sorting

Word will sort items for you, putting them in alphabetic or numeric order. It can sort lists, paragraphs, tables, outline headings, or whatever you have that needs to be sorted.

1. To get ready to try out sorting, set a custom left-aligned tab at 2.5" and type the following table at the end of any document you created:

500 Miles   Davis
(white album)   Beatles
1812 Overture   Tchaikowsky
5th Symphony   Tchaikowsky
18th Century Dances various
5th Symphony   Beethoven
Poems   e. e. cummings

Basic Sort

To perform a basic sort using all the default options, all you have to do is select the items you want to sort, choose the Utilities Sort command, and choose

<OK> in the Sort dialog box (shown in Figure 11.5). The sorted items replace the original items in the selected block.

Tip | If you're sorting a large number of items, save the file first. If Word runs out of memory during a sort, it might freeze up and you'll have to reboot to get out of it.

1. Select the list that you just entered.
2. Choose the Utilities Sort command (Alt,U,O).
3. Choose <OK>.

Are you surprised that "(white album)" comes first? Or that "1812" comes before "500," which comes before "5th"? Let's look at how Word determines the order of items in a sort.

Sort Order

In ascending order, all punctuation characters come first, with a specific order for each one. That's why the entry starting with "(" came first in our example.

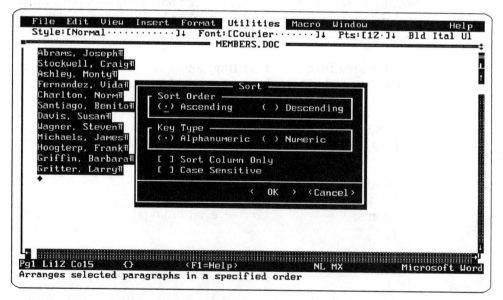

Figure 11.5. Sort Dialog Box

Numbers come next, and letters are last, which is why "Poems" came last in the example—it's the only item that starts with a letter. By default, capital and lowercase letters are equivalent, but you can change that if you wish. International characters with diacritical marks immediately follow their comparable English letters; that is, "ä" immediately follows "a" and "é" immediately follows "e."

In alphanumeric order (the default), each character is treated individually; no consideration is given to the overall values of multiple-digit numbers. In our example, "1812" preceded "500" and "5th" because of their first digits: "1" precedes "5" and "50" precedes "5t."

By contrast, a numeric sort considers only the numbers in an item, and the whole value of a number is used to determine order. Any lines that don't contain numbers are not moved.

1. Choose Utilities Sort again.
2. Turn on the **Numeric** button in the **Key Type** group.
3. Choose <OK> and examine the results.

The "(white album)" still comes out first and "Poems" still comes out last, but all the items with numbers have a different order. Now "5th" comes before "18th," which comes before "500," which comes before "1812."

If you don't like the results of a sort, Edit Undo (Alt+Backspace) will undo it as long as you haven't typed anything else or used any other commands since the sort was completed.

4. Press Alt+Backspace to undo the last sort.
5. Press Alt+Backspace again to restore it.

Other Sort Options

So far, we've sorted everything in ascending order. You can also use descending order, which would exactly reverse the results of the sorts that you have seen. You might want to sort a list of years in descending order, for example, so that the most recent year is first.

By default, Word ignores case when sorting. "A" is the same as "a." But if you want Word to pay attention to case, turn on the **Case Sensitive** field. Then all capital letters precede all lowercase letters; that is, A-Z comes before a-z. The word "Statement" precedes the word "command."

Sorting Tables

When you sort a table, you frequently don't want to use the entire entry as the *sort key* (the data used to determine the order). You want to use one or two fields to determine the order of each row. If you select a column before starting the sort, only that column will be used as the sort key.

1. Position the cursor on the first letter of "Beatles" in your sample table. (You are going to select the entire second column.)
2. Press Ctrl+Shift+F8 to turn on column selection.
3. Move the cursor down and to the right to select the column containing the composer's names.
4. Choose Utilities Sort to sort the column.
5. Turn on the **Alphanumeric** and **Ascending** buttons. DO NOT turn on **Sort Column Only**. (We'll get to that later.)
6. Choose <OK> and examine the results.

Now the table has been sorted based on the names in the second column only. The Beatles still come first, but they're followed by Beethoven, Davis, and so on in alphabetical order by the first characters in this column.

Suppose you want to sort just one column in a table, leaving the other columns in their current order. To do that, select **Sort Column Only** in the Sort dialog box before sorting. Make sure you don't do this by accident; it can really screw up a table.

Sorting Paragraphs

Most of the time, you will sort lists and tables, but you can sort paragraphs using the same techniques. You could use this feature to alphabetize an index or glossary, where the initial word will determine the sort order.

You can also use the sort utility to rearrange paragraphs quickly. Just number the paragraphs in the order you want them. Be sure to place the numbers at the beginning of each paragraph. Then select all the paragraphs and sort them using a numeric sort. The numbers will determine the positions of the paragraphs. Then go back and delete the numbers. This technique is much faster than cutting and pasting a bunch of paragraphs. (You could also use it to sort lists and tables where the order isn't inherent in the data itself.)

Tip | Use the Utilities Renumber command to remove the paragraph numbers after sorting.

1. Number your table in the order shown below (be sure to use the period and space after each number):

3. (white album)	Beatles
2. 5th Symphony	Beethoven
6. 500 Miles	Davis
7. Poems	e. e. cummings
1. 1812 Overture	Tchaikowsky
4. 5th Symphony	Tchaikowsky
5. 76 Trombones	various

2. Now sort the list in ascending numeric order.
3. Choose the Utilities Renumber command (Alt,U,R).
4. Turn on the **Remove** field, then choose <OK>. Word will delete the initial paragraph numbers in the selected block.

1. Open the document named TYPOS.DOC (if it isn't already open).
2. Reverse the order of the paragraphs (except for the heading).
3. Undo the changes you just made to TYPOS.DOC.
4. Open the document named CHARTEST.DOC.
5. Sort CHARTEST.DOC in ascending alphanumeric order.
6. Sort CHARTEST.DOC in ascending alphanumeric order using only the second column as a key. (Sort both columns, however.)
7. To return CHARTEST.DOC to its natural order, sort it in ascending numeric order (both columns).
8. Sort the first column only in descending numeric order.
9. Undo the last sort. Then close both documents without saving any changes.

*To rearrange the paragraphs in TYPOS.DOC, number them in the desired order, then use Utilities Sort to sort them in ascending numeric order. Use Edit Undo to restore the original order. Use Utilities Renumber to remove the paragraph numbers. To sort CHARTEST.DOC, select the entire document and choose Utilities Sort. To use just the second column as a sort key, use Ctrl+Shift+F8 to select just that column, then choose Utilities Sort. To sort just the first column, use Ctrl+Shift+F8 to select just that column and turn on **Sort Column Only** in the Sort dialog box.*

Calculating

The Utilities Calculate function will do basic calculations, displaying the answer on the message line and placing it in the scrap so you can insert it where needed in the document. Figure 11.6 shows an example. We highlighted the expression 2+3*4 and pressed F2. The message line tells us that the answer is 14. Notice in the status line that the braces show that the scrap contains the characters 14.

Use these mathematical operators in your calculate expressions:

%	percentage
/	divide
*	multiply
–	subtract
+ (or nothing)	add

Let's figure out how long Thomas Jefferson lived; he was born in 1743 and died in 1826.

1. Type this sentence in your document: **Thomas Jefferson was 1826 – 1743 years old when he died.**
2. Highlight the expression "1826 – 1743" and choose Utilities Calculate (Alt,U,C) or press F2.

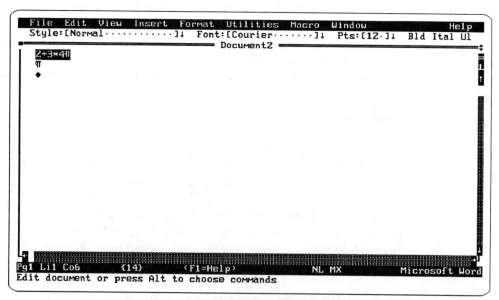

Figure 11.6. Sample Calculation

The answer 83 should appear in the message line and in the scrap.

3. Press Delete to delete the highlighted expression. Don't use Edit Cut here because it would overlay the contents of the scrap.
4. Choose Edit Paste or press Shift+Insert to insert the scrap at the cursor.

Addition with No Operator

You don't need to use an operator when you add. You can just use an expression like 25 17 33 21 94. (The result is 190.) This comes in handy when you want to add up a set of figures that are buried in a paragraph (Word ignores text when calculating).

Tip || If you include a comma in any one of the values, the result includes commas.

1. Type this sentence: **We have 4,130 blue jumpers, 2,235 green, 2,591 red, and 3,194 yellow, for a total of ? jumpers.**
2. Select the entire sentence and press F2.

Word adds all the numbers in the selected sentence and displays the result, 12,150, in the message line and in the scrap.

3. Delete the question mark and insert the scrap value.

This feature also comes in handy when totaling a column in a table. Just use column selection (Ctrl+Shift+F8) to select a column and press F2.

Priority of Operations

Unlike some calculators, Word does not evaluate an expression from left to right. Instead, it uses *algebraic logic*, in which operations are performed in order of their priority. The list of operators on page 298 shows the priority: percentages are done first, then division and multiplication, then addition and subtraction. If an expression involves two or more operations that have the same priority, they are done from left to right.

The example in Figure 11.6 shows the effect of algebraic logic. If you calculated 2 + 3 * 4 from left to right, the answer would be 20. (2 + 3 is 5, and 5 * 4 is 20.) But because Word does multiplication before addition, the result is 14. (3 * 4 is 12, and 2 + 12 is 14.)

You can use parentheses to change the order of operations if you don't want to use the default order. Word does any expressions inside parentheses first. If you calculate (2 + 3) * 4, the result is 20.

Significant Digits

Word can produce results with up to 14 significant digits. If a result is larger than that, an error message appears. (Intermediate results can be larger than 14 significant digits, as long as the final result fits within the limit.)

Negative Numbers

You can use negative numbers in your expressions. Just put a minus sign in front of the number or in front of the parentheses enclosing an expression. For example, the result of 3 * –5 is –15. The result of 2 * –(18/6) is –6. You can use parentheses instead of a minus sign if you prefer, but not in combination with other parentheses. The result of 3 * (5) is –15, but the result of 2 * ((18/6)) is 6.

Fractional Values

Word can handle fractional values in calculations. The result of 4 / 3 is 1.33. The result of 2.175 * 3.992 is 8.683. Notice in both cases that Word rounded off the answer to a reasonable number of decimal places. Even though Word is capable of generating up to 14 significant digits in an answer, it won't give you more than is justified by the problem itself.

1. Calculate the result of 5*25+2/3 and insert the result into your current document.
2. Insert this sentence into your current document: **We have 45,231 outlets in the United States, 3,210 in Canada, 12,503 in Mexico, and 16,302 located elsewhere, for a total of ? outlets.**
3. Calculate the total number of outlets in the previous sentence and insert it to replace the question mark.

Use Utilities Calculate (or F2) to perform the calculations, which can be inserted from scrap. The first answer is 125.67 and the second is 77,246.

Exercise

This chapter has covered the use of several Word utility features that make your work easier, including the spelling checker, the thesaurus, hyphenation, sorting, and calculating. This exercise lets you practice using them.

1. Open a document that has not been spell checked or hyphenated yet.
2. Check the spelling in the document. Correct any incorrect words. Add correct words to the document dictionary.
3. Hyphenate the entire document, confirming each hyphen. Accept, reject, or move hyphens as needed, then undo the hyphenation.
4. Select a multisyllable word in the document. Look it up in the thesaurus. Replace the original word with a good synonym.
5. Start a new document, set appropriate custom tabs, and enter the following table:

Item	Value	Quantity	Total Value
Hammers		3.15	20
Screwdrivers	1.27	113	
Axes	14.28	12	
Wrenches		2.20	42
Total:			

Then calculate the Total Value for each line (Value multiplied by Quantity) and enter it in the appropriate column. You can insert an asterisk before the calculations, then remove them before the next step.
6. Add up the total values and enter the sum in the Total Value column on the bottom line.
7. Sort the item lines in the table in ascending alphanumeric order according to the name of the item.
8. Sort the item lines in the table in descending numeric order according to the Total Value.
9. Close the document without saving it.

To spell check the entire document, make sure nothing is selected and choose Utilities Spelling. Respond to each prompt appropriately, adding at least one word to a dictionary. Use Utilities Hyphenate to add hyphens. Edit Undo (Alt+Backspace) undoes the entire command. Use Utilities Thesaurus to find a synonym for a word.

Use Format Tabs to set up the custom tabs and Shift+↵ to end each table line except the last. Type expressions like «3.15*20» in the Total Value column and select, then choose Utilities Calculate.

Select the entire area to be sorted, then choose Utilities Sort to sort the item lines by the first characters in the table. Use column selection (Ctrl+Shift+F8, then use arrows) before choosing Utilities Sort to sort by the value field.

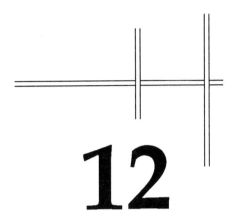

12

Using Nontext Elements

he documents you've created and worked with in Word so far use text but no lines or graphics. In Chapter 8 you learned to use borders and lines to enclose paragraphs using the Format Borders command. In Chapter 10, you learned to place vertical lines with a vertical tab stop.

Some documents, however, benefit from the use of additional lines, including boxes, rectangles, and dividers. Other documents need actual graphics, which are generally stored in another file. These graphics can be clip art, scanned images, graphs, charts, or even screen images. In this chapter, you'll learn to:

- Create line drawings in a document
- Modify the format of the default line draw font
- Manipulate line drawings
- Add text to line drawings
- Import a graphic file into a document
- Arrange the horizontal and vertical positioning of a graphic in a frame
- Modify the size, position, and borders of a graphic
- Capture screen images
- Arrange graphics on a page

Lines in Documents

Word's line draw feature lets you control the appearance and placement of lines in a document. You can specify the type of line and where to place it. You can draw boxes, organization charts, anything made up of horizontal and vertical straight lines. You can draw with a single line, a double line, or with other characters.

What prints, however, depends on your printer. Your printer may ignore characters that it can't handle, or it may substitute some other character. You may have to experiment a bit to get the best result on your printer.

Using Line Draw

Figure 12.1 shows several drawings on screen as produced by line draw. Notice the different characters that make up the lines.

Fonts

The Word program has a default font for drawing lines that is appropriate for the installed printer. This font may be for lines only, such as the LineDraw

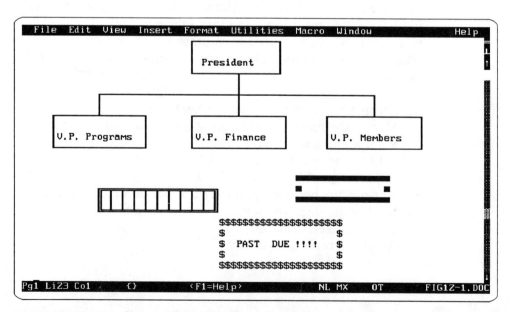

Figure 12.1. Line Draw Samples

font, or it may be a multipurpose font such as Courier or Pica that can handle characters as well.

Which font is used in line draw will determine the outcome. Each line segment must be the same length, so you must use a fixed-pitch font, such as Courier or LineDraw. The default font for this function is always fixed-pitch.

If you don't specify a different font, Word uses the default line drawing font for your printer. Some printers can support more than one font for drawing lines. The *Printer Information for Microsoft Word* book supplied with Word shows the options for each supported printer.

The font size is important too. The default font size may be the only one supported. For example, the LineDraw font is available only in the 12-point size. You can change the font size only if other sizes are shown for the line drawing font in the **Point Size** (or **Pts**) field menu. Only valid sizes will be shown. If you do change the default point size, the line height may not be correct. Make sure the **Line** field in the Format Paragraph dialog box is set for an automatic line height; then Word sets the line height to match the font size. If you have it set for 1 line, Word assumes you have six lines per inch.

Setting the Line Draw Character

By default, Word uses a single line when it draws lines, much like the single border you can create around a paragraph. If you want to use a different character, you can set it through the Utilities Customize command.

1. Open one of your practice documents.
2. Choose the Utilities Customize command.

The **Line Draw Character** field in the upper right shows the current character. The single line is the default. The field menu includes a double line and a hyphen/bar option. The double line is like the double border around paragraphs. The hyphen/bar option is for printers that don't support any line drawing font and can't handle the standard lines. Other characters you can select from the field menu include shading, bullets, and solid blocks; these may be available in various fonts.

If you prefer, you can type any character for use in drawing "lines." For example, you could specify a dollar sign ($), a pound sign (#), or an asterisk (*). No matter what character you use, it is used in lines drawn on the screen.

3. Drop down the **Line Draw Character** field menu by clicking or by pressing Alt+H, Alt+↓.

4. Scroll through the options to see what is available.
5. Choose <Cancel>.

Drawing Lines

To draw lines, you use the arrow keys, Home, and End. Each arrow key draws a one-unit line in the indicated direction. The Home key draws a line from the current cursor position to the left indent of the paragraph. The End key draws a line from the cursor to the right indent of the paragraph. You can't draw lines with the mouse.

The space for the line drawing must already exist in the document. The ⏎ key doesn't work when line draw is in effect. While you are drawing lines, existing paragraph marks may automatically move to the right to make space for the line draw characters. Word wrap is not in effect either; if you try to draw lines beyond the right margin, Word beeps and waits for you to turn a corner or stop. Line draw is always in overtype mode, so you can't insert lines to push over characters. Lines you draw over existing characters on the screen remove those characters.

Line Draw Function. You start the line draw function with the Utilities Line Draw (Alt,U,L) command. The menu name remains highlighted in the menu bar to remind you that a special function is in effect. The characters LD appear in the status bar for the same reason. The line draw font is in effect. Pressing any keyboard keys other than the arrow keys, Home, and End has no effect. To stop line draw, press the escape key or click either mouse button.

1. Insert six or seven consecutive blank lines into the document. Place the cursor in the top one.
2. Choose the Utilities Line Draw command (Alt,U,L).
3. Press → five times.
4. Press ↓ four times.
5. Press ← five times.
6. Press ↑ four times.
7. Press → ten times.

Removing Lines. Drawing over the lines a second time doesn't erase them. And backing up doesn't either. Once you leave line draw mode, you can select, delete, cut, and copy line draw characters as needed. You can even backspace over them.

1. Press ← three times. Notice that the line is not erased.
2. Press the escape key to end line draw. Notice that the menu bar is cleared.
3. Press the delete key three times. The line characters disappear.
4. Select the drawing in the usual way and choose Edit Copy (Ctrl+Ins).
5. Move the cursor to another location in the document and choose Edit Paste (Shift+Ins).

You can place line draw characters anywhere in a document. The line draw characters are always in overtype mode; they don't push characters over. Instead, line draw characters replace any text characters they overlay. If you want to include lines and text on the same line, plan it first. If the text is already there, it's a bit easier to add the lines. If the lines are already entered, turn insert mode off (Ins or Alt+F5) before typing characters to the left.

If you want to place characters inside a box, draw the box first. Then turn insert mode off and place the characters where they belong.

1. Take a little time to practice drawing lines using several of the **Line Draw Character** options.
2. Make line figures of several different shapes just to get the feel of it.

Set the character, then position the cursor and turn on line draw. When you screw it up, press the escape key to turn off line draw, delete the parts that aren't any good, position the cursor, and turn on line draw again.

Adding Text. When you stop using the line draw function, Word leaves the line drawing font in control. If you start typing text immediately after drawing lines, they will look fine on the screen, but you will actually be using the default font. You can tell what font you are using by checking the ribbon once line draw is turned off.

1. If it isn't on, turn on the ribbon with View Ribbon or by clicking the right button on the ruler/ribbon icon.
2. Place the cursor on a line you drew earlier. Notice the values in the **Font** and **Pts** fields in the ribbon.
3. Place the cursor on a nearby character. Notice the values in the same ribbon fields.

If the fonts differ, you have to be more aware of how you end line draw. After you leave line draw, type a character and check the font in the ribbon. Whenever you aren't in line draw mode (no LD in the status line), you want your regular character font displayed in the ribbon for text characters.

1. Insert several more consecutive blank lines into the document.
2. Choose the Utilities Customize command and change the default **Line Draw Character** to a double line.
3. Choose the Utilities Line Draw command.
4. Draw a rectangle about twelve characters wide and five high.
5. Press the escape key to turn off line draw. The box is now shown on your screen.
6. Press Ins to turn off insert mode.
7. Position the cursor inside the box positioned so you can type **President**. If the ribbon shows the LineDraw font, select the word and set the font to Courier using the ribbon or Format Character command.
8. Move the cursor outside the box and turn insert mode back on.

Printing

You print a document containing lines just like any other document. The result, however, may not be what you expect. Your printer's capabilities make the difference. The printer may be able to handle any of the suggested line draw characters in the Utilities Customize dialog box. Or it may be able to handle only a few. If your printer doesn't handle graphics at all, it will be able to use the Hyphen/Bar option, which uses dashes and vertical bars to form its lines, with the plus sign for corners. Or you could specify a character it can print, such as = or # for use in the lines.

1. Print the page containing one of your line draw figures with a single line.
2. If the result doesn't have neat lines, erase the figure. Then change the **Line Draw Character** to the Hyphen/Bar, redraw a figure and print it. This may be all you can handle with that printer.
3. If the result of item 1 looks like it did on screen, print the page containing the double-lined box around the word *President*.
4. Select the word *President* and change the font to 8 points. If the page didn't print as readable characters in item 3, change the font to Courier or a different fixed-pitch.
5. Print the page again.

The box did not print as nicely with the smaller size text inside it. When you use a font of a different size than adjacent or enclosed text, the alignment can get out of kilter. In most cases, just use the same size fixed-pitch font for such text as you do for the line draw characters.

Tip If you don't format the characters following drawing, Word may use the default line draw font. The characters might not be readable in print, even though you see them nicely on screen. Check the format in the ribbon of anything that prints.

Automatic Style

An automatic style is provided for use with the line draw character and applied automatically. If this style hasn't been defined, it has the default format for the installed printer. You can define the automatic style to use a different format if you like, just like you define any other automatic style; these are covered in more detail in Chapter 9. The *Printer Information for Microsoft Word* book provided by Microsoft gives information on what fonts and what point sizes can handle line drawing for all supported printers.

1. Move the cursor to a part of your document that doesn't have drawings, and insert ten blank lines.
2. Create an organization chart like the one in Figure 12.1. Use any line style that prints on your printer.
3. Add some text to each box, then print the result.

Use the Utilities Customize command to set the line draw character. Use Utilities Line Draw to start drawing a line. Remember to position the cursor before starting line draw, and to turn off line draw to make corrections to lines. You'll have to turn overtype mode on to put text in the boxes.

Graphics in Word Documents

Word includes facilities to import graphics of many types into Word Documents with the Insert Picture command. This command doesn't actually pull the graphic into your file, but it sets up a special code and places a graphics paragraph in your file. The special code, which appears as .G., tells Word that this is a graphics paragraph. The graphics paragraph tells Word where the graphic is, what size to make it, and what format it is in. When you preview or print the document file, the referenced graphics file is located and printed as part of the document.

On the screen in text mode, you'll see the code as hidden text, followed by the graphics paragraph. In layout mode, the same line appears in the bottom of the space allowed for the graphic, but you won't see the graphic in document mode. In Print Preview mode, or in a printed document, you'll see the actual graphic in position.

Tip | If you don't see the graphics code on the screen, choose the View Preferences command and turn on the **Hidden Text** field. This makes hidden text display. It still won't print unless you modify the Print Option as well.

Types of Graphics

Word can import many types of graphics, including pictures, charts, screen prints, and clip art, into document files. Each graphic imported must be a separate file. Word can't handle all types of graphics file, but it can handle many of them. You'll find the complete list in *Using Microsoft Word,* your Word reference manual. Here are some of the different file types that can be imported, along with some of the programs that create these file types.

HPGL. HPGL plotter files can be created by such programs as AutoCad, Microsoft Chart and Microsoft Excel. Many common graphics programs can convert their files to HPGL format.

TIFF. Many scanners produce TIFF format files; Word supports the B (black and white) and G (gray scale) TIFF formats. If you have a scanner, have it create images in one of these formats rather than the dithered format. Some graphics programs can convert their files to one of the supported TIFF formats.

PCX. PC Paintbrush produces graphics in PCX format. Many scanners and graphics programs can convert their output into PCX format that can be handled by Word.

EPS. Common graphics programs such as HotShot Graphics can create files in EPS form. Other graphics programs may be able to convert to an encapsulated postscript file.

PIC. Several spreadsheets, including Lotus 1-2-3 and Paradox, produce graphics in PIC format. Word can import these directly.

Captured Images. The Word program comes with a screen capture utility that can make a file containing an image of the current screen. These files can be imported directly into Word document files. You'll see how to use these in this chapter.

Windows Clipboard. If you are running Word as a non-Windows application under Windows, you can use the clipboard to transfer graphics. This is covered in detail in the reference manual.

How Importing Works

Each Word paragraph is contained in a frame (see Chapter 8). The frame forms a rectangle around the text, extending from the top line to the bottom, from the left margin to the right. If you place a border around the paragraph, you see the outline of the frame, but otherwise you don't see it on the screen or in print output. If you change the margins, add text to the paragraph, or delete some of it, the shape of the rectangle changes.

Graphics are placed in similar frames. And just as you can border or position a document paragraph, so you can add borders to a graphic or position it on the page.

When you import a graphic, Word inserts a special code as hidden text, followed by a graphics paragraph. If hidden text is displayed (through the View Preferences dialog box), it shows up on the screen. The graphics paragraph includes the name (and path if needed) of the graphic file, its dimensions, and its format. Here's an example:

```
.G.C:\WORD\PREV.PCX;5.0";3.5";PCX
```

The characters .G. signal a graphic paragraph. The file specification follows. The width and height for the graphic in this document are provided, and the format of the graphic file wraps it up. You provide all this information when you ask Word to import a graphic file.

Capturing Screen Images

The Word software package includes a program named CAPTURE.COM. You can use CAPTURE to capture screen images. These images can then be brought into Word as graphics. The same principles apply to importing other types of graphics. We aren't going to cover all the things you can do with this program; you'll just learn enough to capture a graphics screen for importing into a Word document. Your reference manual includes additional information about this stand-alone program.

CAPTURE.COM captures two types of screen. It can capture a screen as a text file (ASCII) or as a graphics file. Which it uses depends on your video display, the type of image being displayed, and how you have set up the program.

Screens that are captured as text files are given the extension LST; these are treated as text and so must be imported with the Insert File command (covered in Chapter 7). The effect may or may not be what you want when you print the page. You'll have to experiment. The standard Word text mode screen is captured as an ASCII file on a standard IBM display.

Screens that are captured as graphics files are given the extension SCR. These are captured in full living color. The colors are converted to shades of gray for printing, if you have set up the CAPTURE program correctly. The Print Preview screen and graphics mode screens are captured as graphics files. These files are imported with the Insert Picture command.

Setting up CAPTURE.COM

The CAPTURE.COM program is stored in your WORD directory on the hard disk or on Program Disk 1 of your diskettes. Before you can use it to capture screens, you have to set up the CAPTURE program to read your video monitor correctly and tell it how you want screens captured. Once CAPTURE.COM is in memory, you can capture the curent screen by pressing Shift+PrintScreen.

Follow these steps to set up and load CAPTURE.COM so you can capture screen images.

1. Get to the DOS prompt for the directory that contains the Word files and type **CAPTURE /S** to invoke the CAPTURE program with the S parameter for setup.
2. A screen like the one in Figure 12.2 appears.

When you press the indicated letter, a screen appears with further details. It shows you the default setting for the feature and tells you how to change it.

In most cases, you only have to worry about the first item on the list, the display adapter. If that is set correctly, you should be able to capture screens. When you press **D**, you'll see the list of possibilities. If you can't find your exact display adapter type, choose the general IBM adapter. Then type **Q** to end the setup program.

3. Type **D**.
4. On the resulting screen, find your display adapter type. If you can't find a choice that looks better, type **0** to select a general IBM adapter.
5. Type **Q** to leave the setup program.

A message on the screen tells you that CAPTURE is loaded. You can now enter any application and capture screen images. We'll do it in Word, but CAPTURE works until you remove it from memory. To do that, just get back to the same DOS prompt and type **CAPTURE /E**. If you leave it in memory, it takes up about 24K. You can reload the program later without any switches, just by typing **CAPTURE** at the DOS prompt.

Capturing Screens

To capture the screen that is currently displayed, you press Shift+PrintScreen. You may be shown a suggested name. If so, you can change it if you want. CAPTURE automatically generates file names in the form CAPT*nnnn*, starting with CAPT0001. It supplies the LST extension for text screens or SCR for

```
                            CAPTURE.COM
            Screen capture program version 1.0 for Microsoft Word
        (C) Copyright 1989 Jewell Technologies, Inc. - All rights reserved

    Use the menu below to select your display adapter and choose your options.
    When you press a letter for an option, a screen will appear to describe
    the option in more detail.

    TO                                                              PRESS

    Select display adapter                                            D

    Enable/Disable text screens as pictures                           T

    Enable/Disable saving in reverse video                            U

    Enable/Disable clipping                                           P

    Enable/Disable 90 degree rotation                                 R

    Enter number of text lines per screen                             N

    Quit and save settings                                            Q

    -
```

Figure 12.2. CAPTURE Setup Screen

graphics screens. If you prefer a different name, just start typing when the automatic name appears; it will be replaced. CAPTURE supplies the appropriate extension.

When you are happy with the file name, press ⏎. Text and some graphics screens are captured immediately and you hear a beep when they are ready. Other graphics screens are set up for clipping so that you can capture only part of the screen. In that case, you'll see thin lines on the right and bottom edges of the screen. Press ⏎ again to accept the full screen. As soon as CAPTURE has saved the image, you'll hear a beep.

Tip ‖ We aren't covering how to use the clipping feature. But if you disable clipping through the setup program, you won't be able to choose your own file names for captured files.

1. Start Word if necesary, and open one of your practice documents.
2. Choose the Print Preview command. This gives you a graphics screen for capturing.
3. Press Shift+PrintScreen.
4. If a file name appears at the top of the screen, notice what it is and press ⏎ to accept it.
5. If you see a thin line at any edge of the screen, press ⏎ again to accept the full screen.
6. When you hear a beep, the screen is captured in the file. If you don't hear a beep after a minute or two, press ⏎ again.

Now you have a graphic available for importing. While there are many more features of the CAPTURE.COM program, they aren't essential to us now. In practice, you'll probably have some other way of preparing or acquiring graphics for use in your Word documents.

Tip ‖ If you have trouble capturing a screen image, and you don't expect to do this ever again, check your WORD directory. A file named RIBBON.SCR is supplied that you can insert as a graphic.

Importing Graphics

To import graphics, use the Insert Picture command, which brings up the dialog box shown in Figure 12.3. You can select the graphic file name and specify all the formatting information here.

Specifying the File and Format

The first step is to select the file from the **Files** list box or type it in the **Picture File Name** field. If the file name isn't displayed, you may have to change the directory through the **Directories** list box. If you are looking for a particular type of picture file, you can limit the listing of files by typing an expression such as *.SCR or *.PCX in the **Picture File Name** field. Then only files with that extension will be listed.

1. Press the Escape key to leave preview mode, then position the cursor at the beginning of a line in your document.
2. Choose the Insert Picture command (Alt,I,P).
3. Select the name of the file you captured so that it appears in the **Picture File Name** field; this is probably CAPT0001.SCR.

Now you can set up the rest of the information. The **Format** field will show the format of the file if it can tell; it should show **Capture** for this file. It might show PCX, HPGL, Print File, or whatever it thinks it is. If this field is left blank, you'll see a message when you finally choose <OK> to import the picture.

The **Align in Frame** field lets you choose whether the graphic should be aligned with the left or right edge of the frame or centered within it. These all have the same effect if the graphic is the full frame width.

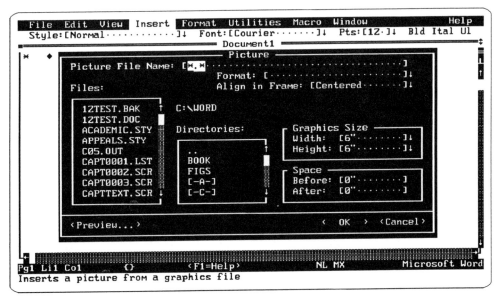

Figure 12.3. The Insert Picture Dialog Box

The **Graphics Size** fields let you specify the **Width** and **Height** of the imported graphic. The width, by default, is the full width of the column. You can make this smaller here, especially if you want the graphic aligned on the right or left. It won't change the width of the frame, just the size of the graphic. The height is in proportion to the width if Word can figure it out. Otherwise, Word suggests the same dimension as for height. You can modify either of these values by typing a different dimension.

The **Space** fields let you enclose extra space **Before** and/or **After** the graphic within the frame. This lets you include white space to arrange vertical positioning of the graphic in the frame.

4. If the **Format** and **Align** fields have values, leave them be.
5. If the **Height** field shows 6, move the cursor to this field and type **4**.
6. Choose <OK>.

If Word has any problems, you'll see a message box. Just choose <OK> if necessary and continue. If you don't see a graphics paragraph in your document, try this series of steps again and insert another SCR file.

The Graphics Paragraph

When you choose <OK>, Word locates the file you specified and inserts a coded paragraph into the document at the current cursor location. The paragraph begins with .G. and is aligned as specified in the Insert Picture dialog box. The file name is followed by the width and height dimensions and the graphics format.

Viewing the Graphic

If you are working in standard document view, you'll see just the coded paragraph in position. If you are working in layout view, however, Word inserts the space it will need for the graphic.

1. Choose the View Layout command to see the other display mode.
2. If it isn't off, turn layout view off.

To see the graphic itself, you have to use preview mode or print the document.

3. Choose the File Print Preview command.

4. If you don't see the graphic, page up or page down until you see it in position.

Printing the Graphic

Whether or not a graphic will print depends on the printer and the settings in your Print Options dialog box. If the **Draft** field is turned on, graphics won't print; a blank area shows where the graphic belongs. You'll want to turn this off before printing graphics. The resolution may affect printing as well. If your printer has limited memory and you see an "insufficient memory" message or your graphic isn't all printed, you'll have to lower the resolution.

5. Choose the File Print command.
6. Choose the <Options> button.
7. Make sure the **Draft** field is turned off.
8. Choose <OK>.
9. Choose <OK> to print the document with the graphic inserted.

Printing pages with graphics takes considerably longer than printing pages that contain only text. How much longer depends on the printer and the complexity of the graphics. If you get an "insufficient memory" message or the graphic doesn't print completely, return to the Print Options dialog box and select a lower value for the **Graphics Resolution** field.

1. Preview the page containing your inserted graphic, then capture this screen.
2. Move the cursor to another location in your document, then insert the graphic you just captured. Use the size 5.5" wide and 3.7" high.
3. Print the page containing the inserted picture.

The CAPTURE program is still in memory, so pressing Shift+PrintScreen should capture the image. You'll have to type the desired width and height on the Insert Picture dialog box. Print the page as usual, but be patient.

Working with Graphics

There are many things you can do with graphics once they are brought into a document. This section covers just a few of the more useful ones.

Move or Copy. Just select the graphics paragraph and use Edit Cut or Edit Copy, followed by Edit Paste, to move or copy a graphic.

1. Select the coded graphic paragraph.
2. Choose the Edit Copy command (Ctrl+Ins).
3. Move the cursor to the end of the document and press ↵.
4. Choose the Edit Paste command (Shift+Ins).

The paragraph has been copied. When the document is printed next, there will be two copies of the graphic.

5. Choose the File Print Preview command to examine the new copy.
6. Press the Escape key to return to the document.

Change the Size. Suppose you want to change the size of a graphic. Place the cursor in the coded graphic paragraph and choose Insert Picture. When the dialog box appears, change the height and width to reflect what you want, then choose <OK>. The codes will change to reflect the new size.

1. Place the cursor on the last graphics paragraph.
2. Choose the Insert Picture command.
3. In the **Width** field, type **4**.
4. In the **Height** field, type **3**.
5. Choose <OK>.
6. Choose the File Print Preview command to examine the effect.
7. Press the Escape key to return to the document.

Add a Border. To have a border around your graphic frame, choose the Format Borders command. The type of border you choose appears around the final graphic. It appears around the coded graphic paragraph when you aren't in layout mode, or around the space when you are.

1. Place the cursor in the last graphics paragraph.
2. Choose the Format Borders command.
3. Turn on the buttons to box the paragraph in whatever style you prefer.
4. Choose <OK>.
5. Choose the File Print Preview command to see the effect.

6. Press the Escape key to return to the document.

The border appears around the graphics paragraph. Notice that the border extends the full width of the column, even though the graphic is narrower.

Add a Caption. A caption is separate text that follows a graphic. To use one, type it in a separate paragraph immediately following the coded graphic paragraph. You can align the caption paragraph and format its characters however you want. To move or position the caption with the graphic, select both paragraphs before choosing the other command.

If you want the caption to be part of the same paragraph as the graphic, change the paragraph mark at the end of the graphic paragraph to a new-line mark (Shift+↵), then type the caption to make the caption part of the same paragraph. This will cause the caption to be positioned with the graphic or included in a border. It also won't be split over a page break.

1. Place the cursor at the paragraph mark at the end of the graphics paragraph.
2. Press Shift+Enter to create a new line in the paragraph.
3. Type **Sample Graphic Position** and press ↵.
4. Examine the effect under preview mode.

Tip ‖ Use preview mode every time you make a change to your graphic formatting. It helps you keep on track.

1. Work with a fairly pure graphics paragraph for this exercise. Give it a one-line caption and copy both to the beginning of the file.
2. Change the graphics size to 3" wide and 1.75" high. Make sure both paragraphs are centered in their frames.
3. Make the frame width 3.5" (for graphic and caption).
4. Add a border and print the result.

Use standard copy commands for item 1. Use Insert Picture to change the size of the imported graphic. Use Format commands to align the graphic, resize the frame, and add a border.

Exercise

This chapter has covered various ways of getting nontext elements into a document. Line draw lets you insert lines directly; your printer and the font determine how the lines print. Graphics, including screen images you capture, can be inserted using other commands. This exercise lets you practice using these features.

---

1. For this exercise, open a file you haven't used yet during this chapter.
2. Draw three or four different diagrams, using different line draw characters. Put text in at least one of them.
3. Capture a graphics screen or locate a different graphic of a type that Word can handle.
4. Import the graphic in a size that extends three-quarters of the way across your page. It should be followed by a few paragraphs of text.
5. Add a caption to the graphic frame, then print the page.
6. Abandon the document or save it as you please.

When you choose Utilities Line Draw, the default font for your printer is used. The arrow keys let you draw lines. You can't erase line portions until you leave line draw by pressing Esc or by clicking. Change the line draw character in the Utilities Customize dialog box.

To capture a screen image, get out of Word, then type **CAPTURE** *at the DOS prompt. Go back into Word. When the screen you want is displayed, press Shift+PrintScreen. Press ↵ once or twice, depending on the screen, to capture it; provide a file name if asked. To insert the captured screen or any other graphic, position the cursor, then choose Insert Picture. Provide the file name when prompted. You can format the inserted paragraph with the Format Paragraph command.*

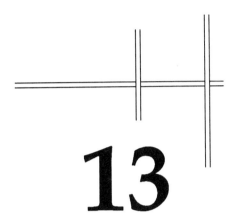

13

Macros

Have you ever wished you could simplify some of the Word functions you do all the time? For example, don't you wish you could print the current file with one keystroke instead of four keystrokes (Alt,F,P,<OK>) or clicks? Well you can—if you create a *macro* to do just that. In fact, you can reduce much longer, more complicated procedures to just a couple of keystrokes if you wish. This chapter shows you how. You will learn to:

- Open a macro glossary file
- Merge a macro file into the current glossary file
- Run a macro
- Remove changes to your glossary file
- Save changes to your glossary file
- Define macros using the macro recorder
- Correct macro definitions
- Adapt existing macros to create new ones
- Interrupt and cancel a running macro

What Is a Macro?

A macro is a function (or a series of functions) that you can accomplish with a couple of keystrokes or by selecting it from a list. For example, you might have a set of macros like this:

Function	Key combination
transpose two letters	Ctrl+T,L
transpose two words	Ctrl+T,W
transpose two sentences	Ctrl+T,S
transpose two paragraphs	Ctrl+T,P

You'll learn to create these macros in this chapter. They're handy to have around. Word's macros can be much more complex than these simple ones. You might, for example, create a macro to seek out all the words surrounded by angle brackets (< >) in a set of selected documents, remove the angle brackets, and italicize the words.

Word supplies several macros with the program. You can use these as they are or alter them to better suit your needs. You can also create an unlimited number of new macros yourself.

Once you get used to macros, you'll probably create new ones all the time. They help to reduce keystrokes, reduce errors, and lessen the tedium of repetitive tasks.

The Macro Menu

The Macro menu contains commands that help you work with macros. You can use this menu to record, run, or edit macros. As you'll learn, you can easily run macros without going through the menu.

The MACRO.GLY File

Just as Word supplies NORMAL.GLY as a default glossary file, it supplies MACRO.GLY as a glossary file. MACRO.GLY contains many sample macros and several sample glossary entries. If you open MACRO.GLY through the Edit Glossary command, you see only the glossary entries. When you are working with macros, you see only the macro entries.

Running Macros

Macros are stored in glossary files, which must be opened to make the glossary entries and macros stored in them available. When you start up Word, the glossary NORMAL.GLY is open. This file does not contain any macros, although you can add them if you wish.

When you open a glossary devoted to macros, it closes any open GLY file. You can merge the macro file into the current glossary file if you want both your macros and your glossary entries available at the same time. However, you can define both macros and glossary entries in the same GLY file as well.

Merging Macro Files

When you merge a macro file into the open glossary, all the commands in both are available to you. If any names are duplicated, the names in the merged (macro) file take over. Here's how to do it:

1. Open any document, if none is open.
2. Choose the Macro Edit command (Alt,M,E).
3. Choose <Merge>.

The resulting dialog box looks just like the Edit Glossary dialog box.

4. Select MACRO.GLY from the file list and choose <OK> or double-click on MACRO.GLY. If this file isn't listed, make sure the directory shows the one that contains your Word files.
5. Word might ask if you want to save changes to the current glossary. Choose <Yes> to save any previous work you have done to the glossary.

This last step saves any changes you made to the glossary file, but has no effect on the merged macros. If you choose <No>, any changes you've made since the last time you saved the glossary file are lost. When you leave Word or change to a different glossary file, you'll have the choice of saving or abandoning changes to the glossary file. Later in this chapter, you'll see how to make these macros permanent in a glossary file or how to remove them from your glossary again.

Figure 13.1 shows the dialog box that remains on the screen. You could edit any of the macros now by selecting one and choosing <Edit>. Most of these buttons work just like their counterparts in the Edit Glossary dialog box.

6. Choose <Close> to close the dialog box. (It doesn't close the glossary file.)

Effect on Glossary File

When you merge a macro file into a glossary, any glossary entries in that macro file are assimilated into the current glossary as well. If their names are the same as in the open glossary, the merged ones will be in effect. MACRO.GLY includes some supplied glossaries. Take a moment to look at them.

1. Choose Edit Glossary.
2. Highlight one or two of the new entries and notice their contents.
3. Choose the <Close> button.

Macro Run Command

Once the glossary file containing macros has been opened or merged into an open glossary, you can run one by choosing the Macro Run command or by pressing the macro's key combination. You can also run the macro just like a glossary. Choosing Macro Run results in a dialog box like the one shown in

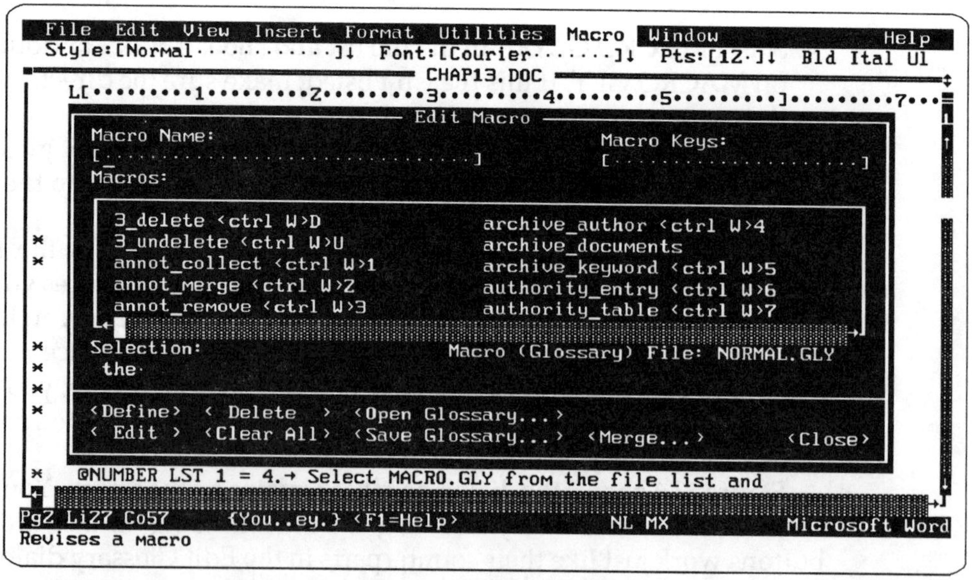

Figure 13.1. Result of Merging Macro File

Figure 13.2. It includes a list of all the defined macros in the currently open GLY file, including any merged into it.

When you run a macro, you must be sure that two specific settings in the Utilities Customize dialog box are the same when you run a macro as they were when the macro was created: **Use Word 5.0 Function Keys** and **Use INS for Overtype Key**. For the macros supplied with Word, these two options must have their default settings (off and on, respectively). If you have trouble running other macros, these field settings are the first things to check.

1. Position the cursor at the beginning of a paragraph.
2. Choose Macro Run (Alt,M,R or Ctrl+F3).
3. From the displayed list of macros, select Filename (use the arrow keys or scroll bar) and choose <OK>, or double-click on Filename.

This macro inserts the name of the current document file (with complete path) at the cursor position. You should see the result on your screen.

When the Run Macro dialog box is on the screen, you can see the macro key combination for each macro. These work much like the optional keys you can define with glossary entries. The macro key combination for the Filename macro is Ctrl+V,7.

4. Move the cursor to any other position.
5. Press Ctrl+V,7.

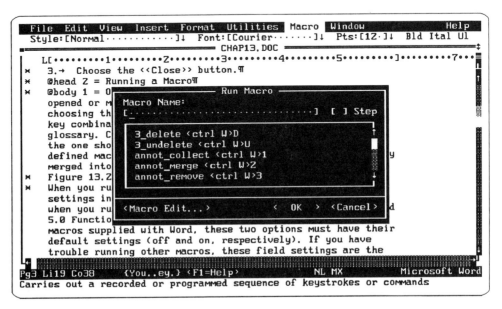

Figure 13.2. The Run Macro Dialog Box

The file name should once again appear at the cursor.

Tip || It's unfortunate, but true: You can't undo a macro.

The Filename macro runs fairly quickly, but many macros take longer to accomplish their tasks. It depends, of course, on how many tasks a macro must do and how many steps each task involves. The message "Running Macro" at the right end of the status bar tells you that a macro is at work even when you can't see any other evidence on your screen.

6. Press Ctrl+V,7 again. Notice the "Running Macro" message.

Macros are stored in glossary files (with extension GLY) and can be run just like glossaries can. Just type the macro name in your document and press F3. The macro is run immediately. To run the Filename macro, type Filename and press F3. As with glossary entries, the case of letters or numbers in the entry name makes no difference to Word.

Word's Macros

As you have seen, the macros supplied by Word are stored in the default file MACRO.GLY. They are briefly described in your Word documentation, and you will need to experiment with them to see how they actually work. We are not covering them in detail here because many of them apply to special situations, some are so simple that they aren't really useful, and some don't always work properly.

Warning: Some of the macros don't work as described, and some can actually do harm. For example, the Manyprint macro closes all open files without saving; this can cause you to lose data.

To remove the merged macros from your current glossary file, close the glossary without saving it. You can do this by opening another glossary or by reopening the same one. In either case, when Word asks if you want to save changes, choose <No> to eliminate the merged macros.

Warning: This will also eliminate any other changes you have made to the glossary since the last time it was saved or the macro file was merged into it.

1. Choose Edit Glossary.

Notice that your entries are here, as well as several additional entries. The glossary entries from MACRO.GLY are available through this dialog box.

2. Choose <Open Glossary>.
3. Choose your current glossary from the list of glossaries.
4. When a dialog box asks if you want to save the changes, choose <No>.
5. Choose <Close> to get rid of the dialog box.

Now you have eliminated the macros that you merged earlier. (They're still in MACRO.GLY, however.) To see that they're gone, examine the macro list.

6. Choose Macro Edit. Notice that the macro list is empty; there are no macros in this glossary file.
7. Choose <Close> to get rid of the dialog box.

Creating Your Own Macros

You can create macros in several ways. The easiest way is to use the macro recorder; then Word does most of the work. You can also modify existing macros and save them under new names or create them from scratch.

Recording Macros

Writing a simple macro is quite easy; you tell Word you want it to remember the steps, then you perform them. And you tell Word when to stop remembering and save the series. You tell Word to turn on the macro recorder to start; choose the Macro Record command. Then you execute the actions you want to make into a macro. Then you turn off the recorder again. The macro recorder can't sense mouse actions, so you have to perform all actions from the keyboard while recording.

Here are the steps in creating a simple macro that transposes two letters:

1. Position the cursor at the second of two characters to be transposed.
2. Choose Macro Record (Alt,M,C or Ctrl+F3).
3. In the resulting dialog box, type **Transpose-Letters** in the **Macro Name** field.
4. Move the cursor to the **Macro Keys** field, then hold down the Control key and press T. Release both keys and press L.

What you see in the field at this point is "<Ctrl T>L."

5. Choose <OK>.

The message on the status line is "Mouse inactive. Press <Ctrl F3> to stop recording macro." That message will disappear as soon as you press any key. But at the right end of the status line is the code "MR" for Macro Recorder, which will stay there until you turn off the recorder by pressing Ctrl+F3. In the meantime, if you try to use your mouse, Word will beep to remind you that the mouse is inactive when the recorder is on.

6. Click your mouse to make the computer beep.

Now the macro recorder is turned on. Word will remember each step you make at the keyboard, whether you type, use commands, delete characters, or whatever. Word even remembers any mistakes you make whenever recording is turned on; you'll see how to correct these later in this chapter. While macro recording is in effect, the command on the Macro menu changes to Stop Recorder; pressing Alt+M,C chooses this command and turns off recording. (Remember you can't use the mouse.) Here are the steps to record a macro to transpose letters:

1. Press Shift+→ to highlight the current letter.
2. Press Shift+Delete to cut the letter to the scrap.
3. Press → to move the cursor to the right one character.
4. Press Shift+Insert to insert the letter from the scrap.
5. Press Alt+M,C or Ctrl+F3 to turn off the macro recorder.

Testing a Macro

The macro is now recorded and you can try it out. To do this, you use the key combination or run the macro from the dialog box. Let's transpose the two letters that you transposed while recording the macro.

1. Move the cursor back two characters, to the first letter that you want to transpose.
2. Press Ctrl+T,L.

You should see the two letters being transposed. If it doesn't work, go back to the Recording Macros section and repeat the steps until you successfully record a macro to transpose two letters. Try it again using the dialog box to run the macro:

1. Choose the Macro Run command (Alt,M,R).
2. Select the Transpose-Letters macro and choose <OK>.

1. Start the macro recorder for a macro named Transpose-Words with the key code Ctrl+T,W.
2. Record a macro to transpose two words. (Alt+F6 selects the current word and Ctrl+→ jumps to the beginning of the next word.)
3. Try out your macro. If it doesn't work, rerecord it until it does.
4. Record macros to transpose two sentences (key code Ctrl+T,S) and transpose two paragraphs (key code Ctrl+T,P). (Alt+F8 selects the current sentence and Alt+F10 selects the current paragraph. Ctrl+↓ jumps to the beginning of the next paragraph. There is no keyboard command to move to the beginning of the next sentence, but you can use Alt+F8 to select it, then → to put the cursor after it.)
5. Try out all your macros. Record them again until they work.

Use Alt,M,C or Ctrl+F3 to start macro recording and to turn off the macro recorder again. Remember to position the cursor at the appropriate point before you turn on the macro recorder. You have to position it again before you run the macro.

Choosing Macro Names and Key Codes

A macro name must follow the same rules as a glossary name: up to 30 characters including letters, numbers, hyphens, underscores, and periods. Notice that spaces are not allowed. If you don't assign a macro key combination, the macro name can be 31 characters long. The key combination counts as part of the 31 characters.

If you specify a name that is already defined for another macro in the same glossary, Word asks if you want to replace the existing macro. If you choose <OK>, the former macro is replaced with the new one. If you choose <Cancel>, you must start the macro definition over again.

A macro key combination can have many different forms. It could be any function key combination (such as F2, Shift+F7, or Alt+Shift+F12), the Ctrl key plus one or two characters (Ctrl+N or Ctrl+1,G), or Ctrl+Shift plus one or two characters. Avoid using a single character with Ctrl or Ctrl+Shift because that limits the number of macros you can create. For example, if you create a macro for Ctrl+D, you can't create other ones for Ctrl+D,A or Ctrl+D,1 or any other combination starting with Ctrl+D.

Be sure to keep track of your key combinations; some are assigned to glossary entries, for example. And if you assign one that starts with one of the speed formatting keys, such as Ctrl+B (for bold), you'll have to use Ctrl+A,B to bold a selection.

Since Alt activates the menu bar, it cannot be used in a key code, except in combination with function keys. Even with function keys, some combinations that include the Alt key (such as Ctrl+Alt+F*n* and Shift+Alt+F*n*) are not allowed. You'll be able to see on your Word template which key combinations are already assigned to functions.

You cannot use punctuation characters (!, @, #, etc.) in any key codes—just letters and numbers. Word beeps when you try to define an illegal key code, but it doesn't care if you redefine a speed formatting key.

If you specify a key code that is already in use by another entry in the same glossary, Word tells you to choose another one. If you specify a key code that includes a speed formatting key (such as Ctrl+B for bold), one of Word's function keys (such as F4 to repeat the last action), or a style key code (such as Ctrl+Shift+H,1 for heading level 1) the new definition overrides the existing one without any warning. You can continue to use overridden key codes by prefixing them with Ctrl+A. You used Ctrl+T,W for a macro earlier in this chapter; if you want to create a hanging indent with speed formatting, you'll have to use Ctrl+A,Ctrl+T.

Saving Your Macros

To save the new macros, save the changes to your glossary file.

1. Choose Macro Edit.
2. Choose <Save Glossary>.
3. Choose <OK>.

Actually, saving the glossary through the Edit Glossary dialog box has the same effect. Whenever you save the glossary, any changes made to glossary entries and macro entries are saved. To abandon changes, open the same or a different glossary and choose <No> when asked if the changes should be saved. You can't save just some of the entries; it's all or none.

Deleting One Macro

To delete a single macro, choose the Macro Edit command, select the macro command to be removed, and choose the <Delete> button. This removes the macro, just as it deletes a glossary entry through the other dialog box.

Editing Macros

Why is it that the minute you turn on the macro recorder, you start making all kinds of mistakes? You don't have to start over to eliminate the errors. You can edit a macro to correct any mistakes or to modify it. You can use some features through the editor that aren't available while recording the macro.

To edit a macro, select it in the Macro Edit dialog box and choose the <Edit> button. The macro is inserted in your document at the cursor. Notice that this is the same effect as choosing the <Insert> button in the Edit Glossary dialog box; in fact, the buttons are in the same location.

1. Position the cursor at the beginning of a new paragraph.
2. Choose Macro Edit.
3. Select the Transpose-Letters macro name in the list box.

As soon as you choose the name, several things happen. Its name and key code are filled in at the top of the dialog box. The codes that define the macro are displayed underneath the list box. And the <Edit> and <Delete> buttons become available.

4. Choose <Edit>.

Now the macro's definition has been inserted in your document. Each item enclosed in angle brackets (< >) is a key that you pressed while recording the macro. First, you pressed Shift+→, which shows up in the macro as <shift right>. That highlights the current letter. Then you pressed Shift+Delete to cut the letter to scrap; that shows up in the macro as <shift del>. Then you pressed →, which shows up as <right>. And finally, you pressed Shift+Insert to insert the letter from scrap, which shows up as <shift ins>.

Now that the macro's definition has been inserted in your document, you can edit it just like any other text. You can delete keys that you pressed accidentally and insert new key codes by typing their names in angle brackets. Table 13.1 shows the names of the various keys. (The keys with single-character names—such as u, &, and 7—are just typed as is, without angle brackets.)

Tip ‖ The key name <alt> does not work in macros when it's not combined with another key. The key <alt F> works, but <alt>F doesn't. To access the menu bar, you must use <menu>.

Let's edit the Transpose-Letters macro so that it switches the current letter with the one before it instead of the one after it.

1. Edit the macro codes so that instead of <right> you have <left>.

Once you have edited the macro defintion, you have to copy the edited version back into the macro file. You do this just like you define a glossary entry—by selecting the macro definition, choosing the Macro Edit dialog box, and selecting the <Define> button.

2. Highlight the edited macro definition.
3. Choose Macro Edit. Notice that the definition you highlighted appears below the list box.
4. Select Transpose-Letters.

Now the definition below the list box is the current one for Transpose-Letters, but Word is still aware of the one that's highlighted in your document.

Table 13.1. Macro Key Names

Macro key name	Key
<alt x>	Alt+x
<ctrl x>	Ctrl+x
<shift x>	Shift+x
<menu>	Activates menu bar; same as pressing Alt
<esc>	Escape
<enter>	↵
<tab>	Tab
<del>	Delete
<ins>	Insert
<home>	Home
<end>	End
<left>	←
<right>	→
<up>	↑
<down>	↓
<pgdn>	PageDown
<pgup>	PageUp
<keypad*>	The * key on the numeric keypad
<keypad+>	The + key on the numeric keypad
<keypad->	The - key on the numeric keypad
<space>	Spacebar (used to select an option in a dialog box; not used for spaces in text)
<backspace>	Backspace
<numlock>	NumLock
<scrolllock>	ScrollLock
<capslock>	CapsLock
<fn>	Fn

Notice that, for the first time, the <Define> button is available. That's because of the highlighted text in your document.

5. Choose <Define>.
6. In response to the confirmation question, choose <OK>.
7. Press Delete to delete the macro definition from your document.
8. Move the cursor to a position where you can try out the revised macro.
9. Try out the revised macro by pressing Ctrl+T,L.
10. Repeat it (press F4) to restore the two letters you just transposed.

It is convenient to remove it immediately following the definition because it remains highlighted. But you can do it later if you prefer.

1. Edit the Transpose-Letters macro again so that it transposes the letters to the right of the cursor.
2. Try out your revised macro to make sure it works.
3. If you made any mistakes when recording your other macros, correct them now.
4. Save your macro glossary file.

To edit the macro, choose Macro Edit, select Transpose-Letters in the list, and choose <Edit>. In the macro definition, change <left> to <right>. Then highlight the entire definition, choose Macro Edit, select Transpose-Letters, and choose <Define>. Remember to press Delete to remove the macro definition from the text. Press Ctrl+T,L to try out the macro. To save the macro glossary file, choose Macro Edit followed by <Save Glossary> and <OK>.

Adapting Macros

Sometimes an easy way of creating a new macro is to adapt an old one that's similar. The process is almost the same as editing a macro, but when you return to the Macro Edit dialog box to choose the <Define> button, instead of reselecting the same macro name you enter a new name and key code in the text boxes at the top.

Let's adapt the Transpose-Words macro into a Delete-Word one.

1. Choose Macro Edit, select Transpose-Words, and choose <Edit>.

2. Edit the macro definition to read "<alt f6><shift del>".

Tip || Since you can't undo macros, avoid pressing the Delete key while recording a macro (when MR shows in the status bar). Use Edit Cut instead to place the value in the scrap (Shift+Delete) instead. That can be undone with Shift+Insert.

3. Highlight the edited macro definition.
4. Choose Macro Edit.
5. In the **Macro Name** field, type **Delete-Word**.

As soon as you type the first letter, notice that the <Edit>, <Delete>, and <Define> buttons become available.

6. In the **Macro Keys** field, press (don't type) Ctrl+D,W. (Since you now know the names of the keys, you could type **<Ctrl D>W** if you prefer.)
7. Choose <Define>.
8. When the dialog box disappears, press Delete to delete the macro definition.
9. To try out your new macro, position the cursor on any word and press Ctrl+D,W. (To restore the word, press Shift+Insert.)

If you decide to use double underline after defining this macro, you'll have to press Ctrl+A,Ctrl+D. Unless you use double underline formatting a great deal, that won't be any problem.

1. Adapt your Delete-Word macro into a Delete-Sentence macro (Ctrl+D,S).
2. Adapt your Delete-Sentence macro into a Delete-Paragraph macro (Ctrl+D,P).
3. Try out your new macros and correct them until they work.

Use the <Edit> button to copy a macro definition into your document. After editing it, use Macro Edit to open the dialog box, enter the name and key code in the text boxes at the top, and choose <Define> to create the new macro. Delete-Sentence should be defined as <alt f8><shift del>. Delete-Paragraph should be defined as <alt f10><shift del>.

Macros Involving Menus and Dialog Boxes

The macros you've created so far have used keyboard shortcuts but no menus or dialog boxes. You can record macros involving those elements just as easily.

Choosing Menus, Commands, and Fields

Once you start the recorder, use the keyboard (Alt followed by the highlighted letter in the menu name) to pull down the desired menu. Choose a menu command by typing its highlighted letter. In the dialog box, move the cursor to specific fields by pressing Alt at the same time as the highlighted letter.

Let's set up a macro to print two copies of the current document, including the summary information.

1. Choose Macro Record or press Ctrl+F3 and name the macro Print2, with the key code Ctrl+P,2.
2. Press Alt,F,P to open up the Print dialog box.
3. Whenever you open the Print dialog box, the cursor is positioned to replace the value in the **Copies** field. Type **2** to request two copies.
4. Choose the <Options> button.
5. Move the cursor to the **Summary Info** field.
6. Press ↵ twice to close the dialog boxes and start the printing.
7. Choose Macro Record (Ctrl+F3) to turn off the recorder. (You might have to wait until the print job is finished.)
8. If you made any mistakes while recording the macro, edit the macro and clean up the errors.
9. Try out the macro by pressing Ctrl+P,2.

How you handle a field menu depends on the menu. Some field menus let you select an item by putting the cursor in the field and typing the first letter of the desired item. Others let you type the entire name of the desired item. In some cases, you might want to press Alt+↓ to drop down the menu, then use ↓ to highlight the item to be selected.

Selecting from List Boxes

Selecting from a list box via a macro can be tricky. Suppose you want to select the same item from the list box every time the macro is run, such as the file named CHARTEST.DOC. Suppose you move the cursor into the list box, press

↓ five times to highlight CHARTEST.DOC, and press Enter to select it. The macro records the five ↓ key presses as <down 5>. But the next time you use this macro, CHARTEST.DOC might be in a different position in the list. The five <down> key presses will select a different file! To avoid this kind of problem, type the name CHARTEST.DOC in the associated text box rather than selecting from the list box. Be sure to include the full path for the desired document; that way, you don't have to worry about which directory is active when you run the macro.

Let's create a macro to print CHARTEST.DOC.

1. Turn on macro recording for a macro named Print-Chartest (Ctrl+P,C).
2. Choose File File Management and choose <Search>.

The only reliable way to get to the same file every time in the File Management dialog box is through the Search option.

3. In the **Search Paths** field at the top of the dialog box, type **C:\WORD\CHARTEST.DOC**. (Adapt the path to designate your Word directory.)
4. Press ↵ to choose <OK> and get back to the File Management dialog box.

The only file listed should be the one whose name you typed.

5. Choose <Print>.
6. In the Print dialog box, type **1** in the Copies field and press ↵ to start the printing.
7. Press the Escape key to close the File Management dialog box.
8. After the document finishes printing, turn off macro recording with Alt,M,C or Ctrl+F3.

The macro is recorded. You can now examine it, modify it, or whatever you want. Here's how to take a look at the macro you just recorded.

1. Choose Macro Edit, select Print-Chartest in the list box, and choose <Edit> to copy the macro definition into your document.

The macro starts with <menu>, which puts the cursor on the menu bar. The following two fs were the letters you pressed to select the File menu and the File Management command. The <alt S> resulted when you selected the <Search> button. Next you typed the name of the file and pressed ↵, which recorded the <enter> key. Then you selected the print button (<alt P>). On the

Print dialog box, you typed 1 in the **Copies** field and pressed ↵. Finally, you pressed Escape to close the dialog box.

You could modify the macro at this point. Since you don't want to, however, take time to delete it before going on.

2. Make sure the entire macro is selected in the document, then press Delete.

Interrupting a Macro

Sometimes you might want to interrupt a macro before it finishes running, perhaps because you started the wrong macro or because a new macro isn't working correctly yet. You can interrupt a macro by pressing the Escape key. A dialog box asks if you want to continue running. Choose <Cancel> to terminate the macro at this point. Choose <OK> if you want it to continue instead.

Tip The dialog box also contains a Single Step option, which you can use to test your own macros.

When you interrupt a macro, you can use Edit Undo to undo the last step performed by the macro. But that won't necessarily undo everything the macro did. You might have to undo other macro actions yourself.

1. Write a macro to print a single copy of the current document. Call it Print1 and give it the key code Ctrl+P,1.
2. Write a macro to open the file named REMEM-AM.COR (File Open followed by the typed name) and arrange it with the other open windows on your screen (Windows Arrange All). Call it Open-Remem and give it the key code Ctrl+O,R.
3. Try out each macro, making corrections as necessary. When the REMEM-AM.COR file opens, type a few words and close it.
4. Run Open-Remem again, but cancel it before it finishes.

Use Macro Record (Ctrl+F3) to record each macro. Press the defined key codes to try out the macros. Press Esc to cancel the macro before it finishes.

Macro Programming

Word includes a collection of special instructions that can be used in macros you define from scratch with the <Define> button, not when recording a macro. They let you perform relatively simple operations such as suppressing menus and pausing for input, as well as complex ones involving decision making and branching. The Word documentation contains a complete list of the available instructions with formats and explanations.

As your macros get more complex, you might need to slow them down while trying them out, so you can see exactly what's happening at each step. To turn on single-step mode, select Macro Run and check the **Step** check box. This causes Word to run the macro one step at a time. You'll find single-step mode useful if you get into macro programming.

Exercise

This chapter covered the use and recording of macros to perform a series of Word commands automatically. You can create one more in this exercise.

1. Record a macro to delete all the BAK files in the current directory. Call this macro Delete-Bakfiles and give it the key code Ctrl+D,B.
2. Try out the macro and correct it as necessary.
3. Examine the macros you have created in the current glossary file. Delete the ones you don't want to keep.
4. Save the glossary file with the macros you do want to keep.

To record the macro for item 1, turn on recording with the Macro Record command; use the File File Management command, then search for all files named *.BAK. Use Ctrl+Spacebar to select all the files shown. Then choose <Delete>. To stop recording, choose Macro Record (or Ctrl+F3). To run the macro again, you'll have to change to a different directory; then choose Macro Run or use the key code you assigned.

Use Macro Edit to remove any macros, then choose <Save Glossary>.

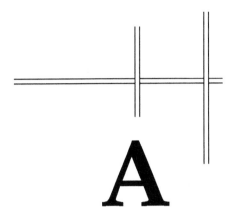

Installation Tips

Installing Word 5.5 is no problem. You insert the Setup diskette in drive A:, get the A: prompt (A:>), and type **SETUP**. The program goes to work, asking you questions about where and how you want Word installed. You answer most questions by selecting the response from a list on screen. The setup program explains how to make choices as it proceeds.

Then it starts to install, prompting you to insert various diskettes from your package. You'll have to be very organized if you are installing on diskettes rather than a hard disk, so as not to get the original diskettes confused with the ones you create. Label everything and stay alert.

You may run into problems answering the questions. This appendix tells you what sort of information you have to provide and gives some tips about what to choose. You can interrupt Setup at any time by holding down the Control key and pressing X. If you do this, the installation is canceled. You'll have to start over from the beginning to install Word.

Specifying the Information

The first part of the Setup program involves your telling Setup what equipment you have and what parts of Word you want available. Setup asks most of the questions before it starts asking you to change diskettes.

Where to Install

The first response you have to make while installing Word tells it what type of installation you want. Word is best installed on a hard disk. If you must install to a diskette, you choose **Set up floppy disk** here. If you have a hard disk, that's where you'll want Word so choose **Set up hard disk**. If you are installing Word on a network, choose **Set up network**.

Word asks you to choose whether you are installing a new version of Word or if you are modifying an existing version. You can run Setup again later to modify the existing version and change your choices if you choose incorrectly or if you change your monitor, printer, or mouse.

If you chose to install Word on a hard drive and your system has more than one, you'll be asked which drive Word should use. You'll also be asked to enter the directory name for your Word files. Setup suggests the directory \WORD, but you can change this if you like.

The Type of Equipment

Once it knows where to put Word, Setup verifies the type of hardware you have. First you choose the type of computer. If none of the other choices describes your computer, choose **IBM PC XT, AT, PS/2 or 100% compatible**. This describes most computers, even if they aren't really 100% compatible.

Selecting the Display Adapter. Next you get to choose the type of display adapter you have. The choice here isn't quite so obvious. Several forms of adapters are listed; choose the best you can. If you can't find a more specific description, choose **IBM EGA or compatible** for an EGA or VGA adapter.

Specifying Printer Information. The printer choice is next; in this section you tell Setup what printer drivers to prepare for you to use. You'll probably want one for each printer attached to your computer; you may even want to install a printer driver for a printer at work or for one belonging to a colleague. Installing a printer driver lets Word use special facilities of that printer, such as italics, bold, variable line heights, even all the features of Postscript printers.

If you choose to install a printer driver, Setup lets you continue to install them until you select **Continue with Setup**. First you'll see a list. You can search through it to find the printer you want; a few fairly generic ones are included as well. If Setup needs more information, you'll be asked to enter or select it. For example, if you select a printer that supports internal and downloadable fonts, you'll have to choose which type(s) you expect to use.

Finally, you'll have to specify the printer port. You must choose the port your printer is connected to; this is usually LPT1: for a parallel printer if your system has only one. If you choose a serial port, Setup reminds you that you have to set various communications settings in the MODE command before you start. But if you use a serial printer, that is probably already taken care of in your AUTOEXEC.BAT file.

Updating the Mouse Driver

If you have a Microsoft mouse or a compatible one, let Setup update the mouse driver with the newest version. If you have a different type of mouse, however, select **Do not update the mouse driver**. If your mouse doesn't work once Word is installed, you may have to check with the mouse manufacturer to get the latest driver. If your mouse works with other recent software, however, it will most likely work with Word.

Installing Optional Features

Word asks if you want to install the spelling checker. In most cases, this is a fine idea. But if you use a different spelling checker or are pressed for disk space, you might not want it. The spelling checker takes about 161K on disk.

Then Word asks if you want to install the thesaurus. Like the spelling checker, this is a handy tool, but it takes up 327K on disk. If you don't expect to use it or if disk space is tight, you might want to choose to bypass it at this time. Remember you can always run Setup again later to install these features.

If you plan to use the Word tutorial lessons on your computer, you'll want to install the Learning Word course. Then you can choose the Help Learning Word command from the Help menu whenever you are in Word. These lessons introduce you to the basics of Word and give you guided practice using its menus and commands. The files that make up the Learning Word course take up about 500K on disk.

Customizing Word

The Setup program offers to let you customize several Word features as part of the installation process. Since you can do all the customization from within Word, we suggest you select **Do not customize Word settings** during installation. Then Word will start with its default setup.

Update the System Files

Several changes may have to be made in the system files (CONFIG.SYS and AUTOEXEC.BAT) in order for Word to run effectively on your system. Setup offers to update them for you. If you aren't altogether sure about this, you can make a copy of these files before running Setup. Then you can restore them later if the automatic update causes problems. Here's how to make a copy:

1. Get to the prompt of your boot disk (A: or C:\).
2. Type **COPY AUTOEXEC.BAT AUTOEXEC.SAV** and press ↵.
3. Type **COPY CONFIG.SYS CONFIG.SAV** and press ↵.

Now you have a duplicate of your system files with extension SAV. You can restore these files later by reversing the file names in the COPY commands above.

If you choose not to let Setup touch your system files, you'll be warned that you have to update them yourself. The updates may not, in fact, be necessary, depending on the contents of these files. If you installed Word on diskettes but boot from the hard disk, you'll have to modify the system files yourself. The required information is explained in detail in the *Getting Started* booklet supplied with Word 5.5.

Switching Diskettes

When Setup has enough information, it remains in memory and asks you to insert other diskettes from the set provided by Word. Just follow the instructions carefully. Based on the information you provided, Setup asks only for the diskettes it needs. If you are installing on diskette, you will be told when to insert blank ones as well. Be sure to label all diskettes that are created.

Modifying Word

Once Word is installed, start it as explained at the end of the Setup program. Any time you want to modify the installation, run Setup again, just as described in this appendix. When asked which drive to install on, select the drive the program is already on. When asked for the directory, use the one that the program is in. When asked whether it is a new installation or a modification, choose modification. Then you can change just the part that needs to be changed.

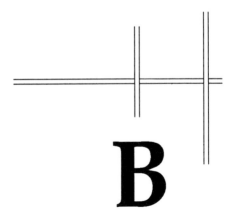

B

Using 360K Diskettes

W ord runs pretty much the same no matter what hardware you use. But if your computer has only 360K diskettes, you have to make some compromises; the entire Word program won't fit on a single diskette of this size. During installation, you'll be told how to label the diskettes you create.

Starting Word

To start Word, you must use the diskette created by the Setup program. Put your Word Program 1 diskette in drive A:. When the DOS prompt is displayed, type **word** and press ↵. The program will start; you'll be prompted when to change drive A: to the Word Program 2 diskette. Any time you use a command that requires parts of Word that aren't on that diskette, you'll be prompted to insert a different diskette. You'll use drive B: to hold your data diskette.

Saving Files

If you don't have a hard disk, Word suggests you save files to drive B:. If your drives support only 360K diskettes, the diskette in drive A: doesn't have room for you to store files. Be sure you have a formatted diskette in the data drive.

Printing Files

To print a file from a computer that has only 360K drives, you have to make sure your printer driver is on the diskette in the B: drive. The Setup program copies a file with extension PRD to the document diskette it creates. You'll have to copy this file to every data diskette you want to print from. Follow these steps:

1. Get to the DOS prompt, outside of Word.
2. Place a diskette containing the PRD file, such as the original data diskette created by Setup, in drive A:.
3. Place a potential data diskette in drive B:. This diskette must be formatted; it can contain data already, as long as it isn't full.
4. At the A: prompt, type **COPY *.PRD B:** and press ↵.

When the A: prompt returns, the printer driver is copied. You can verify this by checking the directory.

5. Type **DIR B:*.PRD**. All files with extension PRD on drive B: will be listed.

You can use any diskette containing the PRD file for your printer to copy it to another data diskette.

Before you print, check the File Printer Setup command. The **Printer Setup** field should show the driver name preceded by B:.

Conserving Disk Space

Word creates temporary scratch files with extension TMP as it works on your documents. These files are stored by default on your Word Program Disk 2 in the A: drive. The disk may get full without your knowing it. To minimize this, save your files often. If you have several files open, close them all and reopen just the one you need at the time. Another option is to divert these files to the data diskette, which may have more space available. Add this statement to your AUTOEXEC.BAT file: **set tmp=B:**. Now any TMP files are sent to the diskette in the B: drive.

You can check the amount of space remaining on a disk with the DOS DIR command from the DOS prompt. Here's how:

1. Get to the DOS prompt, either outside of Word or through the File DOS Commands command.
2. Type **DIR B:** and press ↵.

At the bottom of the directory listing is the amount of space remaining on the disk. You need at least twice as much space as the size of the files you have open (to allow for a BAK file), probably three times as much if you count the TMP files.

If a diskette is full and you have to save a document, you have a few options. You can delete a file from the diskette using the File File Management command or with the DOS DEL command at the DOS prompt.

Alternatively, you can save the file to a different diskette. Here's how:

1. Insert a different formatted diskette into the B: drive.
2. Choose the File Save command.
3. When prompted, switch back to the original diskette. This gives Word access to the DOC and BAK files on the diskette.
4. When prompted again, reinsert the formatted diskette to hold the newly saved file.

As you go through this procedure, don't switch diskettes until Word asks you to.

Various operations cause Word to use memory, both in the CPU and on disk. Whenever you see the message SAVE in the message bar, choose the File Save (or File Save All) command immediately. If the SAVE message starts blinking, memory is dangerously low. If Word runs out of memory, you won't be able to save the document at all.

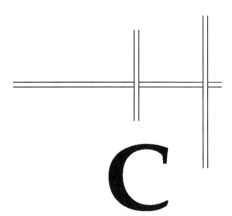

DOS Directory Structure

$\mathbf{D}$OS stores everything on disk in files. If you store a memo, it becomes a file; so does a mailing list, a 50-page report, a letter, and a picture. The Word software itself is made up of many, many files; all of them are stored on disk where DOS can access them as needed.

Every DOS file is specified by a name made up of two parts: the file name itself and an optional extension connected with a period. Valid file names include WORD.EXE, STONE.DOC, CHAP01, and APPENDIX.A. Every DOS file name has from one to eight characters. The extension can have from one to three characters. They can contain letters, digits, and many symbols.

Most people use the file name to indicate the file's contents and the extension to indicate its type. Word applies the extension DOC to files it creates if you don't supply a different extension.

DOS maintains a file directory on every disk, showing each full file name with its location on the disk, its size, the date it was last worked on, and other pertinent information. The directory helps DOS locate files as you need them. A root directory is created by DOS automatically when a disk is formatted. You can add other directories as you need them.

Only one directory on a disk is current at a time. When you use the DOS DIR command, you see a list of all the files in the current directory. When you choose File Open or File Save As within Word, you will see a list of all the files with extension DOC in the current directory. You can change the directory in the dialog box or make it display files with other extensions.

To keep directories from becoming too full to be useful, you can break them into subdirectories. Your hard disk probably has a WORD subdirectory that contains all the files that are part of the Word software. You can place your own document files in this directory or create another to hold them. When files are grouped into meaningful categories, it is easier to find the files you want. DOS finds files faster in shorter directories.

You can create a whole hierarchy of subdirectories, as shown below in the diagram. Your hard disk may already hold such a directory structure. Each box in the diagram represents a directory. The root directory, at the top, contains several files and several subdirectories. Each of these subdirectories contains files, most contain additional subdirectories as well.

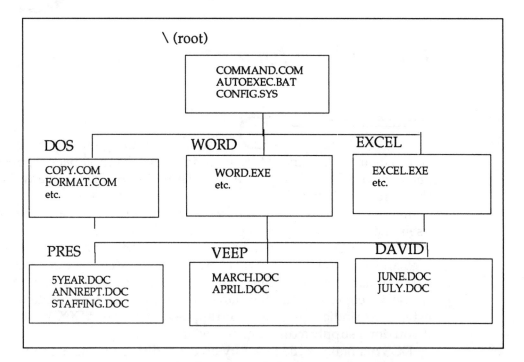

You can structure a disk directory any way you like for your own convenience. Your main objective is to group files that you use together. For example, all the files needed to run the Word software are placed in the same directory during installation; this is named WORD unless you specify a different name. You can create subdirectories under WORD to hold files related to different projects.

A full file reference includes the drive name and the path of all subdirectories from the root to the one that contains the file, separated by backslashes. For example, the full specification for the APRIL.DOC file in the diagram is

For example, the full specification for the APRIL.DOC file in the diagram is \WORD\VEEP\APRIL.DOC. The initial backslash is the name of the root directory. The APRIL.DOC file is in the VEEP subdirectory beneath the WORD subdirectory. A path that begins with backslash (\) starts at the root directory. A path that begins with two periods (..) begins at the parent of the current directory. Other paths begin at the current directory.

Only one directory on each drive is current at any given time; that is the directory whose files are listed when you open a file and to which new files are saved. You can change the current directory by selecting a different one in the **Directories** list box in many dialog boxes. If the directory DAVID is current and you want to open a file named MARCH.DOC in the VEEP directory, you could type **\VEEP\MARCH** or **..\VEEP\MARCH** in the File Open dialog box.

To create a new directory, use the DOS MKDIR command. Follow these steps:

1. At the DOS prompt, make current the directory you want the new one to be under.
2. Type **MKDIR** *name* supplying an eight-character name for the new subdirectory; you can use a period and up to three characters for the extension if you like.
3. Press ↵.

The new directory is subordinate to the current one.

To make a different directory current at the DOS prompt, follow these steps:

1. Type **CHDIR** *path* at the DOS prompt. If the target directory is not below the current directory, type the complete path starting with backslash.
2. Press ↵.

You can change directories within Word as needed. You can also locate any type of file in any directory on any disk using various file management commands within Word.

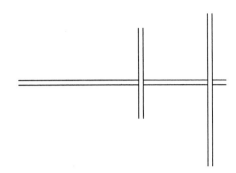

Glossary

AND Logical operator used with file management searches; use it to specify that all entered strings are to be present in located files.

Annotation Special type of footnote that lets you add comments to a document; the reference mark can include initials and the date. Controlled through Insert Annotation and special supplied macros.

Arrange windows Default arrangement of all open windows so they are all shown on screen; Window Arrange all command.

Arrow keys The keys on the keyboard that move the cursor in the indicated direction.

ASCII file A file that contains no formatting codes; produced when printing a file to disk or when you choose the File Save As command.

Automatic style A style that is applied if no other style is specified; it might be applied to a normal text paragraph, to a header, a footer, or a footnote, for example. See *Style*.

Autosave Automatic backup file created at regular intervals by Word; controlled through the Utilities Customize command.

Background printing   Printing that takes place while you continue to edit in Word; controlled through the **Print Queue On** field reached through the File Printer Setup command.

Beep   The sound made by your computer when Word wants to get your attention; controlled through the Utilities Customize command.

Block   A selected amount of text; it can range from one character to the entire document.

Bookmark   An invisible marker that simplifies returning to a location in a document; place it with Insert Bookmark and move to it with Edit Go To.

Borders   Lines at any side or around a paragraph; insert with Format Borders.

Button   Element in a dialog box that you can click on or select with the keyboard.

Calculator   Utility that calculates the result of the selected arithmetic expression or adds the numbers in a selection.

Capture   Method of creating a disk file containing the current screen image. Use the CAPTURE.COM program.

Character format   Any format that affects selected characters, such as font, bold, italic, or size.

Check box   Field in a dialog box that can be on (checked) or off.

Chevrons   Symbols « and », created by pressing Ctrl+[and Ctrl+]; used in macro instructions and fields for merging documents.

Click   Press and release the mouse button (usually the left button).

Close a file   Remove a window from the screen; you'll be prompted to save its file if any changes were made. Controlled through the File Close command.

Close box   The square icon in the upper-left corner of the window; click on it to close the window.

Columns   Type of section formatting that lets you set up a document to have multiple columns; the default is one column.

Command button   Button enclosed in angle brackets that takes some action after you view or modify a dialog box.

Context-sensitive help   Help information related to the active part of the screen; press F1.

Copy The original selected material is unchanged and a copy is placed in the scrap; Edit Copy command.

Cursor movement Positioning the cursor using either the keyboard keys or the mouse.

Cursor speed The speed with which the cursor moves when you hold down a key; modify this with Utilities Customize.

Cut The original selected material is removed from its original location and placed in the scrap; use the Edit Cut command.

Data document File that contains a header record and data records to be merged into a main document.

Data record Records (paragraphs) in the data document that contain information to be merged into the main document when File Print Merge is chosen to print the main document.

Date The date as known by Word; change the format through Utilities Customize.

Decimal character The character in calculated numbers that separates the whole number portion from the fractional part. The default decimal character is a period; change it to a comma through Utilities Customize.

Default A value that is used if no other value is supplied.

Default tabs Tabs at equal intervals across the document width. If you define custom tabs, all default tabs to their left are canceled.

Delete To remove something. To delete one character at the cursor, press the Delete key. If a block is selected, pressing Delete removes it without placing it in the scrap.

Dialog box A box that appears on the screen whenever Word wants information or a response from you. When a menu command is followed by an ellipsis (...), a dialog box is produced.

Direct printing Printing exactly what you type as you type it. Choose it in the File Print dialog box.

Diskette A removable disk 5.25" or 3.5" size; often called a floppy disk.

Display mode Specifies how documents are displayed; choices are text and graphics with different numbers of lines, depending on your monitor. Controlled through the View Preferences command.

Document window Rectangular window that displays a document.

DOS Disk Operating System; the operating system of your computer.

Drag Move the mouse while holding down the left button.

Edit Entering and modifying text; also a menu name.

Extend selection Make a current selection larger or smaller.

Extension The part of a file or directory name that follows the period; it can be from one to three characters long. Word assumes or applies the extension DOC if no other is supplied.

Field separator A comma or tab separating fields in a header or data record in a data document.

File name The name of a file; the first part has from one to eight characters and the optional extension has from one to three.

Floppy disk A removable disk 5.25" or 3.5" size; more accurately called a diskette.

Font A type style; the fonts available to you depend on your printer. Each font may be available in several sizes.

Footer A paragraph that appears in the bottom margin of every odd and/or even page.

Footnote Additional information, usually a reference, that appears at the bottom of the page or at the end of the document, referenced from the regular text. Controlled through Insert Footnote.

Formatting codes Hidden codes embedded in text to control formatting; can be located and replaced through Edit commands.

Glossary A file that contains pieces of text that you can enter into any document with a few keystrokes; controlled with Edit Glossary.

Glossary entry One entry in a glossary; it can be inserted with commands, key code, or F3.

GLY file A glossary file; may contain macro entries as well.

Graphic An image produced by drawing rather than by text characters; create with Utilities Line Draw or import with Insert Picture.

Graphics mode A display mode in which graphics are used to display text and layout in the document so that you can see all the features; controlled through View Preferences.

Graphics paragraph A paragraph containing an inserted graphic instead of text; controlled through the Insert Graphic command.

Gutter margin Inside margin on text to be printed on both sides; allows for binding or punching on that edge.

Hard disk Fixed disk in the computer; may have 40M, 80M, or even more bytes of storage.

Header A paragraph that appears in the top margin of every odd and/or even page.

Header record First record (paragraph) in a merge data document; contains names of fields in data records that are referenced in the main document when File Print Merge is chosen.

Help On-line information about how to use Microsoft Word; use the Help menu or press F1.

Help index Lets you choose what part of the help system you want to use.

Hyphenation Automatic hyphenation of words at the end of lines; controlled through the Utilities Hyphenate command.

Indentation How much a paragraph is indented from each section margin; the first line can be different; controlled through the Format Paragraph command.

Insert mode Standard typing and editing mode; when you type, existing characters are pushed to the right. Switch to *Typeover mode* by pressing the Insert key.

Justified Paragraph alignment that results in all lines ending at the same point on both the right and left; controlled through the Format Paragraph command.

Key code An optional shortcut code assigned to a style or macro; pressing the key code applies the style to the current or selected paragraphs or runs the macro.

Key letter The highlighted or distinctive letter in a menu name or field name; pressing it alone or with Alt activates the menu or field.

Line drawing A drawing created with Word using the arrow keys; controlled through Utilities Line Draw command. The line draw character can be changed through Utilities Customize.

Macro A series of commands and/or keystrokes that can be played back when the macro is run; controlled through the Macro menu.

Macro file Macros are stored in a GLY file, along with glossary entries.

Macro recorder Automatically records your commands and keystrokes to create a macro.

Margins The right, left, top, and bottom edges of the print area of a page; controlled through Format Margins command.

Maximize Making the window as large as possible; controlled through the Window menu or the maximize icon.

Measurement unit The unit of measurement Word uses for a feature; the default is usually in inches or lines. Change it through the Utilities Customize command.

Menu bar The list of available menus on the top line of the screen.

Menu A list of commands; displayed when you click on a menu name in the menu bar or press Alt followed by a menu's key letter.

Merge files Generating documents by filling variables from a data document into a main document; start it with File Merge Print.

Message bar The bottom line on the screen; it contains messages to you from Word or an explanation of an active command.

Mirror margin Margins on right and left pages are mirror images of each other.

Mouse Hand operated device that lets you point, click, and drag the mouse pointer.

Normal style A style applied automatically to a paragraph or section if you don't apply a different one.

NOT Logical operator used with file management searches; use it to specify that the entered strings must not be present in located files.

Open a file Bring a file from disk into memory and a document window so it can be read and edited.

OR Logical operator used with file management searches; use it to specify that at least one of the entered strings is to be present in located files.

Organize mode Mode used for maintaining outlines; turn on or off with Shift+F5 when Outline is active.

Outline Method of viewing and working with documents so that the headings are the main issue; controlled through View Outline.

Overtype mode A typing mode in which the characters you type overlay existing characters at the cursor; opposite of insert mode. OT appears in the status bar; toggle it with the Insert key.

Page break The division between two pages. A soft page break inserted by Word appears as a line of periods. Insert a hard page break with Shift+↵; it appears as a more thickly spaced line of periods.

Page number The number of the page appears in the status line; use Edit Go To to move directly to a page number. To include it on printed pages, use Insert Page Numbers or Format Section command.

Pagination Word can keep track of pages and insert soft page breaks as you type if **Background Pagination** is turned on through Utilities Customize. If a document is not paginated, use the Utilities Repaginate Now command.

Paragraph format The alignment, spacing, and indentation of paragraphs; can also control paragraph positioning. Control through Format Paragraph command.

Paste Insert the contents of the scrap into the document at the cursor; use the Edit Paste command.

Point Place the mouse pointer on an item.

Point size A unit of measure in typography that is approximately 1/72 inch. In Word, fonts are measured in points and can range from 4 to 72, depending on printer capabilities.

Preview Shows on the screen how the document will look when printed; use the File Print Preview command.

Queue A lineup (on disk) of documents waiting to be printed; you can continue editing while they are printing. Controlled with Printer Setup and File Print Queue commands.

Radio button A set of mutually exclusive options; a large dot indicates which one is currently selected.

RAM Random access memory; your computer's internal storage area for running programs and handling data.

Repeat Command that repeats the last command or text entry; controlled with F4.

Replace Search for a specified string or format and replace it with another; use the Edit Replace command.

Resize Change the size of a window; use the Window Size command or the size icon.

Ribbon Formatting device that appears below the menu bar. Turn it on and off with View Ribbon or the ruler/ribbon icon.

RTF files Rich text formatting; files printed to disk in a format that retains most of the formatting.

Ruler A line below the window's top border, marked in 0.1" increments on which you can view and change the current paragraph's indentation and custom tabs; turn it off and on with View Ruler or the ruler/ribbon icon.

Scrap An area that stores the last block of text cut or copied and the results of certain commands. The first and last characters show in the status bar enclosed in braces.

Screen image A disk file that contains an exact image of the screen. You can capture screen images with CAPTURE.COM.

Scroll bar The horizontal and vertical bars that help a mouse control movement through a file. They appear on the right and bottom borders of the window. Turn them on and off through the View Preferences command.

Scroll box The dark rectangle on a scroll that indicates the approximate location of the visible text in the document. Dragging this box with the mouse permits rapid movement through the document.

Search Locate specified text or formatting codes in a document; use the Edit Search command.

Search path The set of paths from which files are listed in the File Management dialog box.

Section A major division of a document, which is made up of one or more paragraphs; each section can have its own section formatting. Use Insert Break and choose Section to start a new section at the cursor.

Section format The margins, columns, page numbering, line numbers, and setup for a section; controlled through the Format menu.

Selection Highlighted text that can be operated on by a command such as copy or assigned a format.

Selection bar Invisible area two characters wide just inside the left window border where mouse can select a line, a paragraph, or the entire document; same area as style bar.

Shading Paragraph formatting option that applies the selected level of shading to a paragraph; shows up in preview or print.

Sorting Rearranging the selected paragraphs or lines in a columnar table in the specified order; use the Utilities Sort command.

Speed formatting Key combinations that let you apply character and paragraph formats with only a few keystrokes.

Spelling checker Utility that checks the spelling of a selection or document; you can correct errors and add to dictionaries.

Status bar Second line from the bottom of the screen; gives information on the location of the cursor and status of Word features.

STY file A style file, which contains a related set of format styles for a certain type of document; it has extension STY. Controlled through several Format menu commands.

Style A defined set of formatting codes that can be applied to characters, paragraphs, or sections.

Style bar Invisible area two characters wide just inside the left window border where applied style key codes are displayed; same area as selection bar.

Style I.D. Name available for use in defining styles.

Style sheet File with extension STY that contains a set of defined styles; can be attached to documents.

Style Type Indicates whether a style applies to a character, paragraph, or section.

Summary information General information attached to a document, such as author, keywords, and creation date; controlled through the Utilities Customize command and maintained through File File Management.

Tables Columnar tables set up by use of custom tabs and new-line characters (Shift+↵); can be sorted by column.

Text mode A display mode in which all information is displayed via text and special characters; no graphics are shown. Controlled through the View Preferences command.

Thesaurus Utility that provides additional words similar in meaning to the one containing the cursor.

Time The system time can be inserted in a document in the format specified through the Utilities Customize command.

Undo Command that undoes the last command or text entry; use Edit Undo or press Alt+Backspace.

Wildcard An * or ? used to let you specify generic file names.

Window panes Split window to show different parts of the same document in each part of the window; they scroll independently. Control with the Window Split command or the split icon.

Wordwrap Automatic wrapping of words to the next line in a paragraph without your having to press ↵.

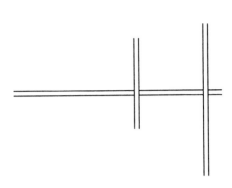

Index

A comprehensive 2-volume tutorial & reference set!

MICROSOFT WORD 5.5
FOR THE PC
Self-Teaching Guide
Ruth Ashley & Judi N. Fernandez

MICROSOFT WORD 5.5
Command Reference
Pamela S. Beason

To receive your $5.00 cash rebate you must show proof of purchase for both the MICROSOFT WORD 5.5 FOR THE PC Self-Teaching Guide and MICROSOFT WORD 5.5 Command Reference. Complete this rebate certificate by hand-printing your name and address and signing below. Mail your rebate certificate together with your receipts of purchase with book prices circled to:

MICROSOFT WORD 5.5 Self-Teaching Guide &
MICROSOFT WORD 5.5 Command Reference
Rebate Offer
P.O. Box 2100
Grand Rapids, MN 55745-2100

Print Name _____

Address _____

City _____ State _____ Zip _____

Signature _____

This certificate must accompany your request. No duplicates accepted. Offer good in the United States and Canada. Offer limited one to a family, group or organization. Void where prohibited, taxed, or restricted. Allow 4-6 weeks for mailing of your rebate. Offer expires **June 30, 1992.**